Resisting Regionalism

Resisting Regionalism

Gender and Naturalism in American Fiction, 1885-1915

Donna M. Campbell

OHIO UNIVERSITY PRESS
ATHENS

Ohio University Press, Athens, Ohio 45701

© 1997 by Donna M. Campbell

Printed in the United States of America

All rights reserved

01 00 99 98 97   5 4 3 2 1

Ohio University Press books
are printed on acid-free paper ∞™

Library of Congress Cataloging-in-Publication Data

Campbell, Donna M.

Resisting regionalism : gender & naturalism in
American fiction, 1885-1915 / Donna M. Campbell

p. cm.

Includes bibliographical references (p.) and index.

ISBN 0-8214-1177-2 (alk. paper)

1. American fiction—19th century—History and criticism. 2. Regionalism in
literature. 3. American fiction—20th century—History and criticism.
4. Masculinity (Psychology) in literature. 5. Femininity (Psychology) in
literature. 6. Women and literature—United States. 7. Authorship—
Sex differences. 8. Local color in literature. 9. Naturalism in
literature. 10. n-us.   I. Title.

PS374.R4C36   1997

813'.40912—dc21   96-45666

CIP

To Chris, Elizabeth, and Madeline

CONTENTS

ACKNOWLEDGMENTS

I am deeply grateful to the Northeast Modern Language Association, its awards committee, and its officers, especially Carol Singley, Laura Skandera-Trombley, and Annette Benert, for their kindness and their generosity in supporting this book.

I also thank the readers for the NEMLA–Ohio University Press Award, and in particular Marjorie Pryse; their insightful suggestions proved invaluable and guided the revision of this work. At Ohio University Press, Holly Panich, Nancy Basmajian, and Helen Gawthrop have provided both patience and timely assistance; Bob Furnish was a constructive and painstaking copyeditor.

Denise Knight, Hildegard Hoeller, and especially Jeanne Campbell Reesman, whose insights on Jack London have informed my own, provided the opportunity to present sections of this work to audiences at MLA, NEMLA, and other conferences. Discussions with Nancy Glazener and Joseph McElrath Jr. have helped to clarify points about regionalism and Frank Norris, respectively; members of the Edith Wharton Society, especially Alan Price, Janet Goodwyn, and most of all Katherine Joslin, have been an unfailing and invaluable resource on Wharton and other matters. My colleagues Amy Doerr and Ann C. Colley were unstinting with their time and advice.

My greatest debt is to Alfred Habegger, at whose instigation I began this project. His insights and suggestions have been instrumental in shaping the work, and his advice and encouragement have been essential to its completion.

Thanks are also due to Craig Werner at SUNY College at Buffalo for funding travel to the Beinecke Library; to Michael Bonin and J. Kevin Waters, S.J., at Gonzaga University for additional travel funds; to the staff of Lockwood Library at SUNY at Buffalo; and to the Interlibrary Loan departments at Butler Library, State University College at Buffalo, and at the Foley Center, Gonzaga University.

The last section of chapter 3 appeared in an earlier version as "Frank Norris's 'Drama of a Broken Teacup': The Old Grannis–Miss Baker Plot in

McTeague," *American Literary Realism* 26.1 (Fall 1993): 40–49, and is reprinted here with the permission of McFarland and Company. Material from chapter 6 on Edith Wharton's short fiction appeared in an earlier version in "Edith Wharton and the 'Authoresses': The Critique of Local Color in Wharton's Early Fiction," *Studies in American Fiction* 22 (Fall 1994): 169–83, and is reprinted with permission.

Resisting Regionalism

[W]hile, therefore, some may choose to decry the substance of the whole [local color] movement on account of its polishing and adornment of the little things of life . . . it is but fair, it is but reasonable, to remember that this same Age of the Carved Cherry Stones brought in the taste and patience to do so much with so little, and to do it with such high art. . . . Or if the historian of our literature should hereafter come severely to regard it as but a thin moss which served rather to hide the deep rocks of American character, still he will never be able to deny that the moss was a natural, a living verdure, and that it grew thriftily and fitly wherever it was planted.

—James Lane Allen (1897)

The New England school for too long dominated the entire range of American fiction—limiting it, specializing it, polishing, refining and embellishing it, narrowing it down to a veritable cult, a thing to be safeguarded by the elect, the few, the aristocracy. It is small wonder that the reaction came when and as it did; small wonder that the wearied public, roused at length, smashed its idols with such vehemence; small wonder that, declaring its independence and finding itself suddenly untrammeled and unguided, it flew off "mobishly" toward false gods, good only because they were new.

—Frank Norris (1902)

I had had an uneasy sense that the New England of fiction bore little—except a vague botanical and dialectical—resemblance to the harsh and beautiful land as I had seen it. Even the abundant enumeration of sweet-fern, asters and mountain-laurel, and the conscientious reproduction of the vernacular, left me with the feeling that the outcropping granite had in both cases been overlooked.

—Edith Wharton (1922)

Chapter One

Introduction
Local Color, Naturalism,
and Gender

· I ·

On 13 November 1901, the *Boston Evening Transcript* printed an essay provocatively entitled "Why Women Should Write the Best Novels: And Why They Don't." While conceding that, like all arts, writing is a "masculine occupation," the author of the piece lists certain advantages that women writers have over their male counterparts, including more leisure, a more extensive introduction to literature and art, and, above all, a more sensitive temperament:

> The average man is a rectangular, square-cut, matter-of-fact, sober-minded animal who does not receive impressions easily, who is not troubled with emotions and has no overmastering desire to communicate his sensations to anybody. But the average woman is just the reverse of all these. She is impressionable, emotional and communicative.[1]

The salient question occurs halfway through the essay: "Why, then, with such a long start and with so many advantages of temperament, opportunity and training should it be that women do not write better novels than men?" (35). The essay suggests that women's frailty, their inability to "grind on steadily for an almost indefinite period" (36), erodes their chances, just as excessive literary training may cause women to polish their work too highly. The crucial issue, however, is that although women may study "real life" through literature, they are barred from direct experience of "life itself, the crude, the raw, the vulgar"(35) by their natural reluctance to force themselves "into the midst of that great, grim complication of men's doings that we call life" (36). For these reasons, "it must be admitted that the ranks of the 'arrived' are recruited from the razor-using contingent" (35).

The martial metaphor implied by "ranks" and "recruited" reinforces the idea emphatically: real literature is the province of real men.

It should be easy to dismiss "Why Women Should Write the Best Novels: And Why They Don't" as just one more entry in the "Woman Question" debates so fashionable in the popular press of the day. But the essay cannot be dismissed. Its author was no hack. He was Frank Norris, one of the country's most promising young novelists, a man whose novels and essays championed the cause of naturalism in America. At the time he published this essay, one of a series he wrote for the *Boston Evening Transcript*, Norris was himself a novelist of the "razor-using contingent" who had joined the ranks of the "arrived" with works like *McTeague*, *A Man's Woman*, and *The Octopus*. In both novels and criticism Norris reiterates similar views, arguing that experience of "real life" and perception exist as necessary complements of one another: without perception, a person becomes a brutish McTeague, and without experience, an artist becomes an ineffectual Vandover. In *The Octopus*, for example, the artist-protagonist Presley recognizes that life, not literature, should govern his writing, and as a result he abandons the conventional romantic epic he had planned to write. Vandover, the aspiring artist of *Vandover and the Brute*, refuses to look outside himself and to regard life as a subject; the puerile, imitative results of his efforts indicate the failure of his method. Norris's comments on women's lack of experience, then, should not be seen as mere misogyny, since he is equally contemptuous of men who willfully shut themselves away from life. Also, since this confident assignment of gender-linked traits characterizes Norris's writing as well as that of such periodicals as the era's *Popular Science* magazine, the essay reflects rather than defies both Norris's own critical preoccupations and the social attitudes of the time.[2]

Yet the essay deserves attention, less for Norris's casual dismissal of women's writing than for his two central assumptions. The first assumption is that of choice. Believing that male artists have access to a larger world and are culpable if they ignore it in their art, Norris refuses to hold female artists responsible for failing to use such sources, since they have virtually no access to "real life." Norris's response is at once chivalrous and damning. Since they have no choice, we cannot blame women for creating inferior literature; but precisely because they have no choice, women cannot create great literature. This first assumption rests on the second, more central one: "real life" is men's life. Left unspoken is the logical corollary to this assumption: if men's life is "real life," the fit subject for fiction, then women's life is, in effect, "not life," and fiction made from it is, at the very least, "not literature."

A scant fifteen years earlier, quite a different judgment on women writers of fiction had been expressed in the February 1887 issue of *Harper's Monthly*:

> An interesting fact in regard to the different varieties of the short story among us is that the sketches and studies by the women seem faithfuler and more realistic than those of the men, in proportion to their number. Their tendency is more distinctly in that direction, and there is a solidity, an honest report of observation, in the work of such women as Mrs. Cooke, Miss Murfree, Miss Jewett, and Miss Woolson which often leaves little to be desired.[3]

William Dean Howells, the author of the essay and one of the country's preeminent men of letters, consistently advocated realism in fiction. As Michael Davitt Bell notes in *The Problem of American Realism*, "It was with the 'Editor's Study' essays, beginning in 1886 and selectively reissued as *Criticism and Fiction* in 1891, that Howells emerged as the primary definer and defender of realism in America."[4] In calling their works "realistic," in praising their observations as "faithful" and "honest," Howells granted his imprimatur to such local color writers as Rose Terry Cooke, Mary N. Murfree, Sarah Orne Jewett, and Constance Fenimore Woolson. During the decade in which Howells's essay appeared, local color fiction reached its peak, appearing in the great literary journals of the day such as *Harper's Monthly, Scribner's*, the *Atlantic Monthly*, and the *Century*. Yet by the turn of the century local color fiction had fallen on hard times. Supplanted on the one hand by the naturalists, who opposed them, and on the other hand by the romance writers, with whom they increasingly joined ranks, the local colorists gradually faded from the scene.

To suggest that Howells and Norris merely existed as opposing ends of a single theoretical continuum, however, misstates the case. Howells himself encouraged younger writers, as he had encouraged the local colorists, and the tales of his kindness are legion, from his helping Hamlin Garland to earn a place in the literary life of Boston to his inviting a hungry Stephen Crane to dinner, and afterward reading to him from Emily

Dickinson.[5] Nor did Howells hesitate to praise the works of younger writers such as Abraham Cahan, Harold Frederic, Robert Herrick, Frank Norris, and Hamlin Garland, and he recognized a special literary kinship with Henry Blake Fuller by writing to him in 1909, "Can't you see it is your duty to write, hereafter, my novels for me?"[6] Howells was also quick to appreciate works as radically different from his own as Crane's *Maggie: A Girl of the Streets*.[7] He encouraged Crane to publish his work and offered Norris one of the few favorable reviews of *McTeague*.[8]

The naturalists in turn willingly acknowledged their early debt to Howells. Hamlin Garland, overcoming his early suspicions that Howells and James were somehow superficial, went on to imitate the former: "I wrote and rewrote, inspired by Howells, whose flexible yet always beautiful style I greatly admired."[9] "I developed all alone a little creed of art which I thought was a good one," Crane wrote to Lily Brandon Munroe. "Later I discovered that my creed was identical with the one of Howells and Garland. . . ."[10] And even Theodore Dreiser, whose attitude toward Howells as a "literary Columbus" is more eulogistic than strictly admiring, wrote the following to him in 1902: "If the common ground is to be credited with the flowering out of such minds as yours I shall not be disturbed to return to the dust."[11] Yet the naturalists' admiration for Howells, even their gratitude to him, failed to overcome their objections to realism itself. The respective positions of Howells and Norris exemplify these objections. Despite Howells's tireless promotion of a distinctly American literature based on realism, Norris dismissed realism in much the same way, and for many of the same reasons, that he had dismissed the idea of women writing novels. "Realism is minute, it is the drama of a broken teacup," writes Norris in a famous passage, "the tragedy of a walk down the block, the excitement of an afternoon call, the adventure of an invitation to dinner. . . . Realism bows upon the doormat and goes away and says to me, as we link arms on the sidewalk: 'That is life.' And I say it is not."[12] Norris's "teacup tragedies" remark seems to have summed up the earlier movement for an entire generation: realism was too tame, too hopelessly uneventful, and far too concerned with superficial problems of middle-class life. Basically, it was too feminine. As late as 1914, Dreiser grumbled that "a big city is not a little teacup to be seasoned by old maids."[13] And Sinclair Lewis's famous Nobel Prize speech, delivered in 1930, echoes the same sentiment. Calling realism "tea-table gentility,"

Lewis uttered the judgment that careless readers of Howells have repeated ever since: "Mr. Howells was one of the gentlest, sweetest, and most honest of men, but he had the code of a pious old maid whose greatest delight was to have tea at the vicarage."[14]

What becomes noteworthy in all these statements is not merely the facility with which Norris's phrase was repeated by other naturalists. The "old maids and teacups" idea implies timidity, an inability or unwillingness to face facts, to look at the "real life" beyond the lace curtains of one's parlor. It also is clearly pejorative, lumping realism with feminine literature in one unfavorable judgment. Nor is the image of the sheltered spinster writer merely an empty epithet hurled at Howells and James, the two realists most commonly tarred with the "old maids" brush. There *was* a school of sheltered spinster writers: the local colorists. As Ann Douglas points out, the female local color writers were largely unmarried or married at a late age.[15] Feeling trapped on the one hand by the "Iron Madonna," H. H. Boyesen's phrase for the pure young girl who comprised the target audience for novels, and on the other hand by a market overrun by female local color writers, the naturalists may well have been expressing their exasperation, not merely at a literature that had run its course, but at a proliferation of the feminine element that had at long last exceeded its bounds. Realism was not all local color, of course, and yet a continual thread of feeling runs through the works of Norris and other naturalists: that "real life," the stuff of literature, was not the same as the realists' teacup tragedies, and that the fit ones to write about real life were men (naturalists), not women (local color writers). It suggests that naturalism grew in part as a gender-based countertradition not only to realism but to female-dominated local color writing. This displacement of the local color movement, and the gender-linked oppositions between naturalism and local color that contributed to it, are the subject of the present study.

· II ·

The displacement of local color fiction and those women who were its contributors occurred as part of a broader shift from realism to naturalism, which in turn marked the passing of a nineteenth-century sensibility and the emergence of a twentieth-century one.[16] Critical studies of each period have scrutinized one or more of the vexed questions inherent in any discussion of realism and naturalism: the endless problems of defining *realism* and *naturalism;*[17] the representation or construction of a carefully crafted and ideologically inflected "reality"; and the oppositions of high culture and low and their metonymic counterparts of the literary East and the roughneck West.[18] Equally significant is the opposition between realism and naturalism based on gender noted by several critics including Eric Sundquist, who posits a further bifurcation: "[E]conomic or political power can itself be seen to be definitive of a realist aesthetic, in that those in power (say, white urban males) have been more often judged 'realists,' while those removed from the seats of power (say, Midwesterners, blacks, immigrants, or women) have been categorized as regionalists."[19] Local color fiction was not, of course, exclusively or even primarily the domain of white, middle-class women writers. As Elizabeth Ammons and Richard Brodhead have demonstrated, local color writing granted a more egalitarian access to the profession of authorship, its characteristic value of inclusivity encompassing the work not only of white male practitioners such as George Washington Cable, Philander Deming, Thomas Nelson Page, James Lane Allen, and Bret Harte but of Charles Waddell Chesnutt, Sui Sin Far, Paul Laurence Dunbar, Alice Dunbar-Nelson, and Zitkala Ša (Gertrude Simmons Bonnin).[20] The naturalists' anxieties about ethnicity tended to be linked to those of class and the threat of proletarianization. Their anxieties about art and writing, on the other hand, pivot on the issue of gender dominance and the encoding of realism and local color as feminine. It is the naturalists' perceptions about local color rather than the actual demographics of its practitioners that inform my argument.

Despite the well-documented opposition between realism and naturalism, the contemporaneous opposition of women's local color fiction and naturalism has received comparatively little attention. Two recent books, Michael Davitt Bell's *Problem of American Realism* (1993) and Richard Brodhead's *Cultures of Letters* (1993), address what Bell calls "a 'woman's place' in American realism" (166), each surveying the gendered inflections of local color fiction and the cultural work it performs before offering a carefully reasoned corrective to the feminist critics and their vision of female community. Bell situates Jewett's primary allegiances not in female community but in her professional identity as an author, an idea that Brodhead seconds with his contextualization of Jewett within genre traditions other than that of women's writing, most notably the "high culture" represented by Annie Fields and her salon and the "topoi of travel writing" within which Jewett's work appeared in the *Atlantic Monthly*. *Resisting Regionalism* differs from these works in that it focuses directly on what is necessarily an ancillary issue for Bell and Brodhead: the ways in which the naturalists' response to women's local color fiction was shaped not only by literary generation or by genre, but by gender as well. Brodhead questions the marginal position ascribed by feminists to local color fiction, and indeed naturalistic works reinforce this idea, suggesting as they do the problems of being young male writers in a literary climate seemingly dominated by elderly female local colorists. Between 1889 and 1901, for example, naturalistic authors Frank Norris and Jack London each published only one short piece in the *Atlantic;* Jewett, by contrast, published thirteen stories and two book-length works in the *Atlantic* alone during the same period. Responding to the tradition of local color "authoresses" such as Rose Terry Cooke, Mary E. Wilkins Freeman, and Sarah Orne Jewett, a loosely defined generational cohort of naturalistic writers such as Crane, Frederic, Norris, London, and Wharton did not hesitate to critique, to rewrite, and ultimately to reject local color's self-imposed limitations of style, form, and subject, and with them the "feminine" values at the heart of the movement.

· III ·

The oppositions that exemplify this radical shift become clear in examining each movement's central ideological premises. Emerging after the Civil War, a time when "[t]he country's internal migration of younger men and women to new urban areas has left behind a ghost world of spinsters, widows, and bereft sea captains," local color fiction celebrates the preservation, through writing, of the lives of humble, ordinary people in an environment threatened by time, change, and external disruption.[21] In part because of these factors, the fiction itself frequently denies or ignores the events immediately surrounding its creation, a strategy to "universalize" the work that results from an unwillingness to dwell on the cause of the disruption and loss that the region had suffered.[22] In celebrating not disruption but continuity, not timely events but timelessness, local color seeks to affirm what is usable about the past and the ordinary: its reluctance to deal with war stems not from a failure to understand war's importance, but from an insistence on the primacy of the enduring world that exists both prior to and as a consequence of war's disruption.

Local color fiction finds strength in looking to the past for its values, seeing in the dying economies and vanishing folkways of its pictured regions an America that never existed. Describing the "cultural work of nineteenth-century regionalism" as "cultural elegy," Brodhead comments that "nineteenth-century regionalism can be said to have manufactured, in its monthly-renewed public imaging of old-fashioned social worlds, a cultural version of D. W. Winnicott's transitional object: a symbol of union with the premodern chosen at the moment of separation from it."[23] As a "transitional object" for the insecure modern age, the local color world resists change, externally by encouraging the isolation of the region from the outside world, and internally by emphasizing community rituals. Much of the literature insists on continuity: revered figures in the fiction of Sarah Orne Jewett, Mary Wilkins Freeman, and Rose Terry Cooke are elderly people who hold the community together by their tales of the old days, passing on stories and traditions to a new generation.[24] Not surprisingly, physical and spiritual endurance in the face of adversity, as shown by these elderly survivors, ranks high both as a virtue and as a theme in local color fiction. It is this combination of values—continuity, community, reverence for the past, and above all endurance rather than defiance in the face of adversity—that many local colorists extolled in their writings, and that the naturalists overturned in theirs.

That these were not the values of naturalistic writers Frank Norris, Stephen Crane, Theodore Dreiser, Harold Frederic, and Jack London should be clear to anyone who has read, however cursorily, a naturalistic novel.[25] "Revelling in the extraordinary, the excessive, and the grotesque in order to reveal the immutable bestiality of Man in Nature," writes Eric Sundquist, "naturalism dramatizes the loss of individuality at a physiological level by making a Calvinism without God its determining order and violent death its utopia."[26] Nineteenth-century local color writers functioned as chroniclers who valued tradition and found in the isolated villages exactly what they sought there: human nature in a less mechanized, hence simpler, state. Influenced by evolutionary theorists Herbert Spencer and Charles Darwin and by French naturalists such as the Goncourt brothers and Émile Zola, naturalistic writers looked not to the rural past for their subjects but to the urban present. They pursued the study of human nature at its most elemental by reaching not back in time as did the local colorists but down in class, working on "a kind of implicit Benthamite assumption that the life lived by the greatest number is somehow the most real."[27] Shaped by a "new journalism" that would make great daily papers like the New York *Sun* and the *World* their "first great school of practical experience,"[28] the naturalists also valued the city over the local color village, for, as Philip Fisher argues in *Hard Facts*, "[A]ny city gives a map of the psyche, a quantitative account of the strength and complexity of the system of human desires at a given cultural moment. . . . Unlike nature . . . within the city anything outside the body is there only because it was projected by will and need."[29] What better place to study elemental man, the naturalists' "beast within," than in the city, where his characteristics are intensified, magnified by projections of his "will and need"; where, as Fisher points out, mirrors are in every direction and "man is for the first time surrounded by himself"?[30] Lee Clark Mitchell locates the essential difference between realism and naturalism in the distinction he draws between realist "selves" with claims to agency and naturalistic "characters" inescapably inscribed within the text: "Naturalism . . . [turned] our attention to fictional worlds into which its characters are absorbed, not to selves that stand somehow free of those worlds. The triumph of naturalism, in short, was to estrange us from the very notion of a self."[31] If the hallmark of local color fiction was its preservation of the self within a matrix of absence and loss, the naturalistic "character," to use Mitchell's formulation, paradoxically faced refraction of the self and ultimately absorption within a culture glutted with possibilities.

Yet the naturalists shared certain objectives with their local color predecessors: a commitment to the accurate and detailed representation of ordinary human beings, a fascination with tracing the workings of heredity, and a belief in the shaping power of the environment. Unlike their local color counterparts, however, naturalistic characters rarely have a "tradition" upon which to draw; instead they have a "past" or an inherited "tendency" that, far from providing them with moral strength in times of crisis, proves instead to be something that they must overcome. Naturalistic characters stumble headlong into their misfortunes, unaware that, as the sage narrative voice tells the reader, they are driven by inherited traits like McTeague's "foul taint" of alcoholism or by Dreiserian "chemisms" beyond their control.[32] More ominously, the overt racism inherent in

Norris's and London's preoccupation with "Anglo-Saxon" blood and in Thomas Nelson Page's plantation fiction finds a more genteel but no less disturbing expression in the local colorists' interest in lines of kinship and descent. For example, in Jewett's *A Country Doctor*, Dr. Leslie praises Nan Prince's potential by weighing her matrilineal past against the patrilineal "taint" of alcoholism (and desire for class mobility) to which her mother had fallen prey: "So far as I can see, she has the good qualities of all her ancestors without the bad ones. Her mother's mother was an old fashioned country woman of the best stock."[33] Cooke's and Freeman's obstinate characters create their own tribulations through a purposeful preoccupation with living up to their "good stock" and a perverse pride in their "morbidly sensitive conscience and overdeveloped will."[34] Further, like Crane's Maggie Johnson or Dreiser's Carrie Meeber, the inhabitants of *The Country of the Pointed Firs* are shaped and defined by their environment, as the emphasis implied by the title makes clear. Writing her impressions of New England in the *Century* (1895), Rebecca Harding Davis noted that New Englanders had "given up the lofty Puritan faith and . . . kept the objectionable Puritan temperament," a transformation attributable to "the effect which a century of insufficient food, narrow interests, hard economy, and superfluous education has produced in them."[35] Heredity and environment in this way have merged, the willful characteristics of decayed Puritanism reinforced by the inhabitants' struggle against the stubborn, rocky land, until land and people seem but manifestations of each other.[36]

Despite this common ground, the naturalists opposed the principles of the local colorists, a position discernable through such points of access as the antithetical themes of self-denial and degeneration, the central metaphor of storytelling, and the inclusion of a self-conscious outside observer. The first two of these, storytelling and self-denial, allow the predominantly female local color characters to wrest a sort of grim satisfaction from their ability to endure the blighted hopes and shattered expectations of local color fiction. Through their endless descriptions of accumulated objects and their ambivalent but frequently admiring portraits of buccaneer capitalists, naturalistic authors, on the other hand, celebrated reportorial immediacy and a kind of experiential excess in behavior, an excess that led to brutishness. Yet even the danger of degeneration into brutishness seemed preferable to intense self-denial and endurance, for these virtues represented the almost suffocatingly insular and feminine outdated world of local color fiction. Indeed, the sheer number of words that they showered on an increasingly receptive public suggests a commitment to overthrowing the small, careful, and limited sketches of the local colorists.

The third parallel between naturalists and local colorists involves the spectatorial distance necessary to the works of both traditions. Naturalistic authors and their representatives within the works typically saw themselves as outsiders or observers; they assumed the stance of interpreters, thereby establishing de facto that the culture they were about to examine was in some way alien to their readers. Underlying the narrative voice or observer's position is always the assumption—sometimes voiced, sometimes not—that these people are objects of study because they are not "like us" in education, class, and ethnicity. The outsider's view becomes not only implicitly normative but an important position, sometimes of privilege, sometimes of exclusion, through which the reader may enter the text. June Howard contends that in naturalistic novels populated by characters whose lack of self-awareness would not otherwise permit reader identification or interpretation, such a position also serves as a safe vantage point for readers: "But although we explore determinism, we are never submerged in it and ourselves become the brute."[37] Howard further argues that "the barrier that separates the privileged spectator from the helpless actor, the free from the unfree, seems to imprison both" (126), for the price of this privileged stance is passivity or paralysis on the part of the observer. Both Howard and Rachel Bowlby stress seeing, not doing, as crucial to this stance, as observation and action (read: intellect and physical being) rarely coexist in naturalism. To consume is to risk being consumed, and if to act is to risk being engulfed by the world of forces, then "just looking" becomes a survival skill in the threatening world of the naturalistic novel, even if it means assuming the racial and class-based biases of the authorially inscribed spectator.

Similarly, in local color fiction the observer-interpreter appears occasionally as a character in the work but more frequently emerges in the persona assumed by the narrative voice. The world of local color fiction is by definition special in that it is self-enclosed and isolated from the larger world by time, customs, and geography. Its people are "characters" in several senses of the word: they do not share the implied audience's sophistication, geographic location, or even ways of speaking, strategies that

Brodhead suggests are a means of acknowledging the threat of the foreign within the "real sounding yet deeply fictitious America" created by local color authors.[38] By mediating between the enclosed world of the region and the larger world beyond, the observer serves as a buffer, exploring, explaining, and protecting the world she studies. At the same time, the very exposure of this world to an outside audience threatens its existence, for drawing attention to a place risks the incursions of others, either the figurative incursions of unsympathetic readers or the actual invasion of travelers.[39] The contradictions embodied in the impulse to write—preservation and destruction—are matched by the conflicting desires of the observer herself: drawn to the local color community, she is finally excluded by the same communal feeling she celebrates. Similarly, the observer recognizes that her modern consciousness, her own sense of the "otherness" generated by class and education, prevents her return to the innocence of such a place, and she carefully removes herself from it, either physically, like the narrator in *The Country of the Pointed Firs*, or by the tone and language she adopts, as in works by Rose Terry Cooke. She embodies both Sylvie and the naturalist in Jewett's "A White Heron": her dilemma is that, to preserve the rare specimen, she must kill it, and this she tries to avoid. Thus the observer's stance in both traditions is not only important, but precarious; and its use by naturalistic and local color authors provides a critical point of access in comparing the two movements.

The gradual decline of women's local color fiction and the rise of American naturalism at the turn of the nineteenth century thus should not, indeed cannot, be seen as discrete events, contemporaneous occurrences that otherwise have little bearing on each other. The rhetoric employed by the writers of the time suggests not a transition but rather a genteelly pitched battle between the two, a conflict ended by the successful subversion and banishment of local color fiction. The second chapter of the present work, "Necessary Limits," lays out some of the battle lines for this genteel conflict, exploring the sources of local color fiction and its parallels with naturalism through the linked themes of self-denial and storytelling. The third chapter, "Opening the Door to the 'Masculine Principle,'" explores the critical reaction against local color fiction, tracing not so much the path of its decline as that of its fragmentation and evolution as it became rewritten into a host of new forms, among them the local color tale of the "Old Folks" that Norris inscribes in his naturalistic novel

McTeague (1899). "Frederic, Norris, and the Fear of Effeminacy," the fourth chapter, examines some ways in which Harold Frederic and Frank Norris expressed their frustration with the dominance of feminine discourse, including the then-current prominence of local color literature, through their portraits of overcivilized men weakened by excessive doses of feminine culture. Reflecting the fluctuating exchange values of urban capitalism rather than the intensely centered, static values of local color fiction, the protagonists of such novels as Norris's *Vandover and the Brute* and Frederic's *Damnation of Theron Ware* experience not only fragmentation but degeneration, a figure for the age's concern with redefining its art and culture along more "appropriate" (i.e., more masculine) lines.

The fifth chapter, "Dreiser, London, Crane, and the Iron Madonna," investigates the naturalists' handling of the alterity of gender as well as class, briefly surveying the fallen woman's redemptive resistance to language before analyzing the ways in which London and Crane use the power of language as a weapon against the "Iron Madonna." The last section of the chapter analyzes *The Monster* as Crane's consummate local color "outsider" story, a story of alienation that inscribes naturalism within the local color world. The sixth chapter, "Edith Wharton and the 'Authoresses,'" explores Wharton's work as a culmination of these ideas, an example of how the literary alliances of a strongly feminine, gender-linked tradition like local color gave way before the imperatives of a predominantly masculine and generation-based rebellion against established forms. As Crane had done in *George's Mother*, Wharton transposes the local color story to an urban setting in "Mrs. Manstey's View" and *Bunner Sisters* (written 1891-1892) to critique the limitations of the local colorists' artistic and social perspectives. In later novels such as *Ethan Frome* and *Summer*, Wharton confronts and rewrites the genre of local color fiction on its own terms, using its settings and characters to disrupt and transform its narrative conventions, the assumptions underlying its iconographic and symbolic structures such as storytelling, preserving, and healing, and its insistence on the value of self-denial. Her work, like that of her naturalistic contemporaries, indicates a consistent, sustained effort to address the problems and limits of local color as a genre, and to demonstrate, through the creation of a new form of fiction, its inadequacies and its dangers as an art form.

CHAPTER TWO

Necessary Limits
Women's Local Color Fiction

· I ·

"The 'eighties in the history of the American short story were ruled by the 'local colorists,'" wrote Fred Lewis Pattee in 1923. "It was the period of dialect stories, of small peculiar groups isolated and analyzed, of unique local 'characters' presented primarily for exhibition."[1] As a literature that treated such seemingly inhospitable themes as absence, loss, limitation, and the past, local color confronted some formidable obstacles in its rise to prominence, a prominence made possible in part by its minute representation of regional folkways and dialects. During this period, local color nonetheless fulfilled some specific needs of the public—for nostalgia, for a retreat into mildly exotic locales, for a semblance of order preserved in ritual, for positively regarded values—and, like other movements, it was discarded once those needs were no longer pressing.

The deeper appeal of women's local color fiction, however, exists both in the possibility of power through restraint with which it tantalizes its readers, and in the strategies of control that it articulates for them. On a community level, these elements involve local color's denial of paternalistic codes of order, especially as embodied in ministers, and its subsequent valorizing of the creation of community through women's rituals. Such strategies, embodied thematically in the repeated, multivalent use of individual self-denial and iconographically in the use of storytelling and preserving, comprise a rhetorical scheme for interpreting local color fiction. An examination of these elements in works by Rose Terry Cooke, Sarah Orne Jewett, Mary E. Wilkins Freeman, and Constance Fenimore Woolson illustrates the varieties of compensations, indeed of pleasures, that these writers offer against local color's great matrix of loss. Women's local color fiction thus provides an antithetical context to naturalistic fiction, a background against which the early naturalists' insistence upon man's aggressive nature, upon natural (rather than man-made) law, and upon the fresh, unmediated reporting of experiences become markers of a rebellion against the literary status quo. Tracing the rise of local color and these significant elements of it thus not only demonstrates some sources of the naturalists' antagonism, but also establishes some sources of the local colorists' power.

· II ·

The literary antecedents of local color are various, but the movement's historians generally credit two traditions as giving rise to it. The first of these, frontier humor, paved the way for local color fiction through its extensive use of dialect.[2] Readers accustomed to the dialect conventions of the frontier humor sketch were less likely to balk at the use of such homely devices in the more serious fiction of the local colorists. Also, the tall-story tradition central to frontier humor gave local color fiction its two characteristic forms, the anecdote and the character sketch.[3] Finally, frontier humor was uniquely American, and writing an—if not *the*—American literature is what the local colorists were after. Though the folklore traditions of many countries include tricksters and tellers of tall tales, the situations and characters of frontier humorists such as Augustus Baldwin Longstreet (1790-1870), George Washington Harris (1814-1869), and Thomas Bangs Thorpe (1815-1878) derived much of their effect from their American context.[4] As frontier humor became domesticated and as one of its permutations evolved into local color writing, the works of the second generation of frontier humorists began to appear in publications with broader circulation instead of in "frontier" newspapers or sporting journals like *The Spirit of the Times*. For example, the crude humor of Mark Twain's (1835-1910) early hoaxes like "A Washoe Joke" and "A Bloody Massacre near Carson" gave way to a more respectable variety in "Jim Smiley and His Jumping Frog," a Western local color sketch later collected as the title story of *The Celebrated Jumping Frog of Calaveras County and Other Sketches* (1867).[5] Twain's sometime friend and longtime rival Bret Harte (1836-1902) published "The Luck of Roaring Camp" in the August 1868 issue of the *Overland Monthly*; widely reprinted, and included in the 1870 volume *The Luck of Roaring Camp and Other Sketches,* Harte's tale helped to establish a market for Western stories.[6] Years later, in "The Rise of the 'Short

Story'" (1899), Harte suggested that American humor freed American literature from the constraints of English tradition, in the process identifying the essential qualities of American humor:

> It was concise and condense [*sic*], yet suggestive. It was delightfully extravagant—or a miracle of understatement. It voiced not only the dialect, but the habits of thought of a people or locality. . . . [I]t admitted no fine writing nor affectation of style. It went directly to the point. It was burdened by no conscientiousness; it was often irreverent; it was devoid of all moral responsibility—but it was original![7]

Though the humorous sketch to which Harte refers is antecedent to local color short stories, his comments apply to the later form, especially since his and others' interest in representing "the habits of thought of a people or locality" grew as the century progressed. Even as they poked fun at American experience, then, these stories helped to define it for their audience, and not incidentally to show how regional differences could be exploited for literary effects.

A second source—the "truth" without the "stretchers"—is the early realistic and local color elements in women's fiction, especially as practiced by Harriet Beecher Stowe (1811-1896) and her contemporaries. Stowe's use of an actual location on the Maine coast for *The Pearl of Orr's Island* (1862) helped to establish the vogue for realistic regional settings, and her depiction of realistic locale, of regional character types, and of accurately observed dialect prefigure later local color works thematically as well, containing, according to Josephine Donovan, "the earliest extended description of a precapitalist, preindustrial matriarchal community—a topos characteristic of the New England local colorists." Not incidentally, *The Pearl of Orr's Island* was "the most influential work [Sarah Orne Jewett] read as a youth."[8] Like her "literary daughters" Jewett and Freeman,[9] Stowe created regional types who exist not merely to interact as characters, thereby exemplifying a moral or emotional lesson, but to reenact and preserve perishable folkways, thus illustrating a cultural-historical lesson as well. For *Oldtown Folks* (1869), another work that adumbrates conventional local color fiction, Stowe drew upon her own experiences in Litchfield (Cloudland), Connecticut, and her husband's childhood in Natick (Oldtown), Massachusetts.[10] Her character Sam Lawson, a "Yankee Uncle

Remus" who, "with his shambling gait and mighty drawl has been called the truest Yankee in fiction," proved popular enough for a sequel, *Sam Lawson's Oldtown Fireside Stories* (1872), a series of short tales in dialect that Sam tells to the eager boys of the village.[11]

Stowe's near contemporary, the Connecticut writer Rose Terry Cooke (1827-1892), was one of the earliest local colorists to confine herself to the form in her adult fiction. Less famous now than Freeman and Jewett, Cooke was celebrated in her own day for her stories of rural New England; as Jay Martin comments, "In the first great issue of the *Atlantic* in 1857, hers was the lead story; and from then until her death [1892] . . . she was its foremost contributor of short stories."[12] Cooke, like Stowe, addressed the effects of a stringent Calvinism on the region and its people, but stories such as "Too Late" present no didactic commentary promising a better future. Her studies of the famously intransigent New England will, such as "Freedom Wheeler's Controversy with Providence," and of drab lives and silent, bitter marital conflicts, such as "Mrs. Flint's Married Experience," anticipate Mary Wilkins Freeman's treatment of similar issues.

The 1870s and 1880s saw a rapid increase in the number of local color stories published, as the new movement began separating itself from the traditions of women's fiction and frontier humor from which it had sprung. As early as 1870, William Dean Howells (1837-1920) had begun promoting local color in fiction. Praising Bjørnstjerne Bjørnson's novels for the "singular simplicity" of the narration and their portrayal of "humble but decent folk," Howells suggests that New England writers study Bjørnson's stories, since "[s]ome of the traits that he sketches are those now of New England fishermen and farmers and of Western pioneers. . . . A conscientiousness also exists in them which is like our own."[13] Later essays in definition, such as James Lane Allen's "Local Color" (*Critic*, 9 January 1886) further helped to explain the movement's purposes. Allen compares the painter's and the writer's use of color, decreeing that, like the painter, "the writer must lay upon his canvas those colors that are true for the region he is describing and characteristic of it." The mere accumulation of colors is nevertheless not enough:

> From an artistic point of view, the aim of local color should be to make the picture of human life natural and beautiful, or dreary, or sombre, or terrific, as the special character of the theme may demand; from a

scientific point of view, the aim of local color is to make the picture of life natural and—*intelligible*, by portraying those picturable potencies in nature that made it what it was and must go along with it to explain what it is. The novelist must encompass both aims.[14]

The first requirement, argue Howells and Allen, is that the stories be flexible and true to their theme, employing formulaic local color elements such as dialect, stock characters, or dry humor not as mere "colorful" decoration, but to explain regional variations in human behavior.

With such encouragement, a new generation of local color stories joined those of Harte, Stowe, and Cooke in the pages of the great literary journals of the time. In New England, Rowland E. Robinson (1833-1900) wrote of the Yankee farmers in the hill country of Vermont in a spare prose similar to that with which Mary Wilkins Freeman (1852-1930) was describing their fellows in western Massachusetts. Sarah Orne Jewett (1849-1909) inherited Stowe's fictional terrain, the coastal villages of Maine, while her fellow New Englanders Alice Brown (1857-1948) and Celia Thaxter (1835-1894) wrote about New Hampshire. In the Midwest, Edward Eggleston's (1837-1902) *Hoosier Schoolmaster* (1871) and E. W. Howe's (1853-1937) *Story of a Country Town* (1883) mixed gritty, realistic details of backwoods life with sentimentalized plots, as did Hamlin Garland's (1860-1940) own first collection of stories, *Main-Travelled Roads* (1891). Constance Fenimore Woolson (1840-1894) wrote of the Michigan lake country in stories such as those collected in *Castle Nowhere* (1875), though works such as *For the Major* (1883), set in North Carolina, and *The Front Yard* (1895), set in Italy, depict other locales. The less innovative short stories of Alice French (1850-1934), who wrote under the pseudonym Octave Thanet, are set in Arkansas and Iowa. Mary Austin's (1868-1934) spare desert stories collected in *The Land of Little Rain* (1903) covered the same Western subjects as autobiographical narratives by Zitkala Ša (Gertrude Simmons Bonnin) (1876-1938).

In the South, the Tennessee author called Charles Egbert Craddock wrote so convincingly with "[t]he severely simple, the robust, the athletic" hand of a man that "his" true identity as Mary Noailles Murfree (1850-1922) came as a shock to Howells. Howells ranked Murfree as "the first to express a true Southern quality in fiction."[15] James Lane Allen (1849-1925) contributed critical articles and sketches of his native Kentucky to *Harper's* and other magazines, publishing several novels about the region in the 1890s.

Another Southerner, Joel Chandler Harris (1848-1908), famous for his "Uncle Remus" stories in black dialect, captured life in postwar Georgia in works such as *Mingo and Other Sketches in Black and White* (1884); the works of Thomas Nelson Page (1853-1922) deal more sentimentally with antebellum life in collections such as *In Ole Virginia* (1887). Closer to the century's end, Kate Chopin (1850-1904) and Grace King (1851-1932) followed George Washington Cable (1844-1925) in their studies of Louisiana's French population. In 1899, Charles Waddell Chesnutt (1858-1932) deftly undercut the racism implicit in the plantation tradition of Page and the dialect tradition of Harris with *The Conjure Woman*, the same year that Alice Dunbar-Nelson (1875-1935) addressed the issues of race obliquely in *The Goodness of St. Rocque, and Other Stories*.[16]

· III ·

The number and the diversity of the local color writers suggest that the reading public was ready for them. Local color fiction gained popularity because of, not in spite of, its fixation on such seemingly inhospitable subjects as absence, loss, limitation, and the past. In exploring these preoccupations, the local color writers offered strategies of control, ways of countering the bewildering array of threats from an increasingly industrialized postbellum world.

The most immediate examples of fragmentation and loss confronting the local color audience were the Civil War and the decline of village life. Critics from Harte to the present day date the roots of the movement to the war, and for good reason: rigid, politically defined regionalism had helped to cause the war; now a literary, nonpolitical version of regionalism would help to heal the nation's spiritual wounds.[17] Although largely silent about the war itself, female regionalists addressed squarely the other major source of change: the loss of village life.[18] They were not alone in doing so: the literary journals of the day consistently featured essays lamenting this decline. For example, in 1897 the *Atlantic Monthly* ran a series on New England villages: Alvan F. Sanborn's "Future of Rural New England" (July 1897) contrasts the decaying town of Dickerman with the thriving one of Indian Ridge, while Philip Morgan's "Problems of Rural New England: A Remote Village" (May 1897) combines character sketch with an elegiac defense of the villagers' "good stock" and the "absolute equality which prevails among us," two of the more frequent staple fictions of local color.[19] In a two-part 1899 *Atlantic Monthly* essay chronicling New England's decline, Rollin Lynde Hartt blames the inhabitants themselves for this decline, citing their proud insularity as well as their habit of inbreeding and producing children of "abnormal heredity." He also faults the outside world for the state of things in the fictional town of Sweet Auburn:

> The hill town is already an anachronism. It confronts an Everlasting No. It cannot maintain itself in opposition to the relentless forces of social reconstruction; and consequently, those who hold all neighborly, ancestral, homely things most dear must witness not merely the aesthetic, but also the industrial, moral, and social decadence of their beloved Sweet Auburn.[20]

Hartt captures perfectly the public's ambivalence toward the long-settled village. Even in its undisputed decay, it represents the last bastion of traditional values, a sentiment metaphorically conveyed by Hartt's description of homely village treasures plundered by antique hunters from the outside world. In a contemporary *Atlantic Monthly* article, Charles Miner Thompson took exception to Mary Wilkins Freeman's portraits of decaying New England villages, charging that she depicted only the negative side of them; Hartt, on the other hand, counters that she is "deficient in artistic audacity; she understates the case."[21]

Because the dying New England villages and the ravaged plantations of the South presented all too grim a spectacle to those who wished to remember better times, local color writers depicted a doubly distanced golden age that remains within the landscape of loss as a significant absence, perpetuating its own myth by daily contrast with the straitened circumstances of the present. The stories thereby constitute the past in two parts: a peaceful golden age of prosperity, projected as always absent from and prior to the second era, the hard times that characterize the recent past. An ever-receding landscape that, like Jewett's Dunnet Landing, stands "high above the sea for a few minutes" and threatens to sink "back into the uniformity of the coast," the glorified past exists primarily, and precariously, through the mythmaking abilities of the villagers and their interpreter, the local color writer.[22] Yet the recent past offers its own myth, one of an unexpected sort. In contrast to the imagined golden age, the local color landscape is frequently one of ruin and desolation, as Ann Douglas has shown in "The Literature of Impoverishment": "In diametric contrast to the lush and fecund fictional world of the sentimentalists, the Local Colorists' imaginary territory is dominated by the laws of scarcity: the wherewithal of life has somehow been withheld and the inhabitants quite literally must get bread from stones."[23] Nor are these inhabitants well suited to the struggle, being disproportionately "women not young and beautiful, but mostly middle-aged and elderly, usually spinsters or widows, usually poor and 'without prospects.'"[24] Within this framework, however, values of simplicity and social harmony replace the prosperity of an earlier era in maintaining a vital community of women.[25] Just as the characters within the stories draw strength from their memories of past glory, so too do the readers of local color fiction find confirmation of another kind of golden age: the reassuring myth that despite the upheavals of the Civil War and increasing industrialization, as well as the threat of immigration, a set of simple, enduring values and an age of moral certainty still existed within the isolated villages described in local color fiction.

Local color fiction also purposefully explores other varieties of absence, notably those of the outside world and physical violence. The economic and social markers of loss parallel other absent elements, including those that would bring the local color world too closely into contact with the "outside" world: specific location of the story in time, overt politicizing, and sensational actions or physical violence.[26] Significantly, overt physical violence is rare in most local color fiction, though there is an abundance of the emotional variety.[27] The physical violence that does exist—the occasional suicide or schoolboy fight—involves individuals acting from personal convictions or intense emotions. An especially suggestive absence is that of a particular kind of violence: the spectacle of men in groups acting against each other for reasons of ideological differences rarely if ever occurs. Local color works thus frequently disregard the usual fictional staples: current politics, violence, youth, romantic love, cities, wealth, fashionable society, world travel, and action-filled, intricate plots.

Working within these limitations, however, women local color writers found a surprising strength. Committed as they were to faithful representation, bound imaginatively by the geographic and temporal restraints of depicting a particular region and its people, they found little necessity for fictional excursions into a larger realm, although their choice for limitation has caused accusations of narrowness and insularity to be leveled against them from the very start. An anonymous *Atlantic Monthly* reviewer, speaking of Jewett's *Country By-Ways* (1881), frets lest he "see her gifts possibly diminish in efficacy by too close a confinement and too narrow a range."[28] Yet although his concern reverberates throughout the criticism of local color, feminist critics have reinterpreted the form's limitations in a more positive light.[29] Millicent Bell, for example, praises local color as a literature of margins. Using dialect, "the language of social marginality," and describing a world populated by women, the local colorists represented this "world on the margins of American society" as nonetheless a source of strength and authentic values, an alternative to the "pervertedness or sterility of capitalist centrism."[30] For Elizabeth Ammons, too, the inherent formal limitations of the sketch constitute a virtue rather than a flaw: "[I]t is the finiteness, the limitedness of the authorial project, brilliant in its detailed concrete accuracy perhaps, but lacking in any pretension to impressive scope, that makes the sketch appealing—as well perhaps as 'feminine.'"[31] In articulating the form of their fiction, the local colorists imposed limitations that forced them to mimic their characters' own struggle. In articulating their themes, they promoted the idea of strength in, indeed through, limitation.

In demonstrating how local color could flourish despite its self-imposed generic constraints, Charles Miner Thompson identified some of the elements of wealth and presence with which the local colorists balanced their visions of loss and absence. In the 1899 *Atlantic Monthly* essay "Miss Wilkins: An Idealist in Masquerade," Thompson catalogues these elements in analyzing the popularity of Freeman's volume *A Humble Romance and Other Stories* (1887):

> It is easy to understand the success of a book which reproduces with a great wealth of accurate and homely detail a life which is still close to the richest and most cultivated of us, and which is of the very fibre of our thought and character,—a book which, in a land where women are the larger portion of the reading public, is written exclusively from the feminine point of view; but I choose to think that it was mainly the insistence upon a fine basic quality of New England character which made A Humble Romance [*sic*] come with all the force of a new revelation of New England to itself.[32]

In other words, local color fiction doubly negates varieties of loss and restraint through its creation of a fictional community of women writing for other women, and through its profusion of "homely detail" that masks the lack of a more sumptuous kind. The local colorists' attention to detail is therefore inseparable from their fictional purposes, indicating as it does the necessity for integrating the whole of life, however seemingly trivial or distasteful, into a coherent moral vision.

In addition to its appeal to a specific feminine audience and its reliance on realistic detail, local color offered a degree of moral definition and certainty, a sense of individual control to counteract the helplessness and incipient anomie of postbellum urban life. As increasing urbanization, industrial and technological growth, and rapid advances in transportation created a sense of uncontrolled and uncontrollable growth, readers welcomed a literature that defined specific parameters and identifiable codes of conduct. Unlike the world of the naturalistic novel, the world of local color fiction presents problems—how to pay a mortgage, regain a lover, preserve dignity in poverty—not only recognizable on a human scale but amenable to human intervention. That many of the protagonists fail to intervene successfully is beside the point. Through the clearly delineated system of values presented in the stories, readers could recognize the inherent pathology in the New England will, or stubborn Southern pride, or parsimonious habits, and reorder or rewrite the protagonist's choice accordingly. The local colorists offered an appearance of order, closure, and humanity in a world that increasingly failed to provide them. Not overtly didactic like many popular women's novels of the 1850s, local color nevertheless presents the same comforting illusion: the opportunity for control in a recent past that, unlike the present, permits not only problems on a human scale but the luxury of choice.

Thus against the great matrix of absence and loss stand the positive kinds of control, including the remaking of a usable past and the careful reconstruction of lives within enforced limitations, that in large measure define women's local color fiction. What critics consider to be its positive values—among them patience, loyalty, responsibility, and compassion—all presuppose not merely the moral capacity to distinguish and choose right over wrong but the willingness to apply this knowledge even against one's own interests. This capacity, and these virtues, are presented as feminine in local color fiction, as is the self-sacrifice necessary to the implementation of these values within local color communities. Yet these are the same values that Kimball King and others find to be literary weaknesses, most charitably described as vestiges of the "conventional feminine virtues" of the "sentimental" novelists.[33] The moment at which such traditional feminine and local color values became literary liabilities intersects one point at which "the feminine" in literature came to be equated with literary inferiority—and, not coincidentally, with the appearance of naturalism as a literary force.

It is precisely at these points of difference between naturalism and local color that the strength of local color as a genre reveals itself. The naturalists considered themselves innovators, bold searchers for the real life beneath the sham and hypocrisy of a community's formal orders and patterns, particularly as those patterns were imposed by the bourgeoisie upon a powerless underclass of lower- and working-class people. Yet the local colorists conducted a quiet rebellion of their own along very much the same lines, showing the hollow, legalistic, often destructive, and finally useless forms imposed by an idealistic male culture (represented often by ministers) upon a community of women. Further, the naturalists admired strength and an active will by means of which man confronts his fate; to become resigned to fate in naturalistic fiction is in some measure to fail. Local colorists, on the other hand, promoted self-denial and acceptance not only as necessary survival tactics but as the means of creating a genuine, if attenuated, satisfaction in life. Finally, the naturalists (in theory, at least) prized spontaneous and random observation. Their storytelling techniques, like those of journalism, promoted immediate, vivid, and comprehensive (rather than selective) reporting of events, all characteristics that tend to presuppose a wide, indiscriminately addressed audience. By contrast, the local colorists, through the motif of storytelling in their fiction, emphasized a homogeneous, empathic audience, insisting that stories are incomplete until they are shared and carefully preserving the story's "essence." Through an examination of some works by Rose Terry Cooke, Mary Wilkins Freeman, Sarah Orne Jewett, and Constance Fenimore Woolson, it becomes clear that these three themes, far from being annoying "weaknesses," are actually used with a complexity that demonstrates both their importance in creating strong local color fiction and some surprising points of contiguity between these ideas and those of the later naturalists.

· IV ·

In local color fiction, misguidedly idealistic characters, particularly ministers and the organized religion that they represent, function more as bastions of moral legalism than as sources of spiritual comfort. In the New England states, this may well represent the dichotomy between a lingering intellectualized Calvinism and the comic misinterpretation of it by uncomprehending country people who, like Mrs. Bonny of *Deephaven* (1877), admire abstruse preaching about "foreordination and them p'ints" (235).[34] Indeed, the churches themselves serve as the focus of community dissension. In Jewett's "Miss Tempy's Watchers," for example, decorating the church building provokes petty squabbles. Sister Sarah Ann Binson and Mrs. Crowe "come as near hard feelings as they could" over the matter of pew cushions, and they are brought together not by the church's influence but by that of the earthly saint Miss Temperance Dent.[35] Not surprisingly, in New England local color fiction, female-dominated community rituals increasingly usurped the church's traditional responsibility for preserving community, and a theoretical religion devoted to empty form was unofficially displaced by a practical one grounded firmly in the quotidian round of earthly events.

The apparent emptiness of church forms parallels the meanness and hypocrisy of godly men like Rose Terry Cooke's deacons. "Mrs. Flint's Married Experience," for example, chronicles the plight of a widow, Mrs. Sarepta Gold, who remarries because she wrongly believes that her presence in their home hinders the happiness of her daughter and son-in-law. Cooke signals the change in the widow's circumstances through her change of name: from the prosperity of being "Mrs. Gold," she marries a man whom Cooke punningly names Amasa Flint. He is indeed a "mass of flint," an intransigent church deacon and secret miser hiding behind a cloak of worthy asceticism. After a few years of near-starvation, Mrs. Flint leaves him and is consequently banished from the congregation and badgered incessantly by the minister, a man "faithful to his dogmas and his education," to return and repent.[36] She does, and she dies; her "married experience" kills her. Miss Celia Barnes, the village seamstress of "How Celia Changed Her Mind," regrets the hasty marriage she makes to avoid being an old maid. More fortunate than Mrs. Flint, she outlives her miserly husband, Deacon Everts, and vows to "keep an old maids' Thanksgivin' for a kind of a burnt-offering" to celebrate "the onmarried" (150). In contrast to the empty formality of love in a conventionally defined marriage—for Cooke makes it clear that Deacon Everts is no different from most men—Celia creates an alternative community of women, one based on genuine feeling. What each of these unpleasant male characters shares is a devotion to the letter and limitations of traditional Christian dogma without any attempt to embrace its concomitant limitless values of love and compassion.

Ministers in local color fiction represent a more complex set of social expectations than do their mean-spirited deacons. In *The Feminization of American Culture*, Ann Douglas describes a mid-nineteenth-century coalition, occurring historically and reflected fictionally, between ministers and women. The coalition eased the transition from a Calvinistic doctrine of salvation by faith to one of salvation by works, and consequently, according to Douglas, "feminized" American culture by valorizing feminine ideals of love, compassion, and charity. Within local color works, the transition has become transmutation: a revolution of sorts has elevated these feminine ideals to the highest spot, in the process discarding the minister, the ally and agent of change common to women's fiction. Describing the local colorists' "condescension bordering on contempt for male figures who are in positions of authority, particularly clergymen," Julia Bader comments, "These men are shown to be especially deficient in using words to soothe, console, and connect people; indeed their verbal hollowness is a sign of emotional emptiness that becomes striking at funerals, weddings, or moments of crisis."[37] Ineffectual men of God such as Parson Stearns of Cooke's "How Celia Changed Her Mind" or Parson Hill of "Mrs. Flint's Married Experience" mean well but fail to consider the real-life consequences of their actions. They represent a departure from the strong figures, like John Humphreys in Susan Warner's (1819–1885) *The Wide, Wide World* (1850), that guided heroines of women's fiction.[38] Wedded to patriarchal values of idealism and legalism, they carry out their official duties unaware that both the changing nature of their communities and the shift from a Calvinistic doctrine of faith to a doctrine of works has rendered them virtually superfluous. Like Sant Bowden, a disappointed military man in *The Country of the Pointed Firs* whom the women laugh at for getting people "all flustered up tryin' to sense his ideas of a holler square" (102), the ministers try to impose a "holler" order on communities that have already created their own.

Mary Wilkins Freeman's "Revolt of 'Mother,'" "A Village Singer," and "A Poetess" illustrate the inability of ministers and their logic to prevail over the powerful feelings of the women they confront. Mr. Hersey, the minister of "The Revolt of 'Mother'" is unable to persuade Sarah Penn to vacate the new barn that she has taken over for her new house: "He could expound the intricacies of every character study in the Scriptures . . . but Sarah Penn was beyond him."[39] Mr. Pollard, the minister of "A Village Singer" is likewise vanquished by the feisty Miss Candace Whitcomb. Removed as chief soprano in the church choir, Candace immediately retaliates, disrupting church services by loudly singing different hymns from her house next door. When Mr. Pollard suggests that they "kneel and ask the guidance of the Lord" (137), Candace tells him off in no uncertain terms and he leaves, his mission unfulfilled. The root of her complaint is that not only manners but human decency and feeling have been violated: "I'd like to know if it wouldn't be more to the credit of folks in a church to keep an old singer an' an old minister, if they didn't sing an' hold forth quite so smart as they used to, ruther than turn 'em off an' hurt their feelin's" (134). By placing artistic standards above human feeling, Mr. Pollard and William Emmons, the choirmaster, transgress an implicit set of values when they put the musically passionless but techni-cally superior Alma Way in Candace's place. The dying Candace becomes reconciled with Alma, but she does reserve one small triumph: as she speaks "it was like a secondary glimpse of the old shape of a forest tree through the smoke and flame of the transfiguring fire the instant before it falls. 'You flatted a little on—soul,' said Candace" (144). Marjorie Pryse reads resignation in these words, finding in them Candace's attempt to warn Alma that she, too, might be replaced.[40] The semi-comic tone of the story surely also suggests, as does the tree metaphor, a lighter interpreta-tion: having forgiven Alma, this is Candace's last small chance to squelch her rival, and she does so with a touch of her old spirit. Her art may have been found wanting, but she dies with her standards of feeling and her sense of her own artistic merit intact.

"A Poetess" presents a darker side to this valorizing of artistic merit over feeling.[41] Betsey Dole writes memorial verse of the Emmeline Grangerford variety, yet she considers herself, and is considered by her community, to be a poet. Betsey's passionate love of her art is instinctive, and, when the minister's chance remark denigrating her poetry reaches her, she initially rages against fate as Candace Whitcomb had done: "I'd like to know if you think it's fair. Had I ought to have been born with the wantin' to write poetry if I couldn't write it—had I?" (194-95). Despair overtakes her, however; she burns her poems and asks the uncomprehending minister to bury the ashes with her. Freeman's story pointedly and ironically contrasts Betsey's artistic passion with the minister's own successful but dispassionate dabbling in poetry. His poetry is good, he allows, because "they did print some in a magazine" (199). What neither Betsey nor the minister questions is that the standards by which Betsey's poetry is judged are the "true" standards, those of an educated male publishing elite. Introduced into this parochial world by the minister, a book-educated but insensitive representative of the outside world, those same standards effectively destroy not only Betsey Dole but by implication her community. The minister does not consider what will happen to those grieving women who, we are told, have come to depend on her verses for comfort in the too-frequent deaths of their children. Betsey fills a spiritually significant niche in the village, for she, rather than the minister, addresses its emotional as well as its spiritual needs. By focusing on rules of art rather than feeling, the minister upsets the village's social ecology. The parallel between Betsey's scorned poetry and the "village art" of the local colorists is obvious, though it does contain some important differences: publishers approved of local color fiction, and it met the outside world's standards as Betsey's poetry could not. Freeman suggests, however, that the imposition of those standards may not only be destructive but irrelevant. Of what use are aesthetic considerations if the emotional needs of the community are not met? Though the canary, an ironic symbol of Betsey's art and its confinement, trills into a "triumphant song" (199) at her death, "A Poetess" clearly mourns the death of feminine sensibilities and community at the hands of a dispassionate masculine aesthetic.[42]

Another confrontation between a minister's dispassionate language and local color's language of community occurs in Jewett's *Country of the Pointed Firs* (1896). The story of Joanna Todd tells of Joanna's determination to become a recluse after committing the Hawthornean "unpardonable sin" of great wrath against God. In her account of the episode, Mrs. Todd shows her increasing exasperation with the inept minister she has taken to visit Joanna:

"'[T]was kind of cold an' unfeelin' the way he inquired. I wished he knew enough to just lay his hand on it [the Bible] and read somethin' kind an' fatherly 'stead of accusin' her. . . . He did offer prayer, but 't was all about hearin' the voice o' God out o' the whirlwind; and I thought while he was goin' on that anybody that had spent the long cold winter all alone out on Shell-heap Island knew a good deal more about those things than he did. I got so provoked I opened my eyes and stared right at him." [*The Country of the Pointed Firs*, 74–75]

Like the bungling ministers of "A Poetess," "The Revolt of 'Mother,'" and "A Village Singer," Mr. Dimmick reproduces the action of reading: as a text is confined within the limits of the printed word and cannot modify itself in order to enter into discourse with the individual reader, so Mr. Dimmick, adopting wholesale the text's unchanging method and merely reproducing its message without modification or interpretation, fails to enter into discourse with Joanna. Clearly uncomfortable, he armors himself by seeming "kind of cold an' unfeelin'," an entirely human response that Mrs. Todd nonetheless rightly despises. Her final comment strikes at the fundamental cause of her irritation: his logocentrism. Neither Mr. Dimmick nor his language appears grounded in the real world of Shell-heap Island, the world in which Joanna has chosen to live, and in which she must face the consequences of her decision. "[H]e seemed to know no remedies," Mrs. Todd concludes, "but he had a great use of words" (77).[43]

By contrast, Mrs. Todd responds to Joanna with the wordless healing "local" language of gesture; "I just ran to her an' caught her in my arms," she tells the narrator and Mrs. Fosdick (75). Offering first a refuge in her own home and then her coral pin, both of which Joanna refuses, Mrs. Todd appears to fail, since she does not succeed in changing Joanna's mind. But in contrast to the Bible Mr. Dimmick offers, Mrs. Todd's gift brings associations of love and kinship. In effect, the coral pin domesticates the sea by which Joanna is surrounded, carrying as it does associations of shaped artistry and domesticity (teething rings, for example, were frequently fashioned of coral) as well as being the "visible sign of female inheritance and attachment."[44] Rejecting the pin itself, Joanna reads its associations as she will not read the Bible, breaking the impassive silence with which she greeted the minister and, through her conversation with

Mrs. Todd, briefly rejoining the human community she has hitherto shunned. Joanna returns Mrs. Todd's expression of feeling with a confession of her own, explaining her refusal to return and telling Mrs. Todd that she feels "'a great comfort in your kindness'" (76). Through their conversation, a form of closure is reached that results in the community's acceptance of Joanna's feelings.

Perhaps the most telling example of linked male idealism and community destruction is Constance Fenimore Woolson's "The Lady of Little Fishing." Meeting accidentally in the ruins of Little Fishing, an island village on Lake Superior, the narrator and Reuben Mitchell share a companionable interlude that is but a pale echo of the community that once existed there. Mitchell tells the story of the Lady who appears in the rough logging town one night and begins to reform it. Her influence is unconscious rather than deliberate, but Little Fishing becomes virtually a parody of an ideal community, with neat houses, flowerbeds, and enthusiastically attended church services. Gradually, however, the town disintegrates when, as the town Doctor tells her, "'our idol came down among us and showed herself to be but common flesh and blood! . . . What wonder (worse than all!) that when the awe has quite vanished, there is strife for the beautiful image fallen from its niche?'"[45] Where women rule by their own power, stable communities exist, but a single woman elevated to power by male idealism is at risk. Created by the men's need to worship her as a saint, the Lady falls from favor when she deigns to love one man romantically rather than the community of men impersonally. Worse, she loves a man who does not love her, thus proving that woman is "'the same the world over'" (45). The men recognize their complicity in this mass delusion, but, significantly, choose to make the Lady rather than their own idealism the scapegoat.

Like other local color communities, Little Fishing depends on a kind of imprisonment in stasis for its existence, but unlike other communities, the imprisonment is not shared by all. The Lady must remain a hostage to idealism in order to preserve the community. She dies begging their forgiveness for her spiritual pride—in other words, for her failure to live up to their idealization of her. After her death the men tear down her house, the temple they had erected to their own infatuation with idealism, and they abandon the town thereafter. Reuben Mitchell, the man who did not love the Lady, considers his thirty years of isolation sufficient punishment for a regrettable accident: "He loved one, not the other; that was his crime" (47). Yet his "crime" occasions some regret, nothing more, whereas the Lady's equally unwitting and unwilling love results in disgrace and death. "The Lady of Little Fishing" testifies to the inadequacy of a male legalistic idealism as an agent of community coherence, and to the disjunction between such idealism and the workings of the real world.

Ministers are not the only figures charged with a failure to understand community, of course; differences in education and class also cause outsiders to misinterpret communities through the misguided idealism with which they approach the life of the region. For example, with missionary zeal Constance Fenimore Woolson's "King David" makes a futile attempt to educate the recently freed slaves, and Mary N. Murfree's John Cleaver, blinded by romanticism and class consciousness, fails (with disastrous consequences) to recognize a mountain girl's love in "The Romance of Sunrise Rock."[46] In Jewett's *Deephaven*, too, Kate's response to the misfortunes of the poverty-stricken family whom she and Helen have befriended strikes a patronizing note: "How seldom life in this world seems to be a success! . . . I find that I understand better and better how unsatisfactory, how purposeless and disastrous, any life must be which is not a Christian life."[47] Heightening as it does the contrast between Kate's youth and wealth and the family's own ill luck, the remark reverberates with unintentional irony: lives can be "purposeless and disastrous" regardless of their Christian content. Though she and Helen, at twenty-four, regard themselves as "two little girls" (12) and their judgments may be forgiven for reflecting a conscious naiveté as well as an outsider's inculcation with patriarchal values, the inadequacy of Kate's conventional Christian interpretation stands out against the powerful funeral scene in the chapter, much as the response of the idealistic ministers has done in other works. Although conventionally religious characters like Kate and the various ministers occur frequently in local color works, their formal efforts at piety and preaching, however sincere, remain ineffectual. Just as the naturalists were to do, many local colorists examined conventional religion, legalistically applied idealism, traditional aesthetic standards, and an unthinking veneration of learning from books over learning from life. And, like the naturalists who prided themselves on their fresh outlook on these subjects, the local colorists weighed the traditional treatment of such themes in the balance and found it wanting.

· V ·

The two sides of self-denial recur frequently in Cooke and Freeman, less so in Jewett and Woolson; but self-denial recurs as a nearly universal element in women's local color writing.[48] Although self-denial may promote satisfaction and acceptance, it may also become merely a means to show off one's vaunted New England "character." Under an economy of depletion such as exists in local color works, many characters learn to value as well as accept loss. They find, through the limits placed on them, that the possibility of ethical choice encourages human dignity; they begin to see an enforced attention to prosaic detail as a means of exercising control by affirming orderliness and harmony. More ominously, however, characters may come to relish self-denial as a way of exercising their "perverted and abnormal wills—baleful forces in characters diseased," the result of their cramped Puritan consciences "exercis[ing] their stubbornness on petty issues," as Thompson said of Freeman's characters.[49]

Thompson's remark cuts to the center of the difference between the types: self-denial and control of will based on realistic expectations confer dignity, whereas destructive, irrational self-denial is a result, not a cause, of willfulness or intellectual pride gone badly awry. Women's realism in such stories again implicitly opposes men's idealism: characteristics linked with the feminine—such as compassion, realism, and a tolerance for adaptability and loss—oppose characteristics seen as masculine—such as idealism, legalism, and an inability to adapt.[50] Yet each set of associations is gender-linked or gender-identified, not gender-specific. In other words, not all women will display compassion, realism, and other virtues designated as "feminine," any more than all men will exhibit the lofty idealism or other "masculine" traits. For example, rigid, mean women do occur in local color stories, including characters such as hard-hearted Deborah Thayer of Freeman's *Pembroke*, meddling Mrs. Simonds of "A Mistaken Charity," and the monstrous daughters of "A Village Lear," or Jewett's careless, brusque caretaker in "The Village Poor." In a similar reversal, male characters reveal admirable traits as they shed legalistic, rigid idealism and move toward compassion. In "A Solitary," Freeman's title character, Nicholas Gunn, gradually abandons his willful isolation to care for Stephen Forster, an ailing outcast from the village workhouse. Woolson's Northerner John Rodman comes to the aid of the embittered Confederate officer Ward De

Rosset in "Rodman the Keeper." A sensitive man, Rodman is aware of the ironic nature of his job: no Southerner enters the "national" cemetery he keeps. Recognizing nonetheless, as the title suggests, that he is indeed his brother's keeper, Rodman overcomes the dying De Rosset's objections and makes his last months comfortable. The two gradually accept that their common humanity provides a bond more vital than the politically imposed sentiments that separate them. Thus if they are to abandon the excessive strictures of will and pride that result in negative self-denial, characters must allow themselves the sort of feminine "weakness" that they have spent their lives fighting: compassion, forgiveness, and compromise. In short, as the local colorists would have it, characters need to adopt feminine values in order to become whole individuals.

Much of what masquerades as a negative form of self-denial in Cooke's and Freeman's work is actually the sheerest self-indulgence. In such cases, not true acceptance but a perversely excessive will manifests itself through self-denial. Because the lingering Puritanism of the culture rewards self-denial as a virtue, those characters who are irremediably attached to it—with negative consequences for themselves and those around them—choose it as a means of display, a spiritual form of conspicuous consumption in a culture that, ostensibly at least, prizes the spiritual over the material. Most of the major characters displaying this quality are brought to some form of redemption through feminine values. They learn to bend, ironically to "deny" themselves the luxury of self-denial, by the end of the work.

Rose Terry Cooke's "Too Late" illustrates several of these points in its portrait of one such initially unrelenting soul. Outwardly cold, Hannah Blair is in fact a veritable "vine-planted and grass-strewn volcano" (219) when her heart is awakened to Charles Mayhew. They become engaged, but on her wedding day, she receives an anonymous note accusing him of "certain lapses from virtue" (232). As she reads, "life, light, love, withdrew their tender glories from her face. It settled into stone, into flint" (222). The images of stone that characterize her throughout the story foreshadow her response: after reading the note, she refuses ever to see him again, enters a loveless marriage some ten years later, and brings up her daughter Dolly to recite "that theological torture—the Assembly's Catechism" (231). Like Joanna Todd, who also loved too much, she craves emotional peace and finds it in staking out her own "Shell-heap Island" of spiritual isolation behind her "cold blue eyes" (231) and "heart of granite" (232). The "chaos" of emotion she fears and represses channels itself into a rigid self-denial, finding an outlet only in the obsessively perfect housekeeping that demonstrates her rage for order.

Hannah's need to control and order her external circumstances, shared in lesser degree by many local color characters, exceeds the boundaries of the usual, since she tries to edit out of her life the one thing that cannot be eliminated: emotion. Yet because she dares not "once let that iron hand relax its pressure" lest "chaos [threaten] her again," Hannah ruins her own life, Charles's (he dies "a lonely, drunken pauper" [232]), and very nearly that of her daughter. Only on her deathbed does she acknowledge to Dolly her mistake, making a confession remarkable for its mixed passion and conventional sentiments:

> "Oh, Dolly!" groaned the smitten woman, "when he stood under my window and called me I was wrung to my heart's core. . . . I was upon the floor, with my arms wound about the bedrail and my teeth shut like a vice, lest I should listen to the voice of nature, and, going to the window to answer him, behold his face. Had I seen him I must have gone down and done what I thought a sin; so I steeled myself to resist, although I thought flesh would fail in the end; but it did not. I conquered then and after. . . . Had I been a meeker woman, having mercy instead of judgment, I might have helped him to right ways. I might have saved him—I loved him so."
> [232]

Ulysses hearing the sirens' call, which this scene faintly evokes, could not have felt a stronger pull. Hannah cannot wholly admit this physical love as her reason, and at the end of the passage couches her regret in conventional and respectable feminine terms, identifying the right response though for the wrong reason: she should have used her feminine influence to be "meeker" and thereby have "saved" him, subduing her masculine force of will and legalistic judgment. These lofty sentiments cannot dispel the image left by the earlier part of her confession, and the triumph of spirit over flesh is obviously a Pyrrhic victory. Dolly tries to console her, saying "try to believe it was all for the best," but Hannah faces the truth: "Dolly, it is too late!" (233).

On her deathbed, Hannah also begins to face the real heart of her problem. She had been swayed from the "voice of nature" by the written word, first by the anonymous note in which she placed more credence than in the feeling of her love for Charles, and second by the catechism that dictates what constitutes sin. When she rejects the "voice of nature" and begins to restructure her life she does so according to the word, and, ironically, brings her daughter up by the same combination of grim Sundays, official church teachings, and self-denial that caused her own unhappiness. When the "voice of nature" struggles for supremacy with "the word," Hannah always chooses the word—note over Charles, rules of sin over voice of nature, and judgment over mercy—and the word fails her every time. By the time she sees her life's outer perfection and inner failure, recognizing a value in "nature" and "mercy," it is indeed "too late." Cooke writes a powerful indictment not only of self-denial but of the corrupting qualities of Puritanism and its reverence for the legalistically applied judgments of "the word."

Negative self-denial in the works of Mary Wilkins Freeman presents itself as an expression of excessive will, as characters in novels such as *Pembroke* (1894) forego what they most desire in obedience to the dictates of their overdeveloped consciences. "Nearly every character," wrote Charles Miner Thompson of *Pembroke*, "is a monstrous example of stubbornness—of that will which enforces its ends, however trivial, even to self-destruction."[51] In *Pembroke*, the main plot traces the relationship between the engaged couple Charlotte Barnard and Barnabas Thayer. On the Sunday night before their wedding, Barnabas (Barney) argues heatedly with Charlotte's father about a minor political point and vows never to return to her house. As the main plot proceeds amid the usual local color complications—Charlotte will not marry anyone else, Barney becomes bitter and twisted—a host of subplots arise from the characters' willfulness. Freeman uses the device of the giving, receiving, and refusing of food as a measure of the villagers' emotional starvation. After eighteen years of courting Miss Sylvia Crane, Richard Alger fails to find her at home one Sunday evening and ceases his attentions, breaking his silence only several years later when the townspeople try to remove the by-then starving Miss Sylvy to the poorhouse. Cephas Barnard, Charlotte's father, decides to "eat the kind of things that won't strengthen the animal nature at the expense of the spiritual" and stubbornly makes indigestible sorrel-and-molasses pies in order to keep his "good" disposition.[52] Deborah Thayer, withholding affection and mince pie from her young son Ephraim on the grounds that too much (or indeed any) would spoil him, finds herself outwitted when Ephraim enjoys the twin pleasures of devouring a pie and going sledding in her absence. The beating she administers for his transgressions indirectly causes his death, but upon learning from the neighbors about the sledding and the pie, "a great light of hope" (201) illuminates her face as she decides that Ephraim's forays into forbidden indulgences, not her corrections of them, have killed him. Only when she is dying of a stroke does she begin to value forgiveness over her absolute righteousness: her last action is to call for her estranged children, Rebecca and Barney.

Barney Thayer, her son, shares her excessive reactions to minor transgressions and her stubborn inability to admit error. Like Jerome Edwards of *Jerome, a Poor Man* (1897), whose thoughtless promise to give away a fortune should he ever be given one nearly destroys his life, Barney lives to regret his hasty words. Struck down ostensibly by rheumatism but actually by "the dreadful warping of a diseased will" (235), his spiritual intransigence manifests itself in the same type of spinal curvature that had plagued his obstinate grandfather.[53] Asked if he has hurt his back, Barney replies, "I've hurt my soul. . . . It happened that Sunday night years ago. I—can't get over it. I am bent like his back" (233). His obstinate vision of himself as being a man of straight, rigid character bends and deforms his back; ironically, only when he learns emotionally to "bend" and loosen his ideas of right conduct will he become physically, and as Freeman suggests, morally straight. A fever that he suffers presents Charlotte with an opportunity to defy Cephas and live in Barney's house while she nurses him back to health. As if to reset their relationship on the track abandoned some twelve years earlier, Barney sends Charlotte home and walks "straight as anybody" to her house, there to be reconciled with "his old sweetheart and his old self" (254).

Freeman explains her rationale for happy endings such as those in *Pembroke* and *Jerome* in her Introductory Sketch to the earlier novel. The work was, she says, "originally intended as a study of the human will in several New England characters, in different phases of disease and abnormal development, and to prove, especially in the most marked case, the truth of a theory that its cure depended entirely upon the capacity of the individual for a love which could rise above all considerations of self" (33). Yet even love scarcely compensates for the wasted youth and misspent energy that attend such excessive outward self-denial. What occurs is even more than a healing through love: it is a stripping away of the pride and will manifested as outward self-denial. In an almost literal destruction of the personality that these characters have built, often and aptly symbolized as "stone by stone," they become reconstructed or reborn under a whole new set of rules. Giving up the superficial appearance of self-denial, they cast aside their will, the essence of their personality and the part most tied up with any person's self-concept. Only then do they really experience "self-denial": giving up or denying one's self the thing that the self most values. The characters must agree, indeed must want, to dwell in the human community, not in a prison of their own egotistic devising.

In a more positive way, self-denial can also provide the character living a circumscribed existence with one of the few means for demonstrating dignity and ethical choice. Freeman, Jewett, and Woolson all present self-denial in this manner, though even viewed positively self-denial can rarely provide unalloyed satisfaction. Freeman's Louisa Britton in "Louisa" shows a commendable dignity, for instance, by refusing to marry Jonathan Nye for his money despite her venal family's wishes, just as Inez Morse of "A Taste of Honey" has no ethical choice but to pay off her family's mortgage, even at the cost of losing her beau and probable future happiness.[54] As a concession to realism in her short stories if not in her novels, Freeman rules out the possibility that self-respect and a traditional romantic happy ending can coexist, despite Granville Hicks's claim that she could not "resist the temptation of the happy ending [and that] her unfortunates are always compensated for their sufferings."[55] On the contrary, her "unfortunates" are well aware of their suffering, taking as their only consolation a knowledge that they have acted ethically and for the good of others. Freeman's "A Moral Exigency" provides one example. Never allowing that Burr Mason might have chosen to love her on his own over her rival, Ada Harris, Eunice Fairweather blames herself for "stealing" him and will not allow herself to keep him. In an ending that reverses the "economy of suffering" solution found in Howells's *Rise of Silas Lapham*, plain girl Eunice gives up her vacillating fiancé Burr Mason to pretty blonde Ada, saying only, "'I want—something.'"[56]

Only Louisa Ellis of "A New England Nun" meets the future with no regrets about what, if anything, she has lost by turning Joe Dagget away. Freeman's narrator comments that "[i]f Louisa Ellis had sold her birthright, she did not know it, the taste of the pottage was so delicious. . . .

Serenity and placid narrowness had become to her as the birthright it-self."[57] Aside from this editorializing, however, Louisa's choice seems wholly positive, not merely ethical but in line with her own desires as well. Louisa's strategy, as Ann Romines points out in *The Home Plot*, is not to break out of domestic confinement but to break "*in*, to secure and perfect her solitary domestic art." Romines asks a crucial rhetorical question about Freeman's stories: "In the world of fixity and routine where the women remain, what can *escape* mean and be?" She suggests that housekeeping creates a "domestic aesthetic" within which Freeman's characters "enact that question."[58] The control granted by housekeeping and its repetitions, like the ethical choices local color heroines make, indicate that control itself generates a kind of freedom beyond the seeming limitations of the domes-tic sphere—or the local color form. In an imperfect world where men are scarce, poverty is rampant, and crotchety parents hold sway, these women make choices that allow them to feel not defeat at the sight of their limited prospects, but a tolerable sense of self-worth and control. To choose freely and responsibly in a world in which they otherwise have no control affirms these women's sense of self and conscience.

Self-denial in Jewett and Woolson assumes an even more positive cast, for they show that it can benefit the community as well as ennoble the individual. Jewett's "Miss Tempy's Watchers" describes Miss Tempy's many acts of self-denial as acts of true charity; she denies herself that others may not want. The stingy, initially nonchalant Mrs. Crowe fears death, but she drops her knitting and symbolically her defenses when confronted with Sister Sarah Ann Binson's matter-of-fact attitudes about it and with Tempy's pervasive kindness of spirit. The story is largely one of Mrs. Crowe's subtle transformation from a woman fearing death and clinging perversely to possessions in order to shelter herself from it, to one who comes to understand the minor place that mere things should hold in one's life and the natural place of death. Jewett uses a great deal of Christian imagery to convey Tempy's Christlike power. Tempy does not curse the tree that will not bloom; instead, as Mrs. Crowe tells it, "she'd go out in the spring and tend to it, and look at it so pleasant, and kind of expect the thorny thing into bloomin'," a talent, as Sarah Ann observes, that she also has "with folks" (251). She heals the girl broken from study, denying herself a longed-for trip to Niagara Falls to do so; she is good to little children; she even provides a communion feast of quince preserves and cake for the women to celebrate her memory. Self-denial makes her life worthwhile, and the memory of her example creates a sisterhood between Mrs. Crowe and Sarah Ann (who also learns some humility) that the church could not.

Another New England woman, Prudence Wilkins of Woolson's story "The Front Yard," denies herself cheerfully on behalf of the Italian fortune hunter she marries and his improvident family. She makes extraordinary sacrifices and, like Miss Tempy, gives up her small store of money as well as her time so that others may benefit. Woolson shows that her limited vision is simultaneously the strength and weakness in her character: Prudence does not perceive that she is being taken advantage of, because as a New England woman she is brought up to do her duty. Ignoring a "magnificent view of the valley, the serene vast Umbrian plain" (185), Prudence wishes only to get a decent New England front yard. When a sympathetic American makes her dream possible, she is wholly satisfied. Despite her love, her adopted family disappoints her by their thievery and selfishness, but on her deathbed, far from the place she still considers "home," she sees the orderly garden planted in her front yard and is content.

Woolson's *For the Major* explores a genuine if peculiarly expressed form of self-denial. The social life of Far Edgerley, a small South Carolina town, centers on the town squire, Major Carroll; his young wife, Madam Carroll; their young son; and Sara, his daughter by a previous marriage. The story is told from Sara's perspective, and the reader initially condemns Madam Carroll for blocking all of Sara's attempts to resume her old intellectual companionship with Major Carroll. Madam Carroll, the "American Hebe" (308), seems at first to be the archetypal vain second wife and sinister stepmother; she dresses and acts far younger than her years, and she controls the Major's every movement, setting up his social calendar and putting words in his mouth. What Sara comes to understand is that the whole family scene is a deception. Her father has lapsed into senility, and through her constant attendance Madam Carroll seeks to protect his reputation in the town. Further, Madam Carroll keeps up the wearisome imposture that she is young in order to keep the Major's spirits up and preserve his faith in her. Her admiration for her stepmother increasing, Sara joins in the conspiracy to keep the Major's infirmity from exposure, and she maintains her faith in Madam Carroll even when the latter takes to mysterious secret walks with a young man, Julian DuPont. Sara loyally sends away her own suitor, the Reverend Frederick Owen, in order to protect Madam Carroll: to still Owen's insinuations, she pretends that DuPont is her own lover. Sara's faith is rewarded. Madam Carroll explains that DuPont is her long-lost son by a previous marriage, and that a combination of the Major's initial misperception of her age and her desperate circumstances had forced her into a life of deception. Released by Julian's death and the Major's stroke, she chooses to resume her true appearance, to the amazement of Reverend Owen:

> Her veil of golden hair, no longer curled, was put plainly back, and fastened in a close knot behind; her eyes, the blue eyes he had always thought so pretty, looked tired and sunken and dim, with crow's feet at their corners, all her lovely bloom was gone, and the whole of her little faded face was a network of minute wrinkles. She was still small and slender, and she still had her pretty features, but this was an old woman who was talking to him, and Madam Carroll had been so young. [355]

By becoming an old, wrinkled woman with hair fastened "plainly back," Madam Carroll emerges from her role as romantic ingenue to assume her true appearance—an elderly, self-sacrificing local color heroine.

Woolson first plays upon and then foils the reader's expectations, inverting stereotypes and prejudices and calling into question rigid definitions. Madam Carroll's golden curls and effortless charm seem at first to place her in the best tradition of superficial nineteenth-century heroines,[59] but her odd behavior arouses suspicion until she arises, a heroine of a new sort, from the ashes of her discarded disguise. Like governess Jean Muir of Louisa May Alcott's "Behind a Mask," who adopts false teeth and youthful curls in order to marry a rich, unsuspecting older man, Madam Carroll feigns youth, but her deception, unlike Muir's, is blameless, based as it is on a selfless motive. The beauty for which she is valued is a lie achieved by art; the intelligence with which she is not credited goes toward making the Major look good. Only Sara, another good woman who loves the Major, can penetrate her facade. Even Frederick Owen, a man of God, is willing because of her youthful looks to believe the worst of Madam Carroll. Her husband's faith in her is based firmly on an illusion, one which he initiated and which she must now continue for his benefit. Woolson, like other local color writers, subscribes to the realistic woman/illusion-filled man idea, but in *For the Major*, she goes a step further than most writers in suggesting that although women must not succumb to illusion, men cannot live without it. In order to preserve the Major's life, Madam Carroll must deny every portion of herself: her past, her age, her lack of youth, and her son. Sara, too, must practice deception, and for both women the ease with which they control the Major and Reverend Owen does not mitigate the strain that their pretense places on them. Yet pretense and strain bring them together, in a bond of love more essential than truth. Its sensational plot revelations aside, *For the Major* celebrates an unusual type of heroism that manifests itself through deception and vanity, and it calls into question the system of social relationships between men and women that forces an undignified pretense of eternal youth on an essentially courageous woman as Madam Carroll.

Denial of the self thus involves much more than symbolic gestures, for to display this showy external virtue is the surest sign that it does not exist within. Instead, self-denial involves the bringing of desire into contact with the real world of the local color community. Its essence lies in remaking the self into an instrument in harmony with the world and its order. As a choice for limitation, self-denial is well suited to the literature of limitations, and the realism it necessitates, the pragmatic moral ethicism it promotes, and the harmony it preserves make it a preeminent local color virtue.

· VI ·

A third characteristic of local color works, and one related to self-denial, is the deliberate conservation of experience, of suspending time through preserving it, that encompasses both a theme and a mode of storytelling in local color fiction. Much of the action in local color stories centers on these activities of preserving and storytelling. Gathering herbs, knitting, making quilts, braiding rugs, distilling essences, and putting up preserves take up a great deal of the women's time, just as storytelling occupies their attention. The parallel between the two goes beyond simple contiguity, however: each is a method of preserving the present for the future, of making and reshaping something into a usable and durable object to be shared.[60] Frequently in local color stories there comes a moment such as Jewett describes in *Deephaven*: Mrs. Kew, the lighthouse keeper's wife, has gone to the circus with the girls, and as she leaves she tells them "that she should have enough to think of for a year, she had enjoyed the day so much"

(174–75). Mrs. Kew and others observe life as it is lived, less as a thing to be analyzed than one to be savored. As Mrs. Fosdick tells Mrs. Todd in *The Country of the Pointed Firs*, "Conversation's got to have some root in the past, or else you've got to explain every remark you make, an' it wears a body out" (61). Experiences count for little unless they can be first enjoyed in company, and secondly remembered, shaped, and saved. The act of preserving is a central one in local color fiction; most stories at least allude to it, describing herb gatherers like Mrs. Todd and Freeman's aptly named Aurelia Flower of "A Gatherer of Simples," preserve makers like Miss Tempy, and the preservationists of less orthodox matter, among them Betsey Dole of "A Poetess" and Madam Carroll of Woolson's *For the Major*. As the number of frame stories and stories-within-stories shows, the act of storytelling itself is central to local color fiction, concurrent with and related to the actions of preserving that the women undertake.

Rarely do the women delight in preserving for its own sake, as Louisa Ellis of "A New England Nun" distills essences or as first Clarissa and then Anne May of "A Scent of Roses" fill potpourri jars to remind themselves of the love they lose. For the most part, storytelling, like preserving, fulfills some broadly defined purposes within local color fiction. First, telling stories functions as a means of cementing community bonds, much as gossip might. The oral tradition of these women contrasts markedly with the bookish irrelevancies and pointless texts of the local color ministers and old sea captains.[61] Yet although both involve oral retellings of incidents, there is a difference between the local colorists' stories and gossip. In *Gossip*, Patricia Meyer Spacks describes gossip's traditional characteristics: malice, current freshness, a lack of forethought in the telling, and a "lack of solidarity with the talk's victim."[62] By contrast, narratives such as those concerning Joanna Todd or Aunt Rebecca of Freeman's "On the Walpole Road" occur long in the past, and are not only told without malice but carefully framed so that the listener can sympathize with the character's plight. In the Dunnet Landing stories of Sarah Orne Jewett, for example, the stories that the narrator hears become a gesture of inclusion, since they become increasingly inaccessible to anyone not privy to community se- crets.[63] In addition to the "very commonplace news of the day," Mrs. Todd "one misty summer night" tells the narrator "all that lay deepest in her heart," such as her love for "one who was far above her" (7). This sharing of personal history precedes the recounting of community history as Mrs.

Todd and Mrs. Fosdick tell the narrator the story of Joanna Todd. Finally, after her return to Dunnet Landing, the narrator is sufficiently trusted to become a "conspirator" in William's courtship and marriage in "A Dunnet Shepherdess" and "William's Wedding," the secret of which is not even shared by the community.[64] A sense of shared experience is implicit in the very idea of telling a story, since traditional oral storytelling of the sort prevalent in local color works exists only where teller and audience are gathered together.

Storytelling further sustains communities by allowing much of the action to take place offstage, thereby distancing the threat implied by too great a passion or too violent an act. By the time the stories have become consolidated into a form suitable for telling, they have none of the freshness of gossip, and more importantly none of its potential to harm the community. Suitably distanced by the "once upon a time" quality of events told but not directly experienced, local color stories permit their listeners to substitute sympathy for an otherwise uncomfortable level of distress, especially since, as we have seen, the conventional religious consolations for poverty, loss, and the like are ineffective. Given the local color community's penchant for order and control, storytelling seems but a natural extension of a community's power to perpetuate itself. Telling stories helps to integrate the unusual with the usual, as the villagers' defense of eccentric Jenny Wrayne does in Freeman's "Christmas Jenny" or as Mrs. Todd's explanation of poor Joanna's reclusiveness or of Sant Bowden's eccentric behavior does in *The Country of the Pointed Firs*. When such distance is not present, as in Freeman's "Up Primrose Hill," complications arise. While they retell the story of crossed love and madness of the Primroses, two inquisitive ladies, Mrs. Rowe and Mrs. Daggett, are preparing to break into the abandoned Primrose house. Like the quince sauce they taste, so fresh that it "ain't lost its strength one mite" (*Selected Stories*, 261), the story is really too fresh to be told or indeed to be concluded. A noise proves to be the "characters" of their story converging upon the house: the last Primrose, Maria, returning to take up a recluse's life in her house; her estranged and now witless lover, to whom she does not speak; and a pair of young lovers who make up after their quarrel. Realizing that they have failed to keep a safe distance from the story they are both telling and investigating, the two women bolt. By isolating stories in time, by insulating them from the merely curious and possibly censorious, and by shaping them for the benefit of listeners, the women in local color fiction control the version of the story that is told. They thereby consolidate a further kind of power over what is remembered or preserved, if not over what happens, in their lives.

Freeman uses the eating of preserves in a similarly symbolic fashion in her late story "Friend of My Heart" (1913). Repeating the plot of "A Moral Exigency," "Friend of My Heart" tells of a middle-aged pair of friends, pretty Elvira Meredith and plain Catherine Dexler, whose emotions and old rivalries are roused by the return of their erstwhile beau, Lucius Converse. In a repetition of her willful earlier refusal of Lucius, Elvira shocks Catherine by rejecting the handcrafted woolwork signifying her status as an older woman in the community. Unlike Elvira, who had earlier destroyed her options unthinkingly, Catherine consumes her options/preserves deliberately. Alerted that her peach preserves will spoil, Catherine is given a "second chance" to scald them, yet she eats them instead of preserving them any further. The eating of preserves ironically signifies her readiness for marriage, for "consuming" experience, but her habit of self-denial proves impossible to overcome. She renounces her would-be husband to the frivolous friend who needs him more.

Storytelling further creates the opportunity for another sort of control: the creation of myth. Jewett's use of allusion, such as her overt references to Mrs. Todd standing like "Antigone alone upon the Theban plain" (49), has occasioned a great deal of critical commentary; for example, Sarah Way Sherman traces Mrs. Todd's connections to a "vague memory" of the Eleusinian mysteries. Yet the community's own tales of courage and endurance, like that of Miss Tempy, or of a Hawthornean "unpardonable sin" like poor Joanna's, adorn a niche in village iconography fully equivalent with, and even more usefully employed than, either allusions to classical myth or the old sea captains' tales of faraway places. As a dispensing agent for cautionary tales and rules of conduct, storytelling fulfills the same need to provide continuity between past, present, and future as community rituals. Like tomboy Nan Prince, who in Jewett's *A Country Doctor* (1884) must learn to make calls on the ladylike and formal Mrs. Graham, individuals must not merely become socialized into a community's present but must be informed about its past if its life is to continue on the same civilized plane. The willingness to defer consumption—of food or of experience—involved in storytelling bespeaks not merely a commitment to community but a recognition of the future. Drawing upon its legends of the past, too often the only available capital in local color communities, characters project a future through the spiritual (through preserving stories) as well as the physical (through preserving food) preparations they make.

On another level, the processes of preserving and storytelling not only coexist and reflect on one another within the local color world, but they function as commentary on the process of local color writing itself. All those dried herbs, jars of preserves, pieced quilts, and braided rugs exist as emblems of a particular kind of sensibility, one that takes life as it comes, whole and in scraps, and distills or pieces experience into a coherent, usable product. It is this sensibility that local color fiction chooses to celebrate.[65] True, the preserved stories are doubly distanced; the interesting stories of Joanna Todd or the narratives of sea captains all occur outside the realm of the narrator's experience. If immediate, local color stories are not, conventionally speaking, terribly dramatic; they deal with a visit, a spinster's trip, a little girl's refusal to tell of a heron's whereabouts, and so forth. If dramatic, like the tale of poor Joanna, the stories are not immediate. This leveling of experience serves to reproduce more closely the local colorists' vision of everyday life, as does the double-distilled quality of some stories. Double-distilling and preserving cannot capture the immediacy of incident and action that the naturalists prize—but it can, as Cooke, Freeman, Jewett, and Woolson can attest, create a concentration of experience in miniature.

In his 1904 essay "The Art of Miss Jewett," Charles Miner Thompson quotes approvingly Sarah Orne Jewett's dictum that "to heartily enjoy the every-day life one must care to study life and character, and must find pleasure in thought and observation of simple things, and have an instinctive delicious interest in what to other eyes is unflavored dullness."[66] Jewett's message stands as a multilayered gloss on women's local color fiction. It cautions against exaggerated expectations of what is to be found within. Perspective is all, she warns, for to expect other than a representation of the "simple things" that comprise "every-day life" is to read with "other eyes" than those for which the fiction is intended. Her remark also reveals, however, an indispensable component of the characters' own perspective on their necessarily circumscribed lives. To enjoy the feast of fiction or of life implied by the antithetical metaphors of taste—"delicious," "unflavored"—requires exactly the sort of appetite one might bring to a country meal. By assuming the pleasures of the quotidian, they do not trade their birthright for a mess of pottage, as Freeman's narrator in "A New England Nun" would have it. The quotidian is their birthright, and, by their acceptance of it and assumption of power within it via the rituals they engage in and transmit to succeeding—in every sense of the word—generations, they are able to transform acceptance into a genuine satisfaction.

CHAPTER THREE

Opening the Door
to the "Masculine Principle"

· I ·

In the 1890s, naturalism began to supersede local color and its doctrine of self-imposed limitations, just as in varying degrees the naturalists themselves moved away from the literary realism preached by William Dean Howells. Although they owed much to Howells, such writers as Stephen Crane, Frank Norris, and Theodore Dreiser adopted the attitude expressed by Dreiser in 1911: "Mr. Howells won't see American life as it is lived; he doesn't want to see it."[1] For the naturalists, the "real life" depicted by the local colorists and the realists had become "not life," a false rather than a true representation of the reality *they* saw. The effects of this change in attitude, along with the relationship between the realists and the naturalists, the ways in which naturalism departed from realism, and a host of possible literary sources and influences on the naturalists, have been thoroughly examined in literary and cultural histories of the time. What deserves more attention is the extent to which this shift in literary taste reflects a rejection of local color as a movement, and the degree to which this rejection resulted from a backlash against what was perceived as feminine domination of audience and literature alike. An examination of some of the documents exemplifying the spirit of the age suggests that this backlash indeed had a substantial component of antifeminine sentiment. The alarm about female-dominated literature spread by writers such as James Lane Allen and Frank Norris played a key part in ending the reign of local color as a serious literary movement.

Despite this antifeminine backlash, however, local color did not disappear; it instead became fragmented, dissolving into a host of new literary trends. As a fitting tribute to the fin de siècle spirit of excess, local color characteristics became exaggerated in a sort of baroque flowering as the movement broke apart. Thus local color's preoccupation with the past merged with, or was transmogrified into, the full-blown retreat into the past represented by the rage for historical romance. The movement's careful concern for the uniquely "local" and its emphasis on preserving regional identity were enthusiastically coopted by Hamlin Garland and Frank Norris into a jingoistic literary nationalism. Its emphasis on "color," on accurately representing the speech, habits, and other "homely details" of the humbler classes of American life, helped to inform both the technique and method of American naturalism. In much the same way, the local colorists' preoccupation with the interdependence of character and region fit readily into naturalism's scheme of determinism by race, epoch, and milieu. As its components became assimilated into other, newer movements, local color vanished as a distinct genre. So complete was this dismantling process that, by the century's end, Frank Norris, one of the chief protesters against a too-feminine literature, felt free to construct the "Old Grannis–Miss Baker" plot as parable of local color's virtues and limitations within his naturalistic novel *McTeague* (1899).

· II ·

That local color seemed, by 1894, nearly unassailable can be seen by the critics' reactions to one man's attempt to rewrite its history. For *Main-Travelled Roads* (1891), the local colorist Hamlin Garland won praise from Howells and condemnation from those who objected to his uncompromising portrayal of bleak farm life in the Midwest. In 1894 Garland tried once again to shock the literary establishment with *Crumbling Idols*, his book of twelve essays on literary theory. This time, reviewers generally refused to rise to the bait of its pugnacious tone, though not for lack of trying on Garland's part.[2] Announcing that the local novel "is sure to become all-powerful" and "will redeem American literature," Garland distinguishes his definition of local color from that of lesser authors: "I am using local color to mean something more than a forced study of the picturesque scenery of a State. *Local color in a novel means that it has such quality of texture and back-ground that it could not have been written in any other place or by any one else than a native.*"[3] *Crumbling Idols* assumes a hostile reaction to the ideas it presents, and within its pages Garland taunts the practitioners of "criticism of a formal kind" (52): "Old men naturally love the past; the books they read are the master-pieces; the great men are all dying off, they say; the young man should treat lofty and universal themes, as they used to do" (53). The lofty critics whom he disdains, however, declined to display, at least in print, the vituperative attitude about his "new" ideas that Garland attributes to them.

The *Atlantic Monthly*'s response to Garland's challenge is typical. In the December 1895 issue, the "New Figures in Literature and Art" feature devoted to Garland and *Crumbling Idols* sounded the keynote: amusement, not outrage. Noting similarities between Garland and the "ideal writer" alluded to in the book, Charles Miner Thompson, the reviewer, gives a tongue-in-cheek portrait of Garland as a "literary anarchist" whose aim as a "literary Jingo" is to promote "[o]ur literature—right or wrong."[4] Though the metaphors suggest radical overtones, Thompson is far from alarmed. Indeed, he finds "the fundamental ideas of the book . . . to be so sound as to appear tame" (840) and dismisses Garland's cherished veritism as the ancient advice given writers to "[w]rite of what you know" (841). The reviewer's judgment that Garland will succeed despite rather than because of his ideas, like his praise of the thirty-five-year-old Garland as a promising young writer, bespeaks the secure and condescending attitude of one who recognizes a grandstander when he sees one. A few months later, the *Atlantic Monthly* essay "Present Conditions of Literary Production" calls for literary idealism and improved academic criticism, a defense of the status quo that Garland had predicted. The essay contains a veiled assault on the limitations inherent in Garland's ideas, yet Paul Shorey, the author, concedes "that the novel of local color . . . [is] the most prosperous [form] of literature to-day and contain[s] the most promise for the immediate future."[5] Far from treating him as an outsider, the critics hailed Garland as one of their own.

There are other reasons for this generally complacent critical response. Garland's ideas, though newly printed in book form, had already attained wide currency, both through their publication in the *Arena* and the *Forum* and through Garland's own series of public lectures. In 1891 Stephen Crane covered Garland's lectures on William Dean Howells for the New York *Tribune*, the beginning of Garland's literary sponsorship of the young author. Garland delivered another talk, "Local Color in Fiction," two years later at the Congress on Literature at the World's Columbian Exposition, and Eugene Field's satiric account of it in the Chicago *Daily News* further spread Garland's ideas. Nor was he a stranger to the literary worlds of Boston and New York: despite his promotion, in *Crumbling Idols*, of the West, particularly Chicago, as a literary center, Garland was practical enough to cede that honor to New York, and he had early sought approval from Howells himself.

The truth is that, as Jane Johnson suggests in the introduction to her 1960 edition of the book, "some contemporaries felt [that] *Crumbling Idols* is unduly bombastic for a book advocating the day's most popular literary form."[6] From the date of its inception at the close of the Civil War, local color literature had been popular, promoted in its infancy by Howells and nourished by the steady exposure given it in such prestigious journals of the day as the *Atlantic Monthly*, *Harper's Monthly*, and the *Century*. Later critical writings by local colorists—such as Sarah Orne Jewett's 1893 preface to *Deephaven* (1877), Bret Harte's "Rise of the American 'Short Story'" (1899), and James Lane Allen's "Two Principles in Recent American Fiction" (1897)—all acknowledge that local color had indeed become, in Edward Eggleston's words, "the most significant movement in American literature in our generation."[7] About regional fiction at least, Garland assumes a radical stance not justified by the essays; he failed to whip up either enthusiasm or outrage because, quite simply, he was preaching to the converted.

By the time Garland wrote *Crumbling Idols*, in fact, the converted were rapidly becoming the disenchanted. Charles Dudley Warner's "Editor's Study" column in *Harper's Monthly* (May 1896) presents a dismissive but succinct account of local color's rise and fall:

> We do not hear much now of "local color"; that has rather gone out. . . . "Local color" had a fine run while it lasted. . . . [and] so much color was produced that the market broke down. It was an external affair, and its use was supposed to serve the gospel of Realism. . . . The author had only to go to the "locality" that he intended to attack and immortalize . . . in order to pick up the style of profanity there current, the dialect, if any existed; if not, to work up one from slovenly and ungrammatical speech, procure some "views" of landscape and of costume, strike the kind of landscape necessary to the atmosphere of the story . . . and the thing was done. As soon as the reader saw the "local color" thus laid on he knew that the story was a real story of real life.[8]

Warner's metaphors are telling: the relationship of writer to subject is that of conquest as the author sets out to "attack and immortalize" his subject, not to "under[stand] . . . without speaking" (54) as Jewett's narrator does with Mrs. Blackett in *The Country of the Pointed Firs*. Gone, too, is the sense of stories shared for their own sake: the text itself enters the realm of naturalistic economic exchange as the writer procures, "works up," and exploits the raw materials of this colonial "locality," afterward mass-producing the commodity until "the market [breaks] down." In such a system of standardized production, a smattering of authenticating "local color" dialect guarantees the middle-class reader a commodity at once safely standardized and suitably exotic. William Dean Howells and James Lane Allen had argued that local color techniques should be dictated by the characteristics of the region, not haphazardly applied for their own sakes, merely to be "colorful," but Warner suggests that local color fiction had by the 1890s indeed fallen into this sorry state.[9] In becoming an entrenched, dominant literary form, local color had suffered the fate of other popular literary movements: the use of style as an expression of substance gave way to a focus on style as a substitute for substance, a downhill road leading from stylistic excess to literary faddishness to dangerous self-parody.

What Garland, Warner, and others such as Frank Norris, Gertrude Atherton, and James Lane Allen came to believe during the 1890s was that local color had to be wrested from its comfortable niche and remade—had in short to be fragmented into the sort of meaning that it was no longer capable of providing. The "remaking" of local color actually constituted its disappearance as a cohesive literary genre, as the elements that comprised its characteristic forms were chipped away or borrowed for new purposes. As the twin monoliths of realism and local color began to crumble, writers were eager not merely to discard what they deemed useless but to salvage what they could from the wreckage they were instrumental in creating.

The audience for local color works was one of the first things to change. During the 1870s and 1880s, it had been a critical commonplace, and frequently a source of critical frustration, that the audience for magazines and novels was predominantly comprised of women, and that publishable fiction should be measured for its impact on the American girl. H. H. Boyesen's essay "The American Novelist and His Public" (1887) attacked this problem squarely, though even Boyesen could promise no solution:

To be obliged to repress that which is best in him, and offer that which is of slight consequence, is the plight to which many a novelist, in this paradise of women, is reduced. Nothing less is demanded of him by that inexorable force called public taste, as embodied in the editors of the paying magazines, behind whom sits, arrayed in stern and bewildering loveliness, his final judge, the young American girl. She is the Iron Madonna who strangles in her fond embrace the American novelist; the Moloch upon whose altar he sacrifices, willingly or unwillingly, his chances of greatness.[10]

Boyesen clearly subscribed to the myth of the headstrong, naively powerful American girl, and, as this essay and "German and American Women" show, he does not approve of her. William Dean Howells took exception to this negative image of Boyesen's "Iron Madonna." He defends the "Young Girl" from the imputation that she has arisen and "seal[ed] the lips of Fiction, with a touch of her finger, to some of the most vital interests of life." Manners in general have improved, Howells maintains, and so naturally there are fewer untoward incidents in novels nowadays. Howells does admit, however, that there is a "tacit agreement" between the publisher and the subscriber that the former "will print nothing which a father may not read to his daughter, or safely leave her to read herself." He recognizes this tacit censorship as a practical issue rather than a strictly moral one: "After all, it is a matter of business," he concludes.[11] Yet Howells, unlike Boyesen, is willing to lay responsibility where it more properly rests: not at the feet of the "Iron Madonna" herself, but on the shoulders of the right-thinking fathers and publishers who sought to protect American women from the sort of novels that women of other countries could read freely. Gertrude Atherton exposed the faulty logic of this approach in a 1904 essay for the *North American Review*:

> It is quite true . . . that the majority of readers are women. . . . It is also true that the genius of any race is determined by the thousand active exceptions, not by the million vegetables. . . . But if no educating force is applied to the million, how are they to advance? If their literature—which being sheep, they meekly accept—tells them only of their own life and kind, if not a hint from the real great world ever reaches them, how are they to deepen and augment their spots [of culture]?[12]

Despite Howells's defense, the caricature of the "Iron Madonna" lingered long after her influence had disappeared. Whereas Boyesen's Iron Madonna lived on, Howells's practical approach to the question of magazine audiences came to be seen as weak-kneed, effeminate capitulation, as in Ambrose Bierce's acerbic 1880 reference to "Miss Nancy Howells and Miss Nancy James," whom he identified in the *Wasp* in 1883 as "two eminent triflers and cameo-cutters-in-chief to her Littleness the Bostonese small virgin."[13] The "Bostonese small virgin"/Iron Madonna reappears, in fact, as "The Titaness," a monstrous caricature of middle-class respectability, born of "the goddess" Louisa May Alcott and raised on her "moral pap" in Thomas Beer's 1926 social history of the 1890s, *The Mauve Decade*.[14] She does not vary from her prototype in Boyesen's work: the Titaness uses her feminine powers to stifle creative male genius as surely as does her predecessor, the Iron Madonna. The threat implied by these stereotypes had some basis in truth: magazine fiction did, after all, have to conform to certain guidelines to be published. But the powerful antagonism underlying these stereotypes obscures the point that the Iron Madonna's own needs and tastes are in fact informed and circumscribed by the same male publishing elite that seeks to grant her power and responsibility for what it publishes.

Although fear of the Iron Madonna's influence lingered into the 1920s, her stranglehold, if it existed, relaxed substantially in the 1890s, despite Frank Norris's 1897 complaint that "the 'young girl' and the family center table . . . determine the standard of the American short story."[15] Changes in publishing, such as the perfection of a photoengraving process that allowed cheaper magazine printing, a new flood of cheap editions, and the great success of popular magazines such as *McClure's*, *Collier's*, and the *Saturday Evening Post* signaled equivalent changes in the audience. The new magazines were not necessarily less prudish than their predecessors, as Christopher Wilson points out in *The Labor of Words*, but their aims were different. The *Century*, the *Atlantic Monthly*, and *Harper's Monthly* had maintained an almost paternalistic interest in guiding and formulating public taste, a sense of mission that obscured, though it never overrode, their commercial objectives. By assuming the high ground and maintaining it rigorously against interlopers, the genteel magazines resembled a club for the aspiring culturant. As if to blur the distinction between authors and readers, the *Atlantic Monthly* even had a feature called "The

Contributors' Club."[16] By contrast, the newer magazines actively sought to broaden their readership through aggressive marketing techniques, less from a desire for democracy than from commercial motives. Recognizing an unmet need in the market, such pioneers as S. S. McClure and Edward Bok developed magazines addressed not to the cultured few but to the marginally lettered many; William Randolph Hearst and Joseph Pulitzer took a similar step in newspaper publishing. The increasing specialization of departments within the editorial structure, the relentless commercialism, the heightened emphasis on pictures and engravings, and the obvious willingness to cater more to the desires than to the intellectual welfare of their audience suggest a different model for the new magazines: the department store. As Edward Bok, editor of the *Ladies' Home Journal* declared, "A successful magazine is exactly like a successful store: it must keep its ware constantly fresh and varied to attract the eye and hold the patronage of its customers."[17] Appropriately enough for two movements that owed much to the age's enthusiasm for rampant capitalist expansion, innovations in magazine publishing and naturalism emerged together in the 1890s, and their audiences grew concurrently.

The shift in publishing and the changing audience signaled a concomitant difference in the public's taste in fiction. No longer constrained by the memory of a recent war, the younger generation of writers and readers sought rather to examine than to obscure the dislocations and paradoxes of a new age. Like Gertrude Atherton, who as an eager young writer had clipped out a picture of Howells's study and placed it above her writing desk for inspiration, writers and audience alike had grown up on Howellsian realism and local color. Now they were eager for a change. When Crane interviewed Howells in 1894, Howells decried "the hosts of stories that began in love and ended a little further on," calling them unbalanced in their perspective. In contrast, said Howells, a realistic novel, or a novel in its "real meaning adjusts the proportions. It preserves the balances." But balance and proportion were emphatically not what the new audience was looking for. As Crane put it in his question to Howells, there had been a change in the last four months: just when "it seemed that realism was about to capture things," Crane says, he noticed "a sort of counter wave, a flood of the other—a reaction, in fact." Howells agreed, saying, "I suppose we [realists] shall have to wait."[18] The realists would have to wait a long time for the triumph of the Howellsian realism to which they refer, for even as they spoke it had already begun to recede as a force, supplanted not only by the "counter wave" of romance to which Crane refers, but by the works of "lurid realism" or naturalism that Crane had even then begun to publish.[19]

The public's taste for adventure stories, love stories, and "lurid realism" shows that the celebration of excess that had characterized life in the Gilded Age had now invaded literature. Howells spoke of "proportions" and "balances," but his was a rearguard action of literary restraint; younger audiences sought extravagance in literature as well as in life. As Frank Norris explained to readers of the *Boston Evening Transcript* in 1901, not realism but romance "is the kind of fiction that takes cognizance of variations from the type of normal life."[20] Local color, realism's sister genre, had employed surface "variations," but, as if to compensate for its mildly exotic choices of locale, the movement had embraced wholeheartedly, and fatally, realism's gospel of limitations. Judged by the standards set by the sensationalistic daily papers, "real life" was more exciting and varied than realism had shown; the reporting of Richard Harding Davis, among others, stimulated a taste for adventure, just as the kind of sordid human interest "sketch" that Crane, Dreiser, and others turned out for the great New York daily papers showed real-life depths that realism had not yet explored. But the lack of balance, the focus on "variations," was all part of the age's outbreak of literary excess, whether manifested through journalism, through naturalism's "lurid realism," or through the "counter wave" of romance that distressed Crane. As Howells commented about *McTeague*, "His [Norris's] true picture of life is not true, because it leaves beauty out. Life is squalid and cruel and vile and hateful, but it is noble and tender and pure and lovely, too."[21] The result was that as the spirit of limitation gave way to excess, realism and local color gave up their dominance of the literary market to disparate and competing factions.

The vogue for historical romances and adventure stories marks a second element in the fragmentation of local color, as the retreat into the recent past suggested by local color became exaggerated into the full-blown escape possible in historical romances. Nationalistic fervor grew as America increasingly engineered the affairs of other countries, and interest in the isolated or backward regions of local color fiction lessened. By contrast, historical romances such as Charles Major's (1856-1913) *When Knighthood Was in Flower* (1898) and George Barr McCutcheon's (1866-

1928) *Graustark* (1901) fed on the public's taste for exciting events set in a situation remote from the present. Such novels as Richard Harding Davis's (1864-1916) *Soldiers of Fortune* (1897) combined exotic locales, adventure, and true-blue American heroes, winning both widespread popularity and the admiration of Crane and Norris in the process. In contrasting the popularity of such bestsellers—which he satirized with the fanciful titles *Buckets of Blood* and *The Flaming Sword*—with the undeserved neglect of Filipino novelist José Rizal's *An Eagle Flight* (1900), Howells underscored the imperialist myth at the heart of the genre.[22] Owen Wister's (1860-1938) *The Virginian* (1902) tapped another sort of American myth, one parodied by Stephen Crane in "The Blue Hotel" and "The Bride Comes to Yellow Sky": the American hero who tames the strange land and hostile characters out West rather than abroad. Noting that "historical romances, in fact, were the major best-sellers on the earliest published lists from 1895-1902," Amy Kaplan demonstrates convincingly that the performance of such fantasies of empire effects the revitalization of masculinity through a nostalgic "escape to a distant frontier . . . that . . . allows the American man to return home by becoming more fully himself."[23] Nostalgia for a redemptive atavism and a regeneration through conquest thus replaces local color's nostalgia for a harmonious, nonviolent golden age.

Confronted by such an obvious shift in taste, even the best of the local colorists did not escape contamination by the rage for romance.[24] In 1900 Mary Wilkins Freeman (then Mary E. Wilkins) published a novel whose title sums up its contents: *The Heart's Highway: A Romance of Virginia in the Seventeenth Century*. A year later, Sarah Orne Jewett came out with *The Tory Lover*. It was perhaps about these novels that an exasperated Henry James wrote to Howells on 25 January 1902: "Mary Wilkins's I have found no better than any other Mary, in the fat volume; and dear Sarah Jewett sent me not long since a Revolutionary Romance, with officers over their wine etc., and Paul Jones terrorizing the sea, that was a thing to make the angels weep."[25] Addressing Jewett herself on 5 October 1901, James tried a more tactful vein, though one that binds Jewett inescapably with her former works: "Go back to the dear country of the *Pointed Firs*, *come* back to the palpable present-*intimate* that throbs responsive, and that wants, misses, needs you, God knows, and that suffers woefully in your absence."[26] But neither Jewett nor Freeman was to repeat the success she had previously gained through her local color fiction. The 1902 carriage accident that incapacitated Jewett rendered moot the question of her burgeoning career as a romance writer, and the decidedly pedestrian quality of Mary Wilkins's romances failed to regain for her the acclaim she had received as a local colorist.

Given the circumstances, it is difficult to blame Jewett and Freeman for what, in retrospect, seems such a spectacularly inappropriate leap from serious, realistic local color to historical romance. By the 1890s, *local color* in its conventional meaning had lost many of its positive associations, as Warner's article shows; when it was not being attacked, it was being co-opted, as in *Crumbling Idols*. Hamlin Garland used the terminology of local color, but he clearly had in mind a variety quite different from the one his detractors scoffed at him for defending. For one thing, his preservationist impulse was scarcely that of a Sarah Orne Jewett. Celebrate regionalism, cries Garland—but he applauds the "[s]wifter means of transportation [that] will bring the lives of different sections into closer relationship" as shamelessly as any force-worshipping naturalist, forgetting that those same factors conspire to destroy the "actual speech of the people of each locality." Further, his enthusiasm for literary impressionism suggests not the quiet realism of the local colorists but modern literary impressionists like Crane.[27]

A third element in the destruction of local color lies ironically enough in the attempt to exaggerate its power; in other words, to grant it a promotion from regional to national importance. Garland presents a comprehensive scheme by which local color may prove its usefulness, indeed its patriotism: by producing John W. DeForest's "National Novel." When by the 1890s the sheer expanse and diversity of the country began to dampen even the most ardent enthusiasm, some observers came up with an ingenious solution. "The 'great American novel,' for which prophetic critics yearned so fondly twenty years ago, is appearing in sections," wrote Edward Eggleston in his 1892 preface to *The Hoosier Schoolmaster*.[28] Norris at first vacillated between being disappointed that American novelists had not written an epic treatment of their great land, and being defensive about the lack of a "primitive" stage that would make such an epic possible. Finally, however, he announced that "[a] Great American Novel is not too remote for discussion. But such a novel will be sectional."[29] Garland took a similar stand, applying his ideas about impressionist techniques to the problem. Just as impressionism utilizes bits of color to form an overall

picture or impression, so bits of regional writing, united by veritist theories of composition and presentation, will create an overall picture of the
nation, a picture presumably more "important," because unified, than individual local color works would be likely to give. In his "Editor's Study"
column in the December 1892 *Harper's Monthly*, Charles Dudley Warner
promotes this idea:

> So, while we have been expecting the American Literature to come out
> from some locality, neat and clean, like a nugget . . . there are coming
> forth a hundred expressions of the hundred aspects of American life. . . .
> And all these writers . . . are animated by the free spirit of inquiry and
> expression that belongs to an independent nation, and so our literature is
> coming to have a stamp of its own that is unlike any other national
> stamp.[30]

Responding twenty years later to Arnold Bennett's attack, Howells, in
"The Future of the American Novel," again invoked Jewett, Freeman,
Garland, and even Norris as "localists who have done and are doing far
better work than any conceivable of a nationalist" (348) before rendering
his judgment: "We for our part do not believe that the novel of the United
States ever will be, or ever can be, written, or that it would be worth
reading if it were written."[31]

Thus the *local* in local color was to be both transformed and subdued,
rendered subordinate to a purpose that it had not sought and could not
support. For both Garland and Norris, the parallel between American
expansionism in world affairs and the creation of a national literature
proved irresistible. With the twin avatars of Theodore Roosevelt and (for
Norris) Rudyard Kipling before them, Garland and Norris set forth to
colonize the weak and unruly islands of local color fiction, suggesting that
local fiction be allowed to exist under the aegis of, as well as for the benefit
of, a truly national literature. Strengthened by the diversity and sheer
number of these "colonies" of regional fiction, a national literature might
achieve a stature that at the very least would bring the United States to
literary parity with other nations. In furthering his "literary jingoism,"
Garland, like Eggleston and Norris, seeks to legitimize as well as to colonize the hitherto self-enclosed islands of local color fiction by uniting them
under an all-encompassing banner of nationalism. By this credo of literary

manifest destiny and his expansionist thinking, Garland thereby inflates, and ultimately obliterates, the movement's original impetus, its lack of pretension and focus on preservation of the individual. Dislocated by the passage of time, by shifting tastes, and now by ideology from the local color movement they had represented for so long, Jewett and Freeman may well have felt that they needed to retreat further into the past to salvage what they could from their original commitment to fiction.

Despite the exaggeration and fragmentation of their movement, including the rejection of limited action, the renunciation of the recent past as a usable subject, and the virtual erasure of their original purpose, the local colorists could, it would seem, still look with satisfaction to the kind of literature they had created. Writing for a serious and cultured audience, they had had the satisfaction, unlike most popular women writers of the 1840s and 1850s, of seeing their work respected. Moreover, they established particular virtues, elements of style, and feminine subjects as fit, indeed desirable, material for fiction. But as the *Atlantic Monthly*'s opening essay for October 1897 shows, all this was to change. Not only was the movement itself to be dismantled, but those elements identified as feminine were to be rooted out and replaced, a process that far outlasted the other exaggerated responses to local color's domination of the literary scene.

In the essay "Two Principles in Recent American Fiction," James Lane Allen reports that literature has become divided into two distinct and opposing "principles."[32] One is traditionally characterized by "Refinement, Delicacy, [and] Grace," to which he adds another trio of qualities: "Smallness, Rarity, Tact" (433). Although the public has now tired of this principle and applauds its passing, according to Allen, for the past twenty or thirty years this movement has dominated American fiction, especially American short-story writing. Its practitioners, whom he avoids naming, were plainly regionalists with a purpose: they "sought the coverts where some of the more delicate elements of our national life escaped the lidless eye of publicity, and paid their delicate tributes to these" (433). "[I]nexorably driven across wide fields of the obvious in order to reach some strip of territory that would yield the rare," they "found themselves impelled to look for the minute things of our humanity" (434). Despite their efforts, however, their work was "inadequate and disappointing, when viewed as a full portrayal of American civilization" (434). With the exception of a possible swipe at Howells and James implied by several of his discussions of "tact" and "consciousness,"[33] Allen obviously refers here to the local colorists. The subject at hand is not local color fiction, but is largely synonymous with it: Allen calls it the "Feminine Principle" in literature.

The "departing supremacy" (438) of this Feminine Principle balances the "approaching supremacy" of its opposite, the "Masculine Principle." Allen's discussion of the Masculine Principle reads like a naturalist's manifesto; indeed, this early essay in description parallels strikingly Malcolm Cowley's "Natural History of American Naturalism," published some fifty years later, long after naturalism had ceased to be an active literary movement. In Allen's view, the Feminine Principle's decline began not a moment too soon, since under its influence American novelists and short-story writers have "succeeded in producing a literature of what kind? Of effeminacy, of decadence. For in the main it is a literature of the over-civilized, the ultra-refined, the hyper-fastidious; of the fragile, the trivial, the rarefied, the bloodless" (438). What is needed to counteract this dangerous tendency is the literature that replaces the feminine virtues with new ones: Virility, Strength, Massiveness, Largeness, Obviousness, and Primary or Instinctive Action. Such a literature will contain "more masculinity and also more passion; and being at once more masculine and more passionate, it is more virile" (439), a trait that Allen approves as a counter-weight to the dangers wrought by the "Age of the Carved Cherry-Stones" (435). The Masculine Principle will promote a more accurate vision of the "Anglo-Saxon race," just as, like the Anglo-Saxon race itself,[34] it already strikes out "boldly for larger things,—larger areas of adventure, larger spaces of history" (440). Those who write from this principle are not afraid to look "from the heights of civilization to the primitive springs of action; from the thin-aired regions of consciousness which are ruled over by Tact to the underworld of unconsciousness where are situated the mighty work-shops, and where toils on forever the cyclopean youth, instinct" (440). The characteristics Allen describes—massiveness, strength, instinct, and the rest—inform both the content and the theme of naturalistic novels, where the physical mass created by words and pages, as well as the often ostentatiously rough prose, mirrors and mimics these characteristics within the text itself.

The observations Allen makes are all the more interesting in that he could not have adduced them from the books that made the major naturalists' reputations. Of the principal naturalists at the time Allen writes, only Stephen Crane was well known. In October 1897 Frank Norris was still working as a journalist for the *Wave*,[35] though he had substantially finished *McTeague*; with *Sister Carrie* still two years in the future, Dreiser had just left the editorship of his brother's magazine, *Ev'ry Month*; and Jack London was about to suffer through the winter of 1897-98 in the Yukon. Allen's expectation that the two principles will merge into a form at once stylistically great and virile, like Rudyard Kipling's "Recessional," further anticipates the influence of Kipling's work—particularly *The Light That Failed* (1890)—on Crane, Norris, and London.[36] But neither Allen's intention nor his method demanded exact proof from the literary scene; he affirms throughout that he writes an exposition or description of the temper of the times, not a polemic. His reflections on the Masculine Principle lack documentation because he assumed that the sentiments expressed were so widespread as to obviate the need for proof.[37] His carefully phrased but damning report on the Feminine Principle and the local colorists rested on the same assumption. Nor was Allen misguided in his beliefs. As late as 1904, the persistent connection between "littleness" and femininity that Allen had so emphasized, and that Bierce had used so cruelly, recurs in Gertrude Atherton's "Why Is American Literature Bourgeois?" Atherton attacks the magazines that promote "anaemic" literature and stifle originality, pausing along the way to ridicule those of "slender equipment" who are "always running about looking for copy, for local color," but whose "eyes are closed to the great things."[38] The equation of "local color" with "copy," suggesting that each is mere fodder for the presses, shows the extent to which the reputation of local color had declined.

As early as the mid-1890s, in fact, the term *local color* itself had undergone a metamorphosis, regaining its more general sense of "qualities of a region" as it encompassed more urban settings. "In Search of Local Color" (June 1894), one of the "Vignettes of Manhattan" series that Brander Matthews wrote for *Harper's Monthly*, depicts just such a cynical process of gathering copy and provides an interesting comparison with the Elijah Tilley episode in chapter 20 of *The Country of the Pointed Firs*: an upper-class, educated writer asks a friend, a native of the region, for an introduction to some of its inhabitants; after meeting a laconic widower employed in keeping up domestic pursuits after his wife's death, the writer learns the story of the man's marriage. Only in these essentials, however, does Matthews's local color story resemble Jewett's: in Matthews's

proto-naturalistic sketch, the literary enterprise is overt, the quest after
"copy" and color highlighted, as Harvard-educated man-about-town Ru-
pert de Ruyter asks settlement worker John Suydam to help him find "a
little local color" for "a series of New York stories for the *Metropolis*" (34).
With some hesitation, Suydam takes him to the Italian immigrant neighborhood known as Mulberry Bend, a neighborhood made famous as the
"foul core of New York's slums" in Jacob Riis's *How the Other Half Lives*
(1890). Like Jewett's narrator, who finds classical analogues in Mrs. Todd's
"look of a huge sibyl" (8) and her standing like "Antigone alone on the
Theban plain" (49), De Ruyter draws upon his classical education to see
"faces . . . of a purer Greek type" in the tenement dwellers. Suydam cuts
him short, however, with the ethnically charged "scientific" observation
that Sicilians are the "hottest tempered Italians" (36). Gone is the tact with
which Jewett's narrator approaches characters such as Elijah Tilley, for here
local color conversation becomes naturalistic observation, and then invasion: the two men throw open the doors of apartments without knocking
because "[m]ost of them [the Italian immigrants] don't know what privacy
means" (38). Finding one such resident at home, the two question him as
he stirs a potful of macaroni and laconically tells them that his wife is dead.
Learning later that the man has killed his wife, De Ruyter feels neither
sympathy nor horror; he is instead satisfied that he now has "lots of color"
(39) and a suitably sensational ending to his tale. Jewett's narrator values
relationships as well as writing; she turns with a sigh to her half-written
page and, despite differences in class, counts Elijah Tilley among her
friends. By contrast, De Ruyter, whose Dutch family name links him with
New York's "old stock," remains distanced from his subject, Pietro
Barretti, by class, ethnicity, and the journalistic detachment that distinguishes naturalistic observation from local color sympathy. In the character of De Ruyter, Matthews censures only the local color hack and the
commodification of experience into fodder for the presses, but the basic
enterprise—the appropriation and inscription of a "foreign" oral culture by
an educated observer—remains the same in both tales. Matthews's tale
indirectly questions in uncomfortable ways the construction of class bias,
"old stock" ethnicity, and the privileged position of the educated author-
observer in local color fiction. Jack London's "Local Color" (*Ainslee's*,
October 1903; collected in *Moon-Face, and Other Stories*, 1906) takes a
satiric approach to the subject as a "copy-gathering" excursion into hobo

life yields "local color, wads of it," including an unflattering portrait of a police judge. When the writer, Leith Clay-Randolph, is mistakenly arrested for vagrancy and appears before the judge, he is told, "Young man, local color is a bad thing. I find you guilty of it and sentence you to thirty days imprisonment."[39]

Thus Garland, Allen, Atherton, Norris, and the rest make the same point repeatedly: for too long a predominantly female audience, or a coterie of cowed, timid editors, had created authors, particularly local colorists, in their own small, pale, tactful image, either restraining or refusing to sanction altogether fiction about real life by red-blooded male authors. Indeed, critics of the Feminine Principle often use the same image to describe the problem. Words denoting the presence or absence of "blood" occur frequently in this debate over the new literature: Allen's "bloodless" and Atherton's "anaemic" are only two examples. In an unlikely metaphor, the editors and magazinists, the local colorists, and the female audience are cast as literary vampires, draining the life out of the corpus of American literature with their insatiable lust for propriety.[40] For example, in a 1907 letter, Jack London lashed out at the timidity of *McClure's* editor John S. Phillips: "In short, he wanted to make me take the guts and backbone out of my stories; wanted me to make an eunuch of myself; wanted me to write petty, smug, complacent bourgeois stories; wanted me to enter the ranks of clever mediocrity and there to pander [to] the soft, fat, cowardly bourgeois instincts."[41] For these writers, women are not "red-blooded"; the only suggestion that they might be, or the closest approach to such an idea, is this comment by Norris: "[G]ive us men, strong, brutal men, with red-hot blood in 'em, with unleashed passions rampant in 'em, blood and bones and viscera in 'em, and women, too, that move and have their being."[42] This last vague phrase scarcely suggests parity with the "red-hot blood" he allots to men.

Naturalistic authors such as London, Crane, and Norris accepted the threat of femininity in varying degrees, complaining about magazine timidity and the reluctance of editors to publish pieces that were true to life. London's own frustrating attempts to be published sharpened his recognition of the hypocrisy that encouraged both yellow journalism and the genteel magazines. Writing to his friend Cloudsley Johns in 1899, he laid the blame squarely on "the 'silent sullen peoples' who run the magazines":

Our magazines are so goody-goody, that I wonder they would print a thing as risque [*sic*] and as good as that. This undue care to not bring the blush to the virgin cheek of the American young girl, is disgusting. And yet she is permitted to read the daily papers![43]

Trying to get an early version of *Maggie* published in 1892, Crane faced a similar resistance in talking with Richard Watson Gilder of the *Century*.[44] Gilder's cautious approach is evident in a letter about Crane's later story "A Man and Some Others": "You may think me over anxious, but I am particularly sorry he [Crane] did not change that 'B'Gawd.' It is difficult to know what to do with swearing in fiction. When it appears in print it has an offensiveness beyond that of the actual word. . . ."[45] As he wrote to Lily Brandon Munroe in 1894, Crane saw himself as "involved in the beautiful war between those who say that art is man's substitute for nature" and those who "can't say much but they fight villainously and keep Garland and I out of the big magazines. Howells, of course, is too powerful for them." But the battle has been worth it, he says, gleefully pointing out that the same stereotypical cabal of female audience and editors, the "parcel of old, cringing, conventionalized hens" that had called him a "'terrible, young radical,'" were beginning to "hem and haw and smile" at his approach.[46] Crane would have relished the turn of events when even Gilder gave way to the Masculine Principle. An October 1902 editorial in the *Century* acknowledged that there were now "two magazine audiences— male and female," and two years later, in an effort to attract more male readers, Gilder paid Jack London $4,000 for the serial rights to *The Sea-Wolf*, which began its run in the *Century* in January 1904.[47]

Of the women who were local colorists, the naturalists had relatively little to say. Judging from his extant letters, Crane apparently did not discuss the principal local colorists, although shortly before he interviewed Howells, Howells had grouped him with Jewett and Freeman as among the best writers that America had to offer.[48] Dreiser, like Norris, had read Freeman; in his column "The Literary Shower" for his brother's music magazine *Ev'ry Month*, he praises the "vigor, beauty, and pathos in her lines" and calls her the "leading woman novelist of America." His comment is not without a touch of envy—or is it wishful thinking?—for he remarks that not only her public but "also the syndicates" appreciate the "vigor, beauty, and pathos" of her work. In the same paragraph, he rebukes Stephen Crane for writing "night and day," unlike the less frequent efforts of Mary Wilkins.[49] Writing about the policies of the *Delineator* in 1909 during his editorship, Dreiser groups Freeman with Margaret Deland and other women "magazinists" in explaining that their fiction is suitable: "The finer side of things—the idealistic—is the answer for us, and we find really splendid material within these limitations." Eight years later, he writes to H. L. Mencken, "Barring Howells, James, Norris, Phillips, Mrs. Wharton, Garland, Herrick and London are there any fugitive realistic works of import. [*sic*] I want a list. I should exclude Whitlock, H. B. Fuller, & Stephen Crane." A week later, he responds to Mencken's list as if to extend it, asking about writers that Mencken did not mention: "Did Alice Brown ever write a realistic work?—or Mary E. Wilkins—one that was good all through?" Mencken claimed ignorance of these local colorists, however, and Dreiser dropped the subject.[50] Although Jack London admired the early work of Edith Wharton and maintained a correspondence with the later Western local colorist Mary Austin, neither the voracious reading documented in his letters nor the library he collected later in life reveals an acquaintance with the principal female local colorists.[51] Whatever their indirect complicity in maintaining the feminine literary climate of the times, the local colorists largely escaped direct censure from the naturalists.

· III ·

The principal exception to this record is Frank Norris, whose signature of "F.N. (The Boy-Zola)" bespeaks a willingness to acknowledge literary models at odds with the reticence of Dreiser and Crane.[52] Norris mentions at least two local color writers. He condemns Octave Thanet (Alice French) as a run-of-the-mill magazinist, but he read and approved of Mary E. Wilkins Freeman. In his 1902 essay "An American School of Fiction? A Denial," Norris finds that "[o]f the latter-day fiction writers Miss Wilkins had more than all others convinced her public of her sincerity. Her field was her own, the place was ceded to her." For Norris, "sincerity" was high praise indeed; it is one of his strongest complimentary adjectives. But Wilkins has apparently forgotten that she "owes a duty to the literature of her native country," a cardinal sin in the eyes of Norris, who believed firmly in what he called "The Responsibilities of the Novelist." He berates her for writing *The Heart's Highway*, saying that in choosing "to succumb to the momentary, transitory set of the tide, and forsaking her own particular work," she has disappointed those "who looked to her to keep the standard firm—and high."[53] From his perspective as one who had never known real poverty, Norris loftily dismissed as motive what was in fact the case—that Wilkins had to write *The Heart's Highway* "for the baser consideration of money"—and concluded that she had deserted her public as a "deliberate capitulation to the clamor of the multitude" (110). That "her own particular work" no longer put bread on her table was not, for Norris, the point; she had deserted her own deserving public for "the multitude" (surely an equally deserving public) and had thus disgraced or in Norris's metaphor "discrown[ed]" herself.[54] Norris also considered Freeman's local color point of view restricted, commenting in a posthumously published essay that "writers of fiction in their points of view are either limited to a circumscribed area or see humanity as a tremendous conglomerate whole; that it must be either Mary Wilkins or George Eliot, Edward Eggleston or William Shakespeare." It seems at first ironic that Norris blamed Freeman for turning to romantic fiction when he himself had written "A Plea for Romantic Fiction" only a year earlier. As might be expected, Norris's conception of romance includes something altogether freer and more all-encompassing than the "Realism [that] stultifies itself" by noting "only the surface of things" or the mundane "cut-and-thrust business" that constitutes conventional romance. For Norris, romance itself sweeps through the house from high to low, gathering material from all quarters, dragging with it both realistic techniques and the tenets of naturalism, both of which it uses unstintingly in order to convey the image of "real life."[55]

As evidenced by his critical writings and by Presley's artistic dilemmas in *The Octopus* (1901), Norris was much concerned with such questions of form and genre. About *Blix* (1899), for example, he wrote to Isaac Marcossen that "[i]t's not naturalism and it's not romanticism; it's just a story." When he wrote *McTeague* (1899), Norris was evidently determined to make it a naturalistic test case, writing to Howells that it "is as naturalistic as Moran was romantic and in writing it I have taken myself and the work very seriously." Taking himself seriously in *McTeague* meant writing a novel of "straight naturalism with all the guts I can get into it," as he later said in comparing *McTeague* to his Wheat trilogy, but it also meant doing something more.[56] Within *McTeague*, Norris planted the story of Miss Baker and Old Grannis, an elderly, genteel pair straight out of local color fiction, turning the novel at one level into a parable of literary choices available to the turn-of-the-century novelist.

As Ernest Marchand pointed out in *Frank Norris: A Study*, "[t]he Old Grannis-Miss Baker love affair has always been a *locus criticus* in all discussions of *McTeague*." Contemporary reviewers, according to Marchand, "seized on it desperately as the only palatable episode in the novel," though with his usual perception William Dean Howells nailed down the problem modern readers have found, declaring that the novel's "one folly is the insistence on the love-making of those silly elders."[57] Following Howells's lead, Donald Pizer finds this subplot to be "thematically and dramatically weak." Other attempts to place the "Old Folks" story line within the naturalistic framework of *McTeague* have ranged from finding them to be absurd, Dickensian caricatures providing comic relief to a more sympathetic view that identifies them as foils or commentary for the McTeague story line; Charles Child Walcutt's rationale that they contribute to the "sense of sociological extremes" and William B. Dillingham's explanation that they serve "as an effective contrast and balance to the main plot" are examples of the latter view.[58] More recent critics, such as George M. Spangler in "The Structure of *McTeague*," have adopted this approach through form, a reasonable one in view of Norris's insistence on symmetry of theme and structure in the novel, although at least one scholar, James B. Stronks, proposes a source for the story in H. C. Bunner's (1855–1896) "Love Letters of Smith" (1890).[59] On another level, reading *McTeague* as a commentary on problems of genre and storytelling provides a further explanation of the presence of the Old Folks story.[60] By first contrasting and finally integrating the Old Grannis–Miss Baker story with that of the McTeagues and the Zerkows, Norris explored the problems inherent in the convergence of three late-nineteenth-century literary movements: realism, naturalism, and women's local color fiction.

The Old Grannis–Miss Baker subplot could have appeared in any number of local color stories, but the two characters bear a particularly striking resemblance to David Emmons and Maria Brewster of Mary E.

Wilkins Freeman's "Two Old Lovers" (*A Humble Romance*, 1887).[61] Freeman's lovers live in the proverbially slow town of Leyden, but David Emmons is slow even for that place. He courts Maria for over twenty-five years, and together they work out an unspoken partnership: he visits her every Sunday evening, she bakes for him, and he brings her vegetables. The ritual quality of their partnership is seldom disturbed, although once when Maria senses that David might finally be "coming to the point," she buys some handsome pearl-colored silk and has it made into a dress for her wedding.[62] When she is sixty-eight and he is seventy, David falls ill and dies, but not before saying the words Maria has wanted to hear for so long: "I allers meant to—have asked you—to—marry me" (12).

Norris's rendition of this type of story in *McTeague* is strikingly similar, but, in keeping with the movement away from local color and toward excess, he exaggerates the elements that Freeman has already stretched to the limits of credibility. Old Grannis, owner of the dog hospital where Marcus Schouler works, and Miss Baker, a retired dressmaker, live side by side in the same building as McTeague. Like Maria and David, the two are over sixty years old and in love, yet whereas David withholds the significant words from his relationship with Maria, Old Grannis and Miss Baker suspend *all* words: "they were not even acquaintances; never a word had passed between them."[63] Silence prevails even though they live closer than Freeman's old lovers: their "rooms" are actually one large room, as Miss Baker discovers to her consternation when she finds that the wallpaper is the same in each. They "keep company" by sitting alone in their rooms with the doors ajar as ritualistically as any local color pair: each sits close to the thin partition, Old Grannis binding books that he does not read and Miss Baker setting out afternoon tea on her "little red table, with its three Gorham spoons laid in exact parallels" (288), as neatly as Louisa Ellis ever did in "A New England Nun."

As in Freeman's work, the intrusion of the outside world is the only element that can disturb the equilibrium of the lovers' arrangement. In the tranquil town of Leyden, only natural forces such as the approach of death function as catalysts for a shift in Maria and David's relationship; few other events in that town are monumental enough to move such intransigent characters. The teeming world of lower-class Polk Street, however, provides a host of events, including Maria Macapa's junk-gathering raids, McTeague's wedding dinner, and Maria's eventual murder by Zerkow, the crazed junk man. Each of these events functions as the intrusion not merely of the outside world but of a particularly excessive emotion—greed or gluttony, for example—into the disembodied emotional world of the lovers. Norris takes care to heighten this contrast, as in the scene at McTeague's wedding feast. Falling into silence and confusion after they speak for the first time, Old Grannis reflects on the incident: "[B]ehold, it had suddenly come to a head, here in this over-crowded, over-heated room, in the midst of all this feeding, surrounded by odors of hot dishes, accompanied by the sounds of incessant mastication" (384). The ascetically minded Grannis is surprised that the fleshly excesses occurring around him should bring out such feelings, but throughout *McTeague* that is exactly Norris's point: at each stage of their relationship, the old lovers are brought together by some (often gross or sordid) occurrence from the outside world of the flesh rather than the placid world of the imagination in which each temperately resides. Old Grannis and Miss Baker's encounter with fleshly excess functions much as does David Emmons's approaching death in "Two Old Lovers," in that a recognition of mortality and the inescapable encroachment of the natural, physical world brings the old lovers closer together. After their inadvertent contact, "[I]n a little Elysium of their own creating," Miss Baker and Old Grannis "entered upon the long retarded romance of their commonplace and uneventful lives" (384).

In the words "commonplace and uneventful lives," Norris provides the key to one of the old lovers' functions in the novel. Of the three pairs of lovers in the work, Old Grannis and Miss Baker represent the almost excessive restraint, manners, asexuality, and spiritual self-denial characteristic of local color fiction, just as the junk dealer Zerkow and Maria signify the excessive passions of Zolaesque naturalism. Despite some naturalistic flourishes, the McTeague plot begins as a story of realism, with its lower-middle-class protagonists striving for respectability and a better place in life. Unlike the steady degeneration through sloth of, say, Zola's Gervaise Coupeau in *L'Assommoir*, Trina and McTeague more or less maintain their equilibrium until dual calamities, in the form of the lottery winnings and McTeague's loss of his license, overtake them. Circumstances and instincts conspire to drive Trina and McTeague to recapitulate Maria's murder and Zerkow's flight; the characters only then cast off the world of realism in which they began and descend to the depths of the novel's Zolaesque underworld. Thus each pair of lovers functions on several levels: as representatives of varying social levels and codes of manners; as unwitting victims of the world of forces; as "owners" in several senses—of money, of passions, of restraint; and finally as characters in plots suitable to the differing genres that the novel explores. Their associations thus resonate with meaning as the varying stories and characters become enmeshed with one another. As Trina slips further into her obsessive miserliness, for example, she visits Miss Baker less and Maria Macapa more, signifying her descent from the restraint and middle-class respectability of realism to the lower-class excess and squalor that characterizes naturalism.

Norris further signals his concern with form and genre through the theme of storytelling. The stories told in local color fiction are elaborate, realistic, and purposeful; they help to foster community coherence and preserve a sense of the past through relating particulars about individual characters and events. In contrast, the stories in *McTeague* are limited, conventional, and unrealistic; they contribute rather to the isolation than to the community spirit of individuals. The more convinced the characters become about the truth of the stories, the more likely they are to withdraw from human contact. In *The Art of Frank Norris, Storyteller*, Barbara Hochman distinguishes between storytelling's actual and apparent functions for the characters:

> Throughout Norris's work, characters repeatedly find that reading, writing, or telling stories affords them at least a temporary sense of order or control, some measure of inner equilibrium. . . . For certain characters, the repetition of a story becomes an adaptive mechanism through which the memory of a particular past experience serves to fortify (or sometimes petrify) the self against the pressures of the present.[64]

By relying on this false "adaptive mechanism" of control, the characters in *McTeague* come to trust fiction more than humanity, and believing fiction instead of life was for Norris one of the problems both of literature and of civilization. In *The Fiction of Frank Norris*, Don Graham analyzes the novel's "aesthetic milieu" and finds that it represents the characters' limited, conventionally defined desires and a nearly inarticulate yearning for beauty.[65] The stories that the characters tell in *McTeague* are of a piece with their aesthetic judgment as Graham describes it, yet each tale reverberates disastrously and out of all proportion to its seemingly innocuous clichés, with social instability, loss, brutality, and murder resulting from the telling. The stories all confuse romance and money: all are tales of wealth magically won or lost, trite fantasies of wish fulfillment that contrast ironically with the real relations between love and money in the world of Polk Street.

The most notable storyteller, Maria Macapa, has two stories, the one she refuses to tell—"had a flyin' squirrel and let him go"—and the one of the gold dishes that she tells obsessively, with elaborations, until it leads to her death. The story of the dishes first substitutes for, then becomes itself the substance of Zerkow's treasure, and when she forgets it after the birth and death of her baby, Zerkow kills her, as McTeague does Trina, in a self-defeating attempt to get at the treasure she hoards. In part, Maria's sordid death suggests the destructive powers of imagination, both hers in concocting the story and Zerkow's in believing it, in a narrow, brutally deterministic universe. For the most part, however, Norris stresses the destructive power of the false story itself, as the tales of unearned wealth, which are really a single—indeed the only—story told by characters in *McTeague*, echo ominously throughout the lives of the other characters. For example, Maria's tale of the gold dishes and lost wealth suggests a fall in station comparable to that which Old Grannis is supposed to have suffered, and anticipates that which Trina and McTeague will suffer. In the same way, the lottery-man's tale of riches showered on the deserving poor comments ironically on the McTeagues' story as well as on Old Grannis's, in that these characters are threatened, not made happy, by their chance acquisition of wealth.

Trina's slow transformation into Maria Macapa, and her entry into the world of naturalism, becomes complete when she, like Maria, becomes a storyteller. She confronts Old Grannis with the truth of his love for Miss Baker, ordering him to "go right in and speak to her just as soon as she comes home, and say you've come into money and you want her to marry you" (482). The happy ending has been signaled, appropriately enough, by Miss Baker's "little fiction" of Old Grannis's aristocratic origins: "They say that he's the younger son of a baronet; that there are reasons for his not coming to the title; his stepfather wronged him cruelly" (275). The sentimentality of the "prince-in-disguise" motif and the happy ending is nonetheless subdued, dampened as in any local color work by the atmosphere of death: Maria's, whose body Trina will shortly discover; Trina's own; and of course that implied by the old people's frailty. For the first time in the novel Trina lies not selfishly to protect her money, but rather to create a happy ending for someone else. Completing the story is her last act of affirmation before she sinks irretrievably into Maria's life, and it is her only selfless act in the novel.

In allowing Trina to "write" a happy ending for the old people, one that because of her intercession does come true, Norris emphasizes the distinction between genres: human intervention counts and happy endings do occur in local color fiction, as they cannot in naturalism. Trina is helpless against the inexorable forces of her own naturalistic world, for when she abandons herself to the excessive passions (in her case, greed) of naturalism and refuses to consider restraint, she gives up all hope of entering the genre where restraint presides. She learns only too late to "read" the conventions of the world she comes to inhabit. Of her miserliness she says, "[I]t's a good fault, and, anyhow, I can't help it" (411). As a self-made prisoner of naturalism, she cannot be author of her own destiny, though her hoarding is a desperate and wrongly conceived attempt to exert precisely that sort of control. Indeed, her miserliness seems a mocking allusion to that most central of local color virtues, self-denial. The parodistically conceived and excessive self-denial registers Trina's willful misreading of the local color example that the Old Folks provide: excess of anything is destructive, not virtuous. By allowing Trina to manipulate others' destiny but not her own, by juxtaposing her disinterested act of kindness with her rapid descent into squalor, Norris heightens the irony of her situation. She cannot follow the conventions of the old couple's local color story, and thus cannot reap the benefits of this genre's predictability. Instead, armed with only limited practical knowledge of how to hump one's back so that beatings don't hurt as much, she must enter the new, dangerous, and unpredictable world of naturalistic fiction.

Trina's story hastens the union of the old lovers, but the crisis of Old Grannis's sudden wealth provides the final push. As in "Two Old Lovers" and other local color works, the crisis is of the "slow Leyden" rather than of the Polk Street variety. For the old couple, routine and ritual become disrupted, and with them the fragile fabric of their relationship. With the sale of his bookbinding method, Old Grannis has wealth but no occupation. He reflects that the "absence of his accustomed work seemed to leave something out of his life. It did not appear to him that he could be the same to Miss Baker now; their little habits were disarranged, their customs broken up" (488). As Hochman points out, the disruption benefits the pair: "Old Grannis's loss of habitual occupation, unlike McTeague's, results in a kind of redemption."[66] Like Trina, however, he cannot redeem himself but must depend on the intercession of Miss Baker, who dares to do something that Maria Brewster does not: on a night when old Grannis feels strongly the disruption and loss of ritual he has suffered, Miss Baker makes the first move toward him, offering the traditional local color consolations of a visit and a talk. She makes a cup of tea and brings it to him; they hesitatingly confess their feelings, and, with the symbolic and actual partition now gone, hold hands:

> "keeping company," but now with nothing to separate them. . . . They walked hand in hand in a delicious garden where it was always autumn. Far from the world and together they entered upon the long retarded romance of their commonplace and uneventful lives. [493]

The repetition here of phrases from chapter 9 functions as a coda, reinforcing with variations the satisfaction and even happiness they find. The reference to the "garden where it was always autumn" hints at mortality ever present but continually held in check, an ending more reminiscent of Freeman's "Conflict Ended" than of "Two Old Lovers," but one still firmly fixed in local color convention.

Seen thus as an exploration of local color fiction, the Old Grannis–Miss Baker subplot does not deserve the condemnation it has received. As recently as 1982, William E. Cain in "Presence and Power in *McTeague*" complained that "Norris bathes the characters in sentimentality and alludes to problems of motivation that he does not explore, or cannot handle, or does not care about."[67] Norris's skill at handling motivation in the local color story is problematic, but that he took such pains to ground his characters in an extant literary tradition should put to rest the idea that he simply "does not care about" the characters. The characters and their story line are limited because Norris felt that the local color form itself was limited. Having allowed the old people to consummate their relationship with Old Grannis's kiss on Miss Baker's "faded cheek" (493), Norris sends them to their room for the remaining four chapters of the novel.[68] Quite simply, as Norris sees it, neither the old couple, their story, nor local color fiction has anywhere else to go. With the local color story effectively packed away, the naturalistic story opens out in all its force, complete with sordid elements of setting and action. It is no accident that only now does McTeague light out for the territories, meeting nature on terms of adventure and disaster on a grander scale than was possible in the cramped rooms of Polk Street. He even meets Norris at the Big Dipper mine, "a tall, lean young man, with a thick head of hair surprisingly gray" (531).[69] Norris, his creature McTeague, and naturalism itself have all moved beyond the stuffy rooms and limited space of local color fiction.

With the theme of storytelling, Norris shows the danger of believing in false fiction and simplistic plots that provide happy endings, particularly if, as is true of Trina and McTeague, one inhabits a more dangerously complex genre. In his story of the Old Folks, Norris pays tribute to the stories of Mary E. Wilkins Freeman. Yet he explores the conventions of local color and judges them to be wanting; he finds the limitations of local color unworkable in the real world of Polk Street. Published in 1899, the novel reads both as a handbook of the novelist's options at the century's end, and as a parable of the path that American fiction was taking. Disdaining, like Norris, the limitations and small rooms of the old lovers, American fiction took its chances with the great world. Beset by calamities and world change, American realism, like the McTeagues, took up residence in the house of Zolaesque naturalism.

CHAPTER FOUR

Frederic, Norris, and the Fear of Effeminacy

· I ·

As the century drew to a close, the split that James Lane Allen described between the "Masculine" and the "Feminine" principles in literature had grown still greater. Literary critics and the reading public alike viewed with suspicion the grimy proletarian presence of the Masculine Principle's "cyclopean youth, Instinct."[1] After all, industrial labor had made the youth impatient with gentility and intent on the physical world and his place in it; worse, it had made him alienated, class-conscious, and strong. Yet his presence in literature seemed to ensure a vigor that made the threat to established forms tolerable, as if only an excess of brutish masculinity could surmount both the imported effeminacy of the British and French Decadent movements and the entrenched native traditions of the "Feminine Principle."[2] Alarmed by what they saw as a gradual encroachment of a feminine ethic in literature, the naturalists did not stop to debate the vast differences between these two ideas. They did not seem to care, for example, that the Decadent movement's indifference to didactic purposes, its broad, often shocking choice of subjects, and its focus on careful observation mirrored and in some cases mocked their own objectives. From their perspective, acknowledging the brute indeed risked admitting a potentially destabilizing force into literature, but defending the status quo was certain to preserve an unhealthy, static predominance of the Feminine over the Masculine Principle.

Allen's essay heralded a more generalized crisis of masculinity in the culture at large.[3] For Norris and the other naturalists, the brute's propensity for violence functioned as an antidote to a greater threat, the "mollycoddle." Besides, as Theodore Roosevelt explained in a 1915 speech before the Panama-Pacific Historical Congress, "In the long run the 'sissy' and the 'mollycoddle' are as undesirable members of society as the crook and the bully. I don't like the crook and the bully. . . . But, after all, there is the possibility that you can reform the crook or the bully, but you cannot reform the 'sissy' or the 'mollycoddle' because there is not anything there to reform."[4] Tom Lutz explains in *American Nervousness, 1903*:

> Roosevelt agreed with Brooks Adams and other writers that the civilized races were becoming soft, flabby, and feminized; he railed against "the ideas of the 'peace-at-any-price' theorists . . . the timid and scholarly men in whom refinement and culture have been developed at the expense of the virile qualities." . . . The cure for such deterioration, like the cure for neurasthenia, he wrote, was the exercise of strength and the cultivation of manliness. Neurasthenia effeminized men, and since effeminized men lacked the fighting edge, neurasthenic cultures were doomed.[5]

Roosevelt's "red-bloods" and "mollycoddles" later learned to write and resurfaced as "redskins" and "palefaces," the two antipodal categories whose opposition, according to Philip Rahv, creates a "split personality" in American literature. Rahv's "paleface" is a "highbrow" who tends "toward a refined estrangement of reality," whereas the "redskin" "accepts his environment" and is "emotional, spontaneous, and lacking in personal culture."[6] Confirming James Lane Allen's prediction, Rahv contends, "The palefaces dominated literature throughout the nineteenth century, but in the twentieth they were overthrown by the redskins."[7]

Fifty years before Rahv's essay and a year before Allen's "Two Principles in Recent American Fiction," Gelett Burgess had burlesqued the distinction between "redskins" and "palefaces" in his November 1896 poem for the *Lark*, "The Ballad of the Effeminates":

> Milk-sop, Willieboy, sissy, dandy, tenderfoot; —
> The best of 'em is tailormade, there's more upon the shelves; —
> Rough, tough, mucker, mick, hoodlum or Bowery; —
> If there's any good among 'em all, they done it all theirselves![8]

Burgess's comically blustering narrator, like Norris (and to an extent like Roosevelt), presents an either-or choice. On the side of culture sit the original hollow men—the Willieboys and sissies with no original ideas, no knowledge of real life, and certainly no grit. Their existence bore out James Lane Allen's warning of a literature dominated by "the over-civilized, the ultra-refined, the hyper-fastidious; of the fragile, the trivial, the rarefied, the bloodless."[9] Opposing them are Norris's "strong, brutal men, with red-hot blood in 'em,"[10] the type that G. Lowes Dickinson called "red-bloods."[11] These rough, uncultured Bowery toughs, the modern, urban version of nineteenth-century noble savages, display true American spirit and scrappy determination. It was far better to be a little rough than to be what Roosevelt in *The Strenuous Age* (1901) called "the timid man, the lazy man . . . the overcivilized man, who has lost the great fighting, masterful virtues."[12] Commenting on this passage, Larzer Ziff notes, "Civilization was not a good of which one simply could not have too much; it was, rather, a middle state between ferocity and pusillanimity, and it was possible to be 'over-civilized.'"[13] Civilization, not the brute, was the greater threat.

With this opposition between the hypothetical extremes of (over)civilized man and the brute, three different courses of thematic development emerged in naturalistic fiction: the triumph of the brute, leading to the degeneration of the individual; the balance of the two opposing forces, leading to the perfect amalgamation of sensibility and "red-blooded" vigor; and an excess of civilization, leading, ironically enough, to a degeneration similar to—and in some cases identical with—that which the emergence of the brute signals. The first of these possibilities represents the conventional plot of naturalistic novels such as Norris's *McTeague* or Zola's *L'Assommoir*. In such works, external circumstances tip characters away from a precarious balance of civilized behavior and respectability toward a slow, inevitable spiral of degradation. Inherited traits (sloth, drunkenness, savagery) combine with environment to effect these characters' degeneration until in extreme cases they become little better than animals. Excessive civilization is no threat here. Indeed, civilization itself is nothing more than a thin covering—a veneer, to use Norris's favorite term—that masks the essential beast within. Not surprisingly, the characters whom the naturalists subjected to this treatment bore a strong kinship to the "types" that Cesare Lombroso had stigmatized in *Applications de l'anthropologie criminelle* (1892). They were presented as the antithesis of the "objective" middle-class naturalists who were describing them, and their inevitably sordid ends could thus be observed with equanimity. In choosing the brute as a subject for their stories of degeneration, the naturalists strained their audience's patience by graphically portraying sordid scenes of lower-class life. They did not, however, violate the most serious of all contracts: the elevation of author and audience alike to a position superior to that of the brutish characters.

Within the other two courses of development, however, even this taboo is broken. The second type of plot exploring the opposition between civilization and the brute is exemplified in works such as Norris's *Moran of the* Lady Letty (1898) and Jack London's *The Sea-Wolf* (1904). In each of these works, delicately nurtured males like London's Humphrey "Sissy" Van Weyden confront their more primitive selves, and, as Joseph McElrath, Amy Kaplan, and James R. Giles have noted, redeem themselves with the aid of a courageous "New Woman." Contact with brutishness, initially that of others and thereafter his own, does not prove disastrous; rather, it allows overcivilized man to balance both sides of his nature in order to become a complete human being. In "Beneficial Atavism in Frank Norris and Jack London," James R. Giles proposes that location makes the difference between this plot pattern and the first one. The distinction "between beneficial atavism and destructive atavism . . . rests upon the setting of the stories—if the reversal occurs in the city, it is usually destructive; while a similar reversal on the high seas or on any 'frontier' is generally beneficial."[14] Writing of historical romances, Amy Kaplan further refines this concept: "In the 1890s the lament for the close of the frontier loudly voiced such nostalgia for the formative crucible of American manhood; imperial expansion overseas offered a new frontier, where the essential American man could be reconstituted."[15] The principal determinant of redemption for Norris and London must nevertheless be located within the characters rather than the frontier setting; race, not region, finally emerges as the crucial determinant. These overcivilized tenderfeet, who must be forced into learning the strenuous life, are saved because, unlike McTeague, they come from "good stock," and their experiences serve to reawaken what the naturalists identified as an "inherited" brand of "Anglo-Saxon" courage and endurance.[16] As Sister Soulsby tells Theron Ware in another context, contact with roughness "scours the rust and mildew" off those made of "scythe-steel," although it destroys those who, like Theron, are made of "razor-steel" or lesser stuff.

This honing process was in fact the "underlying motif" of *The Sea-Wolf*, as London explained to his friend and editor George P. Brett:

My idea is to take a cultured, refined, super-civilized man and woman, (whom the subtleties of artificial, civilized life have blinded to the real facts of life), and throw them into a primitive sea-environment where all is stress & struggle and life expresses itself, simply, in terms of food & shelter; and make this man & woman rise to the situation and come out of it with flying colors.[17]

Like Norris's socialite Ross Wilbur, who learns of necessity to be strong when the *Lady Letty* is attacked by Chinese pirates, Humphrey "Sissy" Van Weyden turns into the hardened able seaman "Hump" when shanghaied into a world altogether more violent than his own. Under the sadistic tutelage of Captain Wolf Larsen, Hump learns, in the central image of the book, to stand on his own rather than on his father's legs. Through his own efforts he makes a place for himself in the brutal social system of the *Ghost*, a society that Larsen defends as an inescapably Darwinian microcosm of the world that Hump has been too insulated by privilege, hence too blind, to see before. When Maud Brewster comes aboard the *Ghost*, London suggests that Hump has by his exposure to brutishness become a fit mate for her. A man daring and resourceful enough to execute their escape, Hump is respectful enough of womanhood to build separate huts when they reach Endeavor Island. Whereas Wolf Larsen uses philosophy merely to justify his own savagery in everything from murder to an attempted rape of Maud, Hump adopts only enough of Larsen's ideas to preserve his own life and thus leaves his humanity intact. Contact with both the brute without (Larsen) and the brute within (his murderous rage at injustice) forces him to be strong at the same time that it teaches him the necessity for control.

The third possibility, surrendering to overcivilization or the feminizing effects of too much culture, presents the greatest threat. In both *Vandover and the Brute* and *The Damnation of Theron Ware*, the protagonist's indulgence of his taste for refinement may paradoxically cause his animal nature to triumph, so that he becomes a brute in taste and outlook in Theron's case, and a brute in fact in Vandover's. Furthermore, Theron Ware and Vandover exhibit symptoms of effeminacy as part of their process of degeneration; seduced and abandoned by their own devotion to the false ideals of civilization, they fail as men.[18] Although of a naturalistically defined and class-based "good stock" like Ross Wilbur and Hump Van Weyden, they are not redeemed by the other men's trial by sea. Never forced to assume a different, less civilized perspective, they do not learn the meretricious powers of civilization until they "consume" an excess of it. In actuality, both men misread their culture's dichotomous, rigid messages about gender roles. By fulfilling certain expectations, such as adaptability to circumstances and a love of culture and ideas, that are nominally but not actually set forth for men and women alike, they lose a certain primitive strength and ferocity that the naturalists considered essential to masculinity.

· II ·

As Austin Briggs, John Henry Raleigh, and others have suggested,[19] Harold Frederic's *Damnation of Theron Ware* or *Illumination* (1896) provides a virtual compendium of nineteenth-century intellectual currents ranging from biblical higher criticism, aestheticism, feminism, and contemporary theories of racial types to Jamesian pragmatism and empirically based scientific method.[20] The novel's power, however, resides less in its exposition of those ideas than in its ability to invoke their dark underside—secularism and apostasy, racial and class-based chauvinism, overcivilization, effeminization, and degeneration—and, by so doing, enmesh both Theron and the unwary reader in a world of crumbling certainties and inevitable anxiety. In part, Frederic elicits this anxiety through raising the disturbing possibility that both genre and gender distinctions exist in a state of flux, or, more specifically, collapse. A brief overview of the stock character of the local color minister, followed by an extended examination of the portrayal of Theron as a "hybrid female," reveals Frederic's exploration of realism through his character's progress from the conventions of sentimental and local color fiction to the harsh realities of naturalism.

Although the character of Theron Ware owes much to the "sinning minister" characters of earlier authors, notably Hawthorne,[21] Frederic's portrait of the unaware, impotent, self-important minister recalls similar local color clergymen such as Rose Terry Cooke's Parson Stearns ("How Celia Changed Her Mind") and Parson Hill ("Mrs. Flint's Married Experience"); Mary Wilkins Freeman's Mr. Hersey ("The Revolt of 'Mother'") and Mr. Pollard ("A Village Singer"); and Sarah Orne Jewett's Mr. Dimmick (*The Country of the Pointed Firs*). Instead of the opposition between male authority and female community common in local color works, Frederic explores the affinity between the social roles of ministers and women, namely their true powerlessness in a society that professes to exalt and obey them. Ann Douglas describes this phenomenon in *The Feminization of American Culture*:

> The similarities and dissimilarities between ministerial and feminine roles were exposed and exaggerated by the potent fact that the two groups perforce kept company: the nineteenth century minister moved in a world of women. . . . Female "influence," whether he liked it or not, was the minister's chief support.[22]

Within Frederic's unsparing critique, however, Theron exists as a doubly isolated character through his ambiguous status as a "hybrid female." Rendered powerless by his culture's inscription of his ambiguously gendered profession, he is further deprived of the informal, woman-centered web of relationships both by his sex and by that community's traditional opposition to legalistic Christianity represented by the local color minister, whose idealism, like Theron's, cannot prevail. As Lisa MacFarlane notes in "Resurrecting Man: Desire and *The Damnation of Theron Ware*," "The disordering of gender identity is therefore part of how the male minister negotiates his own political and economic positions within patriarchy, not evidence of how he is aligned with women to challenge it."[23] As Theron explores the feminine role into which he is initially forced, he finds that his own and others' expectations change until he becomes the role he plays. Posturing, adapting, trying desperately to please, he misinterprets the complex rules of the "civilized" society he tries to adopt and retreats into a game of expectations he cannot help losing.

The relationship between Theron and his church establishes this powerlessness from the outset. The grim-faced patriarchs of the Nedahma Conference wield absolute power over the "livings" (in several senses) available to the preachers under their command. Despite his brilliant preaching and wish to remain in the up-and-coming town of Tecumseh, the patriarchs arrange for Theron to be shunted off to Octavius, where the people are "jest a trifle close in money matters."[24] During a meeting with two of the mortgage-holding, interest-gouging members of the Board of Trustees whose names—Pierce and Winch—suggest their approach to finances, Theron's true position becomes apparent. Drawn to serve Methodism by a romantic "wave of religious enthusiasm" (19), he now finds himself bound into an arranged marriage with the intolerant church of Octavius and its intransigent board, whose money and position give them absolute power over him.

Like any nineteenth-century wife, Theron has limited options: he can capitulate, as he does when he agrees to make Alice remove the roses from her bonnet; he can threaten with little effect, as when he says he will take matters to the Quarterly Conference; or, as Sister Soulsby teaches him, he can dissemble, selling his ideals—in one case, what's left of his friendship with Levi Gorringe—for the sake of a hundred-dollar raise in his salary. What he cannot do is defy them openly or divorce himself from them, for, as Sister Soulsby points out when he threatens to quit the ministry, he lacks economic power: "How could *you* earn a living? What trade or business do you suppose you could take up now, and get a living out of? Not one, my man, not one" (175; italics Frederic's). Even the worldly Father Forbes recognizes the practical issues involved; he himself does not publicly ruffle any feathers with his private, freethinking sentiments, and he tells a rebellious Theron, "It is a pretty serious business to make such a change at your time of life" (283). Lacking even the nominal authority granted to local color ministers, Theron, like the women around him, finds himself possessing gifts on which his society places no intrinsic economic value, and thus he must perfect the arts of pleasing his exacting congregation—his "spouse."

As a consequence of his social and economic powerlessness, Theron is also denied the usual male avenues of redress; he cannot escape by going fishing, nor can he take out his aggressions in sharp business dealings or fights with Levi Gorringe. In fact, his defensive arsenal throughout remains that of a nineteenth-century heroine of domestic fiction. When expostulation fails, he resorts to a rhetoric of sentimental gestures: fainting, illness, and weeping in various combinations. According to Ann Douglas, Theron's use of illness as an avoidance technique is not unusual:

> The cultural uses of sickness for the nineteenth-century minister and lady are undeniable. To stress their ill health was a way for both punitively to dramatize their anxiety that their culture found them useless and wished them no good; it supplied them, moreover, with a means of getting attention, of obtaining psychological and emotional power even while

apparently acknowledging the biological correlatives of their social and political unimportance. [109]

Thus as Theron begins to be seduced by the works of Renan, he avoids his hard-shell Methodist parishioners at the Wednesday prayer meeting, insulating himself from their demands by claiming a "bad headache" (131). He shuts out unpleasant conjectures about Alice and Levi Gorringe's relationship by taking refuge in the classic nineteenth-century woman's defense against upsetting news: he faints dead away at the "love feast," spending the rest of the week in a dangerous attack of "brain fever" (164) and feigning sleep to avoid Alice. When Celia dismisses him after her seductive Chopin concert, he challenges her control in words that the strong heroes of conventional romances have taught him: "Things don't end that way!" (204). Theron cannot maintain his role of romantic hero, however, for immediately after this challenge he relapses into the one more familiar to him—romantic heroine: "A sharp, blinding spasm of giddiness closed upon and shook him, while the brave words were on his lips" (204). Here as always, excessive emotion makes him tremble and feel faint. If, as Tom Lutz proposes, the advent of neurasthenia invokes a "ritual space" or a "liminal discourse . . . available to individuals involved in a broad variety of passages and changes . . . [including] reinforcing or transforming traditional roles," then Theron's version of the disease signals the gendered nature of his distress and his assumption of the sentimental heroine's gestures even as it provides a coded reference to his participation in the "disease" of encroaching modernity.[25]

Theron's tears represent an escalation of his ineffectual gestures toward control. Unlike Alice, who swallows her sobs so that she will not cry at his coldness (295), Theron frequently resorts to extravagant tears, particularly when he is crossed in love. In his excessive self-solicitude, he again collapses a significant local color distinction: rejecting the tradition of shared consolation, Theron isolates himself further by unsuccessfully assuming the roles of both comforter and comforted. When he seeks Celia out for the first time, his eyes fill with tears as he feels "tender compassion for himself" (189). Celia rejects him a second time in New York, whereupon he "sank in a heap upon the couch, and, burying his face among its cushions, wept and groaned aloud" (329). A few days later he gives way to another fit of tearful self-pity before Sister Soulsby: "His quavering voice broke off in a gust of weeping, and his face frankly surrendered itself to the distortions of a crying child's countenance, wide-mouthed and tragically grotesque in its abandonment of control" (342). With his tears he abandons all pretense at strength or dignity, becoming a "crying child" whose distressed passivity invites the other characters to act in forceful, "masculine" ways. At first genuinely helpless and innocent, he soon learns like any nineteenth-century heroine to feign those characteristics that others expect of him, and his pose becomes his primary means of manipulating the other major characters in the novel.

Moreover, Theron's increasing reliance on tears and other feminine gestures signal his naturalistic degeneration long before Celia points it out to him. William James, according to Eugene Taylor, explained to his 1896 audiences that degenerative types "show fear, anger, pity, tears, and fainting . . . they are 'oversensitive' and show an 'excessive response' which can include neurasthenia and dependency." From a nineteenth-century psychological perspective, Theron's self-pity, his anger at Alice, his tears, his fainting fits, his excessive dependence and, perhaps most significant, his two mental breakdowns all indicate male pathology, but, with the exception of the anger and the breakdowns, the same symptoms suggest the temperament of a normal, if "high-strung," nineteenth-century woman. As Tom Lutz notes, "the diagnoses and cures [for neurasthenia] were based on [women's] assumed weaknesses and on an explicit understanding that women's natural, healthy state differed not in kind, but only in degree, from their diseased state."[26]

If Theron seems but dimly aware of the implications of the illness, weeping, and other sentimental gestures he enacts privately, he is all too aware of the social, public constructions that inscribe his position as an ambiguously gendered minister. Alice generally views him as lover and comrade, but she often treats him as she might a child or a woman friend, "putting the hat on his head and smoothing back his hair behind his ears" (55). She also advises him to carry an umbrella in the hot sun, saying, "I don't see why a minister shouldn't carry one as much as a woman carries a parasol" (116). Her choice of words is instructive, for she does not say "man" but "minister," a nuance that Theron quickly picks up: "I suppose people really do think of us as a kind of hybrid female" (117). Indeed, Theron thinks of himself as a "hybrid female." Like a woman protecting her reputation, he frets too much about public opinion, certainly far more than the other men in the book. Before he meets Celia, he worries that an Irish servant might tell tales of his home life; when he wishes to visit Father Forbes, he "loiter[s] aimlessly about . . . until dusk" before he goes to the rectory (64), presumably so that he will not be seen by members of his flock. At the picnic, he assumes the privileges of a woman, hoping that "some one would bring him out a glass [of beer], as if he were a pretty girl" (240). Assuming these privileges, however, also confers upon him a less desirable responsibility, that of placating public opinion. When Harvey Semple, Levi Gorringe's office boy, finds him sitting with Celia in the woods, Theron panics, fearing that his reputation will be ruined: "In my position I am a thousand times more defenceless than any woman" (263). Given his narrow-minded congregation, Theron's fears are justified, but his choice of words shows a cowardice that contrasts unfavorably with Celia's indifference to gossip.

Although he cowers in alleyways lest the town comment on his visit to Father Forbes, Theron ostentatiously seeks public approval when he luxuriates in the experience of buying paper from Thurston's department store for his projected book on Abraham. In Rachel Bowlby's terms, he becomes a "willing consumer" in the "available ideological [merchandising] paradigm of a seduction of women by men, in which women would be addressed as yielding objects to the powerful male subject forming, and informing them of, their desires. The success of the capitalist sales project rested on the passive acceptance or complicity of its would-be buyers."[27] Theron later recalls with satisfaction that "he had followed [the clerks] unresistingly. . . . He indulged to the full his whim that everything entering into the construction of 'Abraham' should be spick-and-span" (58), thus exemplifying Bowlby's consummate (female) consumer.

Neglected by Theron and critics alike, Alice Ware both reflects and illuminates this process of Theron's transformation, encoding a set of stabilizing references to ordinary reality and realistic fiction against which both her rivals and the oscillating gender relationships within the novel may be judged. Like Howells's Marcia Gaylord Hubbard in *A Modern Instance* (1882), Alice is a plain-spoken woman married to a man whose ethics she begins to deplore. Her often-belittled talents, like playing the piano and speaking her mind, exist as realistically depicted counterweights to the more fantastically depicted traits of Celia Madden and Candace Soulsby, whose abilities surpass hers even as their characters strain credulity. Alice prefigures these two other important women in Theron's life: her height, commonplace speech, homely metaphors, and pragmatism anticipate those of Candace Soulsby, just as her flowered hat (an emblem of spirit and sexuality) and isolation from her family suggest Celia. Before the Soulsbys appear, Alice advises Theron about managing the trustees, warns him about maintaining an appearance of piety, and hints that, as Sister Soulsby and Levi Gorringe separately tell him later, he would be better off to "move along smoothly and not fret" (174). Like Celia, whose name anagrammatically reverses her own, Alice is pretty, educated, musically inclined, and rich; in short, she is the best catch in town. For ministers and women, success depends on making a "good match"—to a wealthy spouse, to a prosperous, open-handed congregation, or to both. As George Spangler points out in "Theron Ware and the Perils of Relativism," "the attraction of wealth strongly influences Theron's response to Celia, and when the time comes that Theron feels he must act on his wishes, Frederic makes the economic motive perfectly explicit."[28]

Further, Alice functions as a foil to Theron's repressed masculinity and his ever-decreasing humanity. Steven Carter cites his cruelty to her as evidence of his "hard, masculine" side, and, as MacFarlane observes, "As Theron's attraction to Celia intensifies, his construction of Alice's femaleness as inferior becomes more complete, and his need to assert his own dominance as a man increases."[29] He becomes a "street angel, house devil" kind of man, a hypocritical clergyman in the tradition of Deacon Everts in Rose Terry Cooke's "How Celia Changed Her Mind."[30] Reinforcing his masculinity, however, means not only distancing himself from Alice but from the humanity that she had encouraged in him. As Theron grows increasingly deluded about his own intellectual worth, his misapplied "critical standards" cause Alice to suffer by comparison with her more talented and devious rivals. After Celia's virtuoso performance of Chopin and Sister Soulsby's intelligent application of Chopin melodies to religious lyrics, Alice's playing seems only "very good—for her" (237). With the "intelligently warmed" butter of her flattery (144), Sister Soulsby fosters Theron's conceit by belittling Alice, calling her "a kind, sweet little body . . . devoted to you, and it isn't every intellectual man that gets even that much" (146), a barbed compliment that even Theron understands. Early in the novel, Theron remembers that Alice taught him to laugh and reflects that she has "enriched and humanized" him (20), teaching him the "human, the warm-blooded side of things" (99) that the Forbes-Madden-Ledsmar group values in him. In shedding Alice and innocence, Theron believes that he stands "forth, so to speak, in a new skin" (207), never recognizing that the new skin is that of the "long, slim, yellowish-green lizard" (230) that Dr. Ledsmar has named for him. Theron thinks he has attained the "wisdom of the serpent" (144) extolled by Sister Soulsby, but he has really only succeeded in assuming the serpent's changeable reptilian character. Only through Alice can he maintain contact with the supremely ordinary humanity, free from Celia's romanticism and Sister Soulsby's cynicism, that is the best part of himself.

Theron's increasing gender anxiety manifests itself further through the repeated motif of hands and handshakes. At first, he literally and figuratively makes contact with the community and presumably with the rest of humanity by shaking hands with virtually all who cross his path, a series of encounters that mark his progressive alienation from the rest of the book's characters. For example, Theron initially refuses to shake Father Forbes's "outstretched hand" (45) because he fears that he has intruded upon the wheelwright's deathbed and is at first drawn to Levi Gorringe, who shakes his hand with "an excess of cordiality" (121) when Theron visits his office. Later, Gorringe will not "take his hands from his pockets" (275) at Theron's approach, just as Dr. Ledsmar pretends to have an aching shoulder (229) so that he need not shake Theron's hand either. Their refusal to shake hands with him anticipates his isolation at the end of the novel, when "even the little child in the car, playing with those two buttons on a string, would have nothing to do with him" and he sees himself as "alone among awful, planetary solitudes which crushed him" (328).

For Theron, the hands of the women in the book serve not only as markers of character but as gauges of his sexual attraction to them. Theron notes with a newly awakened class-based distaste Alice's "red face and arms bared to the elbow" (52) when she brings him the boiled dinner, since they remind him not, as earlier, of his happiness in Tyre but of the hired girl there. In contrast to his own and Father Forbes's soft hands, the hands of Celia and Sister Soulsby are large and masculine, objects of erotic fascination for Theron. Sister Soulsby, who "wears the breeches" (123) and kisses Alice "in a masterful manner" (137), holds out her hand in a "frank, manly fashion" (146) even as Theron appraises her small wrist, swelling forearm, gold bracelet, and the "delicate, significant odor" that surrounds her (146).

That same combination of delicacy, strength, gold, and implied sensuality attracts him to Celia. The "frank, almost manly vigor" in Celia's handshake startles him almost as much as her "large, robust hands" (102). During the Chopin concert, Theron shifts his gaze away from the cold and incomplete sexuality implied by the half-draped "armless woman in marble" to the complete, warm sexuality implied by Celia's "white, rounded forearm which the falling folds of this strange, statue-like drapery made bare" (202), a contrast Frederic emphasizes through the adjective "statue-like." Although Celia speaks of ideas, Theron ignores her words as he glances at "an extravagantly over-sized and sumptuous bed" and then stares again as though hypnotized at "the mingled delicacy and power of the bared arm and the shapely grace of the hand" (205), an overt connection that supports Frederic's metonymic use of the hand as sexual symbol.[31] Like Father Forbes's "white fat hands" (285) that seem to do no work, the hand here sheds its connotations of work and exists as an aesthetic object, a symbol of sex and leisure. Indeed, one marker of Theron's own degeneration is his purchase of "a small book which treated of the care of the hand and fingernails" (236). This intricate pattern of approach and avoidance figured through Frederic's symbolic use of hands underscores two of the novel's themes: Theron's growing alienation from the rest of humanity, and the movement from the inscribed gestures and gender roles of sentimentalism to the morass of both gender and genre uncertainties, where codified responses no longer reap a predictable result.

Whereas hands, gestures, and attitudes mark the ambiguous and shifting nature of gender identity within the novel, only one major constant exists for determining masculinity or femininity. Theron sees essential masculinity as the confident *possession* of both culture and heretical ideas, femininity as the quest after such culture and ideas. Already reversing traditional gender roles, Dr. Ledsmar, Celia Madden, Father Forbes, and Sister Soulsby also reverse tradition by trying to "convert" the minister to their forbidden philosophies: Celia discourses on Arnold and aestheticism, Father Forbes on the higher criticism and anthropology, Dr. Ledsmar on the biological sciences and Darwinism, and Sister Soulsby on pragmatic religion—the religion of "sabe."[32] The ideas themselves, however, are scarcely the point, for Frederic makes it clear that Theron has only the most hazy understanding of what he reads or is told. Because his church in essence forbids both sexuality and ideas, the two become merged into one exciting and illicit pleasure for him. Theron frequently confuses the two repressed pleasures, interpreting sexual attraction as the intellectual variety, and Frederic emphasizes the point by describing Theron's frequent intellectual attractions in sexual terms: "The very thought that he was on the way now to know [ideas], too, made Theron tremble. The prospect wooed him, and he thrilled in response, with the wistful and delicate eagerness of a young lover" (134). The trembling and eagerness of this first infatuation with ideas soon fades, as Theron begins to toy with ideas "as a woman of coquetry might play with as many would-be lovers" (236); unfaithful to Methodism, he now promiscuously accepts competing belief systems. Ironically, for Theron sophistication implies not a broader, more discriminating outlook but one that is narrowed to the trivialities of sexual gossip.

Of the four characters who attract Theron, Father Forbes provides the best example of Theron's penchant for confusing masculine with feminine, sexual with intellectual. Father Forbes is from the beginning a figure of great power and equally great sexual ambiguity for Theron. For one thing, Theron's rampant narcissism interprets Forbes as an idealized projection of his future self. Like Theron, he is a "hybrid female" by virtue of his calling, a fact doubly reinforced by his celibacy, and the absence of sexuality implied by this celibate state allows Theron's increasingly sexually obsessed imagination free rein. Despite his "masculine bearing," Father Forbes carries his "erect, shapely, and rounded form . . . with the natural grace of a proud and beautiful belle" (68), a combination that fascinates Theron. The femininity implied by such physical characteristics as his "rounded form" and skirtlike soutane is offset by the intellectual vigor that Theron interprets as masculine; moreover, the mixture of danger, intellect, and indeterminate sexuality that the priest represents attracts Theron. Seeing Father Forbes at the bedside of the dying man, "Theron felt his blood tingle in an unaccustomed way" (42). Later, upon hearing Father Forbes discourse on Celia as a type of ancestral Celtic mother, Theron replies, "I love to hear you talk" (285), echoing Alice's words to him during their courtship. He feels, in fact, "as a romantic woman must feel in the presence of a specially impressive masculine personality. It was indeed strange that this soft-voiced, portly creature in a gown . . . should produce such a commanding and unique effect of virility" (285–86). The feminine, even eunuchlike implications of "soft-voiced," "portly creature," and "gown" here are offset by a virility born of Father Forbes's wide-ranging knowledge. Nevertheless

Theron does not necessarily accept any of Forbes's ideas, any more than he really accepts Celia's. He focuses instead on style, preferring to wreathe both characters in his own romantic fantasies rather than to understand their beliefs. Hearing passionately held ideas, he mistakes medium for message and thus seriously misjudges the attitudes of those around him.

Theron hastens his own downfall when he betrays his own commitment to language of any sort. Although Celia, despite her dilettantish ways, begins several projects, he accomplishes exactly nothing on his book about Abraham and is shown repeatedly daydreaming as "the book lay unopened on his knee, and his eyelids half closed themselves in sign of revery" (16). He turns from the reality of "that beautiful pile of white paper, still unstained by ink" (59), to a vision of his completed book in much the same way that his naturalistic contemporary Vandover of Frank Norris's *Vandover and the Brute* endlessly contemplates the empty canvas for his projected masterpiece, *The Last Enemy*. Production becomes for Theron not an expression of ideas, a redemptive return to masculinity, but instead merely a means of facilitating further consumption, as he envisions the book selling "like hot cakes" (62). Theron further fails by misunderstanding the intellectual masculinity of Father Forbes: uninterested in the Higher Criticism that Forbes and Ledsmar discuss, Theron seeks out heartwarming stories about Abraham's personal life, traditionally a woman's concern. In a similar way, he misinterprets Levi Gorringe's ominous story of the girl that got away, ignoring Gorringe's interest in Alice to praise the tale as "full of human nature" (125). Unlike the women in local color stories, Theron does not use stories to cement his community relationships. His anger at Alice's "trivial" concerns, such as getting a large enough table to seat all their company, shows that he does not yet understand the "wisdom of the serpent" that Alice learns from Sister Soulsby. Like the women in local color stories, they recognize, as Theron does not, that the sharing of food and talk is essential to fostering a spirit of community.

As his grandiose, word-intoxicated "illumination" reveals itself to be, in Celia's terms, "degeneration," Theron is cast adrift. Cut loose from rigid teachings and devoid of the faculties of intellect that would allow him to make his own, better rules, he, like Vandover, resorts to a fatal adaptability. He notes that "there was a sense of the luxurious in this position [of choosing among ideas] which softened bodily as well as mental figures. He ceased to grow indignant at things below or outside his standards" (236). He begins, in fact, to see himself as a victim of impersonal forces and to measure things by only the most elemental laws of nature: greed, self-interest, and sexual attraction. The education of this local color minister has led him only into a self-delusional justification of the naturalistic brute within.

Frederic's use of local color conventions in *The Damnation of Theron Ware* thus serves several transformative purposes. By evoking the gestures of sentimental fiction, a precursor genre to local color, Frederic systematically insists on Theron's innocence, a process necessary to emphasize the contrast presented by his final degeneration. Mimicking the stereotypical life of a nineteenth-century woman, Theron exists in a hothouse of public opinion, is denied access to any real economic or social power, and is forced to depend on those in power for his very sustenance. Kept artificially innocent and sketchily educated, he succumbs to the lure of ideas and sexual knowledge without a true understanding of them, focusing too intently and exclusively on sexuality as a key to understanding everything, from Sister Soulsby's checkered past to Celia's "real" relations with Father Forbes. In effect, his position as minister requires him to play this role, and the novel doubly insists on performance: Theron's own as a gifted speaker, and the reader's recapitulation of Theron's experience.[33] The moral growth implied by the sentimental bildungsroman, the self-denial of the local color tale, and the principled "rise" of Howells's characters such as Silas Lapham, however, here become inverted. Theron's ultimate growth into knowledge results in his choosing not self-abnegation but self-aggrandizement: he embraces a ruthless commercial individualism and turns his back on the domestic and communal ideology of earlier fictional forms, developing an embryonic Babbitt-like self through the most cynical kind of theatricality.[34] Frederic had originally intended to make Theron a suicide,[35] and whether his fate is indeed worse than death, as some have suggested, is open to question.[36] For Theron, the theatrical representation of sympathy that Sister Soulsby teaches him is less dangerous than its true enactment: to maintain his masculinity, he must shed the gestures of a sentimental heroine and the trappings of the local color ministry that occasion them, along with the innocence that they signify, in order to reconfigure his identity as a modern man in the realm of naturalism.

· III ·

Like *The Damnation of Theron Ware*, *Vandover and the Brute* (1914) presents a chilling portrait of degeneration. Unpublished until twelve years after Frank Norris's death, it is one of Norris's first novels, originating in his student themes at Harvard (1894–1895) at about the same time as *McTeague* (published in 1899) and *Blix* (serialized March through August 1899 in *Puritan*; published in book form 1899). *Vandover and the Brute* is the story of Vandover, a young artist who dreams of studying in Paris but settles instead for Harvard, where he learns to appreciate drinking, "Van John" (vingt-et-un), and "fast girls." Upon returning to San Francisco, he dabbles in art and the fashionable vices until "three great catastrophes" overtake him in the course of a month: the suicide of Ida Wade, the girl he had seduced and left pregnant; the wreck of the *Mazatlan*, the ship on which he was traveling; and the death of his father. After his return, Vandover attends a production of *Faust*, and, deeply affected by the music, assesses his life: "Religion could not help him, he had killed his father [by his responsibility for Ida Wade's suicide], estranged the girl ["good girl" Turner Ravis] he might have loved, outraged the world, and at a single breath blighted the fine innate purity of his early years."[37] Remembering his art, he reconsecrates himself to it, only to find that it is too late: his talent has fled. He begins a Jekyll-and-Hyde existence when "the brute"—Vandover in a state of "lycanthropy mathesis"[38] (523)—emerges against his will. Vandover also begins to display some of the characteristics of psychological degeneration described by William James in his 1896 lectures on exceptional mental states, including neurasthenia and the *"folie du doute"* behavior that today would be described as obsessive-compulsive disorder.[39] The brute increasingly determines Vandover's level of existence, and Vandover degenerates steadily, following his earlier pattern of initial decline, fitful resolve, and ensuing greater degradation. He is swindled out of a part of his fortune, and he drinks and gambles away the rest. He ends up a seedy, self-pitying vagrant, scrubbing rental houses for his onetime friend Charlie Geary.

In several senses, the degeneration in *Vandover and the Brute* marks a departure from that of Frederic's novel: Theron deteriorates morally, whereas Vandover does so both morally and physically. Too, the causes of their downfall are different. The threat to Theron Ware is very much of the homegrown variety, Celia's and Dr. Ledsmar's European ideas notwithstanding, and it is native American ideas of culture, the ministry, and feminine roles that get him into trouble in the first place. Vandover's quandary, on the other hand, suggests to a certain extent the period of decadence that followed the Aesthetic movement, and his delight in sensuous indolence and reckless indulgence owes something to the spirit embodied in the *Yellow Book*, Joris-Karl Huysmans's *À Rebours*, and Oscar Wilde's *Picture of Dorian Gray*. Indeed, *Vandover and the Brute* bears some striking parallels with Wilde's portrait of degeneration. Like Dorian Gray, Vandover is an artist deflected from his original purpose into a life of sensual indulgence, a life that despite repeated resolutions he at first will not, and finally cannot, give up. Norris uses the image of the brute that Vandover becomes (always behind closed doors) in much the same manner that Wilde used the hidden portrait: as a metaphor of an even deeper and more horrifying degeneration than is visible on the surface. Plot parallels also exist, notably the suicides of the seduced women Ida Wade and Sybil Vane. Yet as an opponent of Wildean decadence and effeminacy, Norris criticized the tendency of his fellow San Franciscans Gelett Burgess and Les Jeunes to indulge in a whimsical approach toward the *Yellow Book*'s excesses. In the May 1897 issue of the *Wave*, he uses the *Boston Evening Transcript*'s glowing remarks against them,[40] castigating the group for ignoring their responsibility as writers: "Yes, there are Les Jeunes, and the *Lark* was delightful—delightful fooling, but there's a graver note and a more virile to be sounded. Les Jeunes can do better than the *Lark*."[41] They would "do better," he goes on to say, to "grip fast" upon the real life happening around them. "It's the Life that we want, the vigorous, real thing," he concludes, "not the curious weaving of words and the polish of literary finish."[42] The story of Vandover's failure is largely that of his refusal to "grip fast" upon real life and sound a "graver and more virile" note, both as an artist and as a human being.

What hinders Vandover in his art and in his life is an inability to transcend the conventional feminine attitudes that his culture has inculcated in him, an inability compounded by his tendency to exaggerate and to parody those feminine attitudes in his life and in his art. In "Frank Norris's *Vandover and the Brute*," Joseph R. McElrath Jr. explains that Vandover's fall results less from a pro forma determinism than from his inability to see that the "paradoxes, incongruities, and absurdities that characterize reality . . . invalidate his naive dual vision."[43] Both McElrath and Barbara Hochman have noted Vandover's rigid dualistic thinking, yet in this respect he reflects, indeed epitomizes, the caste-bound perspective of San Francisco's upper middle class. The problem is not simply that Vandover shares its views but that, lacking a realistic outlook, Vandover takes his cues from the dichotomous views of masculinity and femininity presented and misreads both of them. He "reads" too literally, for, like Theron Ware, he is essentially an innocent who believes in the righteousness of the forms he is taught. Again like Theron, he maintains a rigidity of belief even when he tries to reinterpret the rules of his society in more "sophisticated" terms. Continuing McElrath's point about Vandover's naive dualism, Lee Clark Mitchell explains, "'Artistic' and 'brutal' dispositions are treated as if they were mutually exclusive, instead of as jointly informing perspectives on a range of human behavior."[44] Vandover's attempts to mediate the disparity between the genteel and the real prove futile: they lead him not only into misreadings but into exaggerations or perverse versions of traditional masculine and feminine behavior. Consequently, his efforts to negotiate for himself a viable position within such a rigidly gender-defined society meet with disaster.

To show the impossibility of reading "correctly" (i.e., nonparodically), Norris undercuts the traditional systems of values that the novel presents. These systems are embodied in the three men who comprise the novel's moral spectrum: Dolliver "Dolly" Haight (moral absolutism), Charlie Geary (situation ethics and pragmatism), and Vandover's father, the "Old Gentleman" (rules of a bygone era). Dolly, as the diminutive of his name suggests, is at the "feminine values" end of the scale. Vandover's better self and guardian angel, Dolly rescues his friend from the hysterical fit of barking that overtakes him at the Imperial, the restaurant whose air of destructive sensuality is indicated by the "French picture representing a *Sabbath*, witches, goats, and naked girls whirling through the air" (316; italics Norris's) that hangs above the bar. Dolly gambles little, drinks less, and consorts not at all with Flossie and the other prostitutes. He objects to Vandover's chasing Ida Wade, since he argues "that one should never care in any way for that kind of a girl nor become at all intimate with her" (321). He alone believes that good girls want men to keep to a single standard of virtue, opposing Vandover's cynical view that "what they want is that a man should have the knowledge of good and evil, yes, and lots of evil" (365). Yet Norris destroys an easy belief in such values by proving

94

Vandover right and Dolly wrong. Turner Ravis, the novel's stick-figure "good girl," much prefers Vandover until he puts himself completely beyond the pale by causing Ida Wade's suicide. She only becomes engaged to Dolly because girls "really love the man who loves them the most" (458), a high-flown sentiment that combines an attitude of passive feminine responsiveness and noble sacrifices with a desire for power and economic advantage in a relationship. Further, Dolly does not win Turner's lukewarm affections for long. With Hardyesque irony, Norris has Dolly cut his lip on a glass and then be kissed, very much against his will, by Flossie, the prostitute. Despite all his virtue, Dolly contracts the same syphilis that causes Vandover's paresis and will probably meet a similar death. By creating in Dolly Haight an emblem of unjust fate, Norris rejects the assumption of conventional virtues as a possible means of salvation.

If Dolly Haight is the novel's "mollycoddle," then Charlie Geary is its "red-blood." A practical businessman, Geary resembles amoral entrepreneurs like Curtis Jadwin of *The Pit* and Dreiser's Frank Cowperwood (*The Financier*) rather more than principled tycoons like Howells's Silas Lapham. He makes no secret of his intention to get ahead despite the consequences for others. For example, whereas Dolly Haight stays strictly away from fast girls and Vandover, respecting to some degree their humanity, becomes emotionally entangled with them, Geary uses them solely as objects and says that they can fend for themselves—and to make sure of that, he never tells them his last name. Of all Vandover's friends, only Geary is linked with him throughout the novel, a relationship marked by Vandover's consistent dependence. For instance, at Harvard Vandover allows Geary to arrange his course schedule, suggesting only that Geary choose "something easy, all lectures, no outside reading, nice instructor and all that" (295). This action foreshadows Vandover's later relationship with Geary over the loss of the block in the Mission district. Threatened with a lawsuit by Ida Wade's father, Vandover is distraught until Geary, who has been retained to represent Mr. Wade, agrees to help Vandover sub rosa. At first he intends merely to make Vandover lose the case, but he soon conceives a better plan: extortion. Geary will pay Mr. Wade an $8,000 settlement, in return for which Vandover will give Geary his property in the Mission district.

During his lycanthropic spells, Vandover may resemble a wolf, but, as such a scheme suggests, Geary is the novel's true carnivore. After a "fine long sleep of eight hours" he eats, as is his custom, a "thick underdone steak" (498) for breakfast (suggesting, perhaps, the pound of flesh he's about to exact from Vandover) before presenting the plan to his erstwhile friend. Dazed by guilt and by his failed suicide attempt of the night before, Vandover accepts the inequitable plan readily. Late in the novel, Vandover also swindles a friend by passing a bad check to Dolly Haight, the only character in the novel more defenseless than himself; but the obviousness of the swindle and the paltriness of the sum ensure that Vandover cannot take his place with big-time swindlers—or as Sinclair Lewis's George F. Babbitt would say, businessmen with Vision—like Geary. As the novel's spokesman for social Darwinism, Geary is much given to self-justifying interior monologues, including this one just before his penultimate meeting with Vandover:

> Every man for himself—that was his maxim. It might be damned selfish, but it was human nature: the weakest to the wall, the strongest to the front. . . . To lag behind was peril; to fall was to perish, to be ridden down, to be beaten to the dust, to be inexorably crushed and blotted out beneath that myriad of spinning iron wheels. [568-69]

That Geary cannot be trusted as representing a balanced or correct viewpoint is shown by his extravagant use of naturalistic clichés: "strongest to the front," "inexorably crushed and blotted out," "spinning iron wheels." Yet in theory, at least, Geary triumphs, preying successfully on weaker foes and carrying off Turner Ravis as his prize. By making Geary so morally repellent, however, Norris undercuts the nature of his triumph, as if to suggest that in a world of rapacious Gearys and superficially moral Turner Ravises, the game is not worth winning.

The third member of the group, the Old Gentleman, would seem at first to provide useful, stable values for his son; in fact, Donald Pizer suggests that he is virtually an allegorical representation of "Home."[45] The Old Gentleman's role is limited, however, by his lack of knowledge about Vandover's world, the two men quite literally leading separate lives. Vandover's father rarely leaves the house; in scene after scene he occupies the same padded leather chair in his den, a comfortable sanctuary within which he remains insulated from Vandover's life. In addition, his social mores are distinctly those of an older generation—in fact, very nearly the generation of his fellow businessman Silas Lapham. "[N]early sixty" (283) in 1880 when Vandover turns thirteen, the Old Gentleman would have grown to manhood in the decades prior to the Civil War, and, if he shares that generation's love of tradition, he also shares its healthy respect for business. When he does leave the house, he pursues business as Vandover pursues pleasure. Business being the metaphor through which he understands the world, his characteristic response to Vandover's artistic accomplishments is to pay his son for achievement.[46]

Yet however tender the Old Gentleman might be with his family, he is actually an entrepreneur of the Charlie Geary type. Like the reprehensible Geary, the Old Gentleman makes his fortune by speculating in real estate, building cheap houses to rent and mortgaging them to the hilt. Ignorant until his father's death of such practices, Vandover looks upon his father much as he looks upon Dolly, as a combination of conscience and confessor, and one of his continuing laments is that he has failed to live up to the values his father represents. Vandover does not see, though, that he in fact embodies those values. Among his father's legacies, quite apart from tangible assets, is a taste for speculating, for living not only on borrowed time but on a borrowed sense of his own potential and ability to manage. Lacking the ability to control circumstance because he cannot manage himself, Vandover misreads the message of his father's life. He gambles recklessly but, lacking a businessman's sense of how necessary the controlled risk of a high-stakes investment can be, asks his lawyer for an investment "that's secure . . . [a] good, solid investment, don't you know, with a fair interest" (427), to which the lawyer drily replies, "'I've been looking for that myself ever since I was your age'" (427). The same wrongheaded desire for safety makes him squander his most precious capital, his artistic ability, by waiting indefinitely for his "stock" to rise, deferring the production of his "masterpiece" until a set of impossibly perfect conditions exist for recouping his artistic investment.

From his contact with these three men, Vandover hypothesizes a model of masculinity that is at once accurately observed and breathtakingly wrongheaded. His encounters with Dolly convince him that a single standard of sexual behavior is not only impossible but pointless, since "good" girls really don't care about enforcing it, and, if Dolly's example is any guide, sexual fastidiousness is no proof against illness or misery in any case. Yet Vandover still believes in this standard, even if he does not act on it.

He knows that he is leading a double life, thus widening rather than bridging the gulf between accepted and outlawed behavior, the "genteel" and the "real" worlds that had shown themselves at his mother's death. Unlike Jack London's Martin Eden, whose intellect thrives on perceiving differences between the "real" world he knows and the "genteel" world Ruth Morse represents, Vandover cannot tolerate the division between the two. He feels fragmented, dissociated from both realities by his sense of moral inadequacy.[47] Alternating between halves of this dual vision does not present him with an opportunity to step outside its constraints and consider that "[i]n following his instinct[s]" both sexual and self-preserving, Vandover "performs what turns out to be the 'right' action."[48] He *sees* that Dolly is wrong, but he *feels* that Dolly is right, and this feeling helps to unleash his brute.

Vandover likewise misperceives Geary and his father. He interprets their lessons literally rather than metaphorically, never understanding that their activities (speculating, and, for Geary, drinking and seduction) are mere counters, metaphors for the far more important underlying messages about the rapacity, self-interest, and competition that determine "success" in life. Rather than expressing the predatory part of himself figuratively through business as Geary does, he does so literally, choosing another traditionally masculine proving ground: women. Time and again the others chaff him because he can't "leave the girls alone for one hour in the day" (360). The most striking example of his compulsive behavior occurs when he suspects Ida's pregnancy, fights back his guilt, and chases after "the girl of the red hat," Grace Irving—the same girl he rejects after she smiles invitingly on the ship. Norris surely suggests a double perversion here. First, Vandover's society cleaves the world into good and bad women, madonnas and whores; having done so, it further distorts nature by punishing those who put their drive and energy into natural channels such as sexual pursuits. By contrast, harnessing or sublimating that appetite in the service of business reaps rewards. For Geary, it includes winning the most prized woman in the book, Turner Ravis, who, though technically more virtuous, is as amenable as Flossie to having her attentions bought by the highest bidder.

In a similar way, Vandover fails to understand the message of gambling. With his eyes firmly fixed on the cards before him, on the details of life rather than upon the big picture, he scatters his energies in small ways instead of making the bold sweep into speculation that his father and Geary do. Inheriting his father's taste for controlled risk but failing to understand that men must use that ability in business, not pleasure, Vandover fatally misinterprets the figures of bold, rapacious masculinity before him. Moreover, Vandover must lose at the game of forming relationships with women as he loses at Van John. If he acts on his instincts and allows the brute full sway, he brings down upon himself the miseries of lycanthropy; if he exercises self-denial, that preeminent local color virtue, he risks winning only the ambiguous success of a Geary. The irony is that he studies details of the life around him only in ways that will do him no good with his art. In Norris's terms, Vandover can see individual details and thus be "accurate," but he cannot make of those details a vision that is consistent, logical, and "true."

A second way in which Norris presents this fatal misreading of culture is by describing the extremes of behavior Vandover exemplifies. His drinking, gambling, and womanizing establish him as a man-about-town, yet Norris bestows on him several feminine characteristics. His sexual innocence, for example, is initially akin to the "natural intuitive purity" that Dolly Haight describes (367). During Vandover's time at Harvard, a pair of girls, one of whom wears a "red cape" (298)—signaling, like Grace Irving's red hat, sexual availability—try to pick up Geary and Vandover. The latter's response is instantaneous: "Vandover's gorge [rises] with disgust" (299), and he hurries away from them. Later, "moved by an unreasoned instinct" (300), he seeks one of them out and stays all night with her, but he is nonetheless "overwhelmed by a sense of shame and dishonor that were almost feminine in their bitterness and intensity" (300-301). With few exceptions (e.g., turning down Grace Irving's invitation when he is on the ship), he learns not to "dodge" the opportunity but to seek it out, yet regardless of how jaded he becomes, he never loses that sense of disgust. His womanizing becomes one of the compulsive behaviors that signal his degeneration.

Vandover also displays a feminine kind of dependence. Rather than learning to be a strong masculine figure, Vandover consistently turns to such characters for help. The first of these is his father, to whom he confides the news about Ida Wade's suicide: "It was as if it had been a mother or a dear sister. The prodigal son put his arms about his father's neck for the first time since he had been a little boy, and clung to him and wept as though his heart were breaking" (376). In the context of a local color story, the tears and the embrace would signify healing and new growth. Within the world of the naturalistic novel, however, such sentiments reinforce only weakness. Rather than learning strength from this encounter, Vandover seeks to recapitulate the experience in his deteriorated state near the end of the novel. Geary, the other strong masculine presence in his life, takes advantage of Vandover's "veritable feminine horror of figures" (540) but is by no means willing to stand in a tender familial relation to him. Moreover, unlike the Old Gentleman he is an impatient confidant and an unwilling dispenser of funds. In Geary's office, Vandover tells the story of his degradation and begins "to cry, very softly, snuffling with his nose, his chin twitching, the tears running through his thin, sparse beard" (570), but Geary only shouts, "Be a man, will you?" (570). There is, of course, no "man" that he can be, no model on whom he can base his behavior: his father lacks knowledge of the modern world, Dolly lacks strength, Geary lacks ethics, and Vandover himself lacks will.

In addition to character portrayal, Norris uses spatial description to reinforce his themes, including that of Vandover's bifurcated and inadequate view of his culture. *Vandover and the Brute* presents an unusually large number of carefully described rooms. One way in which Norris indicates each step of the decline is to show Vandover's adaptability to various rooms and apartments, as he removes himself from the muted luxury of his father's house, to his imitative artist's apartment, to the impersonal sterility of the Lick House hotel, to the dirty rooms at the Reno House.[49] Besides establishing Vandover's decline, these spatial descriptions indicate the ways in which Vandover compartmentalizes his life as he does the rooms he inhabits. Because he conducts most of his drinking, gambling, and womanizing in the larger, masculine world of the Imperial and other places away from his apartment, he maintains his apartment as a shrine to his more feminine self. Barbara Hochman demonstrates convincingly that, traumatized by the early loss of his mother, "one of Van's few purposive activities is his search for the comfortable environments that he provides for himself," within which he slumbers "like a too-protected baby."[50] Here too, in the rooms where he alone has control, he is content to spend his time in a perverse version of the exacting housekeeping rituals demanded of the era's women: winding the clock becomes "quite an occurrence in the course of the day"; making exactly two hundred "'lights,' tapers of twisted paper to be ignited at the famous stove" (439), takes two solid days; and "there was hardly a minute of the day he was not fussing with [his tiled stove]" (439). He becomes a votary of the stove, tending his hearth as carefully as any vestal might. The disposition of the rest of his time also suggests some monstrous parody of a society woman's activities. In contrast to businessmen like his father and Geary, he often lolls in the bathtub much of the morning. In the afternoon, "he read a novel, wrote a few letters, or passed an hour in the studio dabbling with some sketches for the Last Enemy. . . . In the afternoon he read or picked the banjo or, sitting down to the little piano he had rented, played over his three pieces" (438). Vandover's three repeated pieces of music recall the "six lugubrious airs" that McTeague plays on his concertina, and, like McTeague, he is content within his rooms to be a creature of his lulled and stupefied senses. The impression of limitation, of decorative parlor arts rather than the serious, difficult variety, suggests not time spent, but time wasted. Nevertheless the repetition of his actions lends a ritual quality, as of placation to the lares and penates guarding that immense hearth of a stove. Outside his rooms he can afford to flout convention, because inside them he has created expiatory rites of the home. He does not need to marry Turner Ravis; he is his own "angel in the house."

By this point in the novel, Vandover's compulsive behavior patterns (drinking, gambling, womanizing) and his creation of exacting rituals suggest psychological degeneration of the sort that William James describes. In addition to the aforementioned hypersensitivity to emotions ("'fear, anger, pity, tears, and fainting'") and inappropriate dependence, these can include neurasthenia; "'mysophobia,' or fear of contamination," which leads to compulsive washing; *"folie du doute,"* or doubting mania, which is "the compulsion to repeat an act that has already been successfully repeated"); *recherche angoissante du mot*, or the attempt to recover lost words or names; and "'oniomania,' or the pathological condition of money-spending."[51] Vandover's actions fit several of these categories: obsessively counting the tapers he makes, despite a "veritable feminine horror of numbers" suggests arithmomania, or the morbid desire to count, just as the heedless extravagance with which he squanders his inheritance could be termed oniomania, or the urgency with which he bathes when he is in some (sexual) trouble recalls mysophobia. Also, like Theron Ware, Vandover indulges in morbid reflections on nuances, which, like obsessive thought patterns, indicate that his is a true case of degeneration.

Further, Vandover's physical symptoms match those of others suffering from the disease. After Dolly brings him home from his lycanthropic fit at the Imperial, Vandover "was dropping away into a very grateful doze when a sudden shock, a violent leap of every nerve in his body brought him up to a sitting posture, gasping for breath, his heart fluttering, his hands beating at the empty air" (548) as "confused ideas, half-remembered scenes" race uncontrollably through his mind. His case is much like James's example of the patient who, in response to obsessive thoughts, "jumped out of bed sweating profusely; he said later that he had felt 'squeezed,' his chest had become like an oven, he could not breathe and felt as if he were suffocating."[52] Most significant, perhaps, is Vandover's attempt, through the kind of ritualized, repetitive behavior of touching common to such disorders as *folie du doute* and *recherche angoissante du mot*, to retrieve the lost figure or key that would allow him to complete *The Last Enemy*. Although he eventually loses hope of finishing the picture, he does not abandon the obsessive thought patterns that characterized his relation to it. Instead, Vandover transfers his monomania to his own lycanthropy, a disease that Norris seems to regard as both physical and psychogenic in its origins. Like the patient James describes, who, fearing hydrophobia, experiences its symptoms when she is distressed, Vandover broods continually on his brute within, an activity that probably increases rather than decreases the number of his lycanthropic attacks. He will gradually drop his ritual behaviors when they come to signal not a welcome defense against the brute within, but impediments to his contemplation of and communion with it.

This process of psychological degeneration accelerates from the moment Vandover chooses the apartment with the large sitting room and small studio over the one where those dimensions are reversed. Norris plays a complicated game with the concepts of interior and exterior: initially, Vandover's brute is safely caged within and he must leave his home to release it; but the distinction between inside and outside collapses until the brute invades his house and finally his appearance. Safe in his first set of rooms—where the rough blue wallpaper and "Assyrian bas-reliefs" that Vandover has copied from his lawyer's house show that he still possesses a recognizable sense of self, albeit an imitative one—he manages to keep the brute far from his sacred hearth, isolating him in the Imperial or in brothels. There are hints, however, that this safe isolation will change.

Vandover's jumping out of the bath "naked and dripping" when Geary tells him of Ida's death both suggests causes for his decline and presages the later time at the impersonal Lick House when his friend Ellis sees Vandover in a wolfish fit, "perfectly naked, going back and forth along the wall" (523). The elaborate fetishes of his first apartment have vanished by this time, and Vandover attempts to evoke them by means of "little placards which he had painted with a twisted roll of the hotel letter-paper dipped into the ink-stand. 'Pipe-rack Here.' 'Mona Lisa Here.' 'Stove Here.' Window-seat Here'" (526). In *The Gold Standard and the Logic of Naturalism*, Walter Benn Michaels reads Vandover's placards as signifying "a model for representation without illusion and for a flatness that isn't simply a shallow three-dimensionality. . . . the art not only of a brute but of a brute that can write"—an art wholly material, representing only itself.[53] Being, as Michaels comments, "neither *trompe l'oeil* nor raw material," the placards are so far removed in the chain of referentiality as to lose their meaning and their power. Despite their ritualized placement, and their status as written word (which should signify spirit but, Michaels suggests, here does not), they no longer protect Vandover against his brute.[54] After one prolonged attack of lycanthropy, "[n]aked, exhausted, Vandover slept profoundly . . . beneath two of the little placards, scrawled with ink, that read, 'Stove here'; 'Mona Lisa here'" (553). The feminine sanctities of the hearth and the masculine powers of art have both failed him. He blends invisibly into his surroundings, his "fatal adaptability" and "state of absolute indifference" contributing to his "mere passive existence, an inert, plantlike vegetation, the moment's pause before the final decay, the last inevitable rot" (524). The rooms in which his final disintegration takes place suggest what is in fact the case: since his suicide attempt, he exemplifies the naturalistic self that cannot exist apart from its environment.

The final instance of Vandover's misreading occurs in the realm of art. The mere fact of his degeneration should not prevent Vandover from becoming an artist; indeed, contemporary psychology linked neurasthenia and creativity, as did at least two experts on degeneration: Max Nordau held "that genius is allied with 'hysteria,'" one of the symptoms of degeneration, and Cesare Lombroso, whose works influenced Norris, theorized that "genius is a degenerative neurosis allied with epilepsy and moral insanity."[55] But like William James, who scornfully dismissed both the degeneracy-genius theory and the faulty statistics used to prove it, Norris refuses to grant Vandover such an excuse for failure. Without an infusion of red-blooded vigor or the ability to look at life, the neurotic symptoms of degeneration, supposedly akin to the receptive nature of the artist, remain just that—maladaptive neurotic symptoms, nothing more. Vandover thinks that his art might have saved him, but, as Don Graham has demonstrated, Vandover's natural talent is corrupted by the banalities of the *Home Book of Art*. His painting and sketching do not reflect the great world, as Norris thought a man's art should. It is instead the feminine art of the parlor—derivative, circumscribed, artificial, and, like the ideal head of Flora he draws for his father, and the "pen and inks of pretty, smartly dressed girls, after Gibson's manner" (438) that he gives to his friends, meant primarily to please. Influenced by the *Home Book of Art*, the art magazines he leafs through, and novels such as *Ben-Hur*, Vandover conceives his "masterpiece," *The Last Enemy*, a painting of a desert, a dying horse, and a predatory lion.[56] Even before any signs of his deterioration occur, the derivative quality of Vandover's imagination sends a warning that Norris would later make again and again in his criticism: Vandover refuses to look at life, preferring instead to dwell on the tame possibilities of life filtered through another's imagination. In his failure to step outside the stock responses and tired conventions of an effete, exhausted tradition, he must fail because he looks to literature for his models.

Only on his sketching trip to Maine does Vandover seem to fulfill his potential as an artist, but Norris makes it clear that Vandover must get beyond drawing this Eastern landscape, which is, after all, the imaginative realm of such local colorists as Sarah Orne Jewett, and, even earlier, Harriet Beecher Stowe. Noting that Vandover "taps some important energies" when he really looks at the landscape in Maine, Graham identifies the real crux of Vandover's problem with art: "Had Vandover directed his attention to the landscape before his eyes, especially to the urban landscape that Norris the painterly novelist describes in vivid detail, his art might have truly developed into something of value."[57] Repeatedly Vandover is shown looking out the window onto the crowded, sometimes dirty life of the city—scenes reminiscent, in fact, of the ordinary life of Polk Street in *McTeague*—and then turning away to yet another abortive sketch for *The Last Enemy*. Vandover's artistic nature may help him to respond sensitively to music such as *Faust*, but he never seems to hear the "prolonged and sullen diapason" that marks "the whole existence of the great slumbering city"; it passes before him "in one long wave of sound" (482) that he neither perceives nor appreciates. Had his ear been keener, his gaze longer, his imagination fresher, he might have become another John French Sloan or Everett Shinn, artists of the "Ashcan School," whose pictures recreated in oils what Norris attempted in his novels. The real talent he showed in painting the Maine seacoast degenerates to the point of parody when he paints blurry conventional seascapes on iron safes, becoming a "safe painter."[58]

In addition to a steadfast unwillingness to reflect "real life" in his art, Vandover displays several other traits that Norris identified as characteristic of another sort of artist—women novelists—in "Why Women Should Write the Best Novels" (*Boston Evening Transcript*, 13 November 1901). Vandover, convinced that his art has left him, tries after a long absence to sketch *The Last Enemy*. Nervous and restless, he leaves the studio, only to return because of "a sudden feminine caprice, induced, no doubt, by the exalted, strained, and unnatural condition of his nerves" (480). Because he cannot draw, he becomes numb and giddy: "hysteria shook him like a dry, light leaf" (481). The "right" path, as Norris develops it in *Blix*, would be to persevere in another mode: Condy Rivers, the initially lazy artist-hero of that work, does exactly that when he gives up on having his early romantic fiction published and writes the true story told to him by an old sailor. Vandover, however, abandons art altogether. He follows exactly, in fact, the pattern Norris describes for women novelists:

> A man may grind on steadily for an almost indefinite period, when a woman at the same task would begin, after a certain point, to "feel her nerves," to chafe, to fret, to try to do too much, to polish too highly, to develop more perfectly. Then come fatigue, harassing doubts, more nerves, a touch of hysteria occasionally, exhaustion, and in the end complete discouragement and a final abandonment of the enterprise. . . .[59]

Vandover also shares with Norris's hypothetical women novelists an inability to use his knowledge of the life that he does see, two examples being the fire in chapter 5 and the wreck of the *Mazatlan* in chapter 9. Norris, a conscious artist, makes the fire a focus of several paragraphs of description, but Vandover lacks here as elsewhere the artist's interest in observation. His thoughts are instead fixed on the "will she or won't she?"

issue of whether Ida Wade will go with him to the Imperial. The wreck of the *Mazatlan* shakes him more profoundly, although he still does not learn the necessary lessons. He confronts his own desire for self-preservation and loses faith in Divine Providence when a "Salvation Army Lassie" (395) is struck and killed minutes after she tells Vandover that Jesus will save her. In the overcrowded lifeboat, he recoils at the "half-clad women, dirty, sodden, unkempt" (404), and sits silent when, after his initial protest, the others throw off "[t]he little Jew . . . writhing and grunting" (402) who clings to the oar in a vain hope of being admitted to the boat. As if alluding parodically to his earlier work, Norris allows the shipwreck to represent a potential turning point for Vandover. In *Moran of the* Lady Letty and London's *Sea-Wolf*, life at sea provides a look into the Darwinian struggle for existence, hence a necessary corrective to the overcivilized softness of men like Hump Van Weyden and Ross Wilbur. Living in the brutal world aboard ship, both Van Weyden and Wilbur arrest the progress of their descent and become more balanced human beings. Vandover, however, observes the same struggle for survival and concludes not that he wants to be strong enough to survive, but that he wants to get back to his comfortable home as soon as possible.

Even given such tried-and-true material for art as the shipwreck, Vandover fails to rise to the challenge. What he finally creates out of his experience of the sea voyage is not "The Open Boat," or even a better subject for painting than *The Last Enemy*, but another masterpiece of cliché:

> He even made up some comical pieces [for his banjo and mandolin] that had a great success among the boys. . . . a third had for a title "A Sailor Robbing a Ship," in which he managed to imitate the sounds of the lapping of the water, the creaking of the oarlocks, the tramp of the sailor's feet upon the deck, the pistol shot that destroyed him, and—by running up the frets on the bass-string—his dying groans, a finale that never failed to produce a tremendous effect. [441]

His terror, his misery, and the elemental expressions of human nature he had seen are all ignored in Vandover's quest for the perfectly trivial and surefire crowd pleaser. He may appreciate music, but the music he composes, like the pictures he paints, represents the triumph of parlor art.

In several ways, then, Vandover has failed to comprehend his society's complex rules. His mistakes, particularly his exaggerations, arise from the theory that reconciling the warring perspectives of genteel and real, feminine and masculine, is possible. Vandover's misprision of what constitutes art serves as Norris's fictional indictment of the Feminine Principle. The insistence on telling a (hackneyed) story, on trivializing one's material, on presenting conventional subjects, on overpolishing one's work, and especially on taking one's subjects from literature and other artists rather than from life all suggest the Feminine Principle, and, equally important, they all mark Vandover as a failed artist, and a failed human being, before he ever sets charcoal to canvas. Caught between old artistic principles and new, he becomes the brute that the new age demanded without any of the brute's traditional vitality.

· IV ·

One of the most prevalent themes running throughout much naturalistic literature is that of fear, an uneasy anxiety about vaguely defined and scarcely articulated dangers. One acknowledged threat is the brute and the possibilities of proletarianization he represents. Equally pervasive, however, are the linked concerns over the age's increasing effeminization and consequent degeneration, themes that underlie much of *The Damnation of Theron Ware* and *Vandover and the Brute*. Frederic and Norris examine the problems of effeminization from several perspectives. First of all, gender roles may shift or be reversed. Theron's varying social roles as a "hybrid female" and bullying husband demonstrate such reversals, as do Vandover's transformations from a womanizing man-about-town to the fussy, domestic "angel in the house" of his carefully ordered flat. Secondly, rules that define the roles may be misperceived, as happens with Theron's view of culture and Vandover's concept of masculinity. Finally, the roles' limitations may be revealed through exaggeration or parody, much as Theron's tears and passivity come to be first a manipulative, then a losing, gambit, and Vandover's dependence, ritual housekeeping, and conventional art bespeak his failure as artist and man.

The heart of the matter is, of course, the fear that losing gender identity leads to degeneracy. The naturalists worried about the personal and literary degeneration that adherence to effete traditions like feminine culture and local color literature seemed to render inevitable. Describing the degenerate personality, William James might almost be discussing the spirit of the age: "Too much questioning and too little active responsibility lead, almost as often as too much sensualism does, to the edge of the slope, at the bottom of which lie pessimism and the nightmare or suicide view of life."[60] "Too much questioning and too little active responsibility" combine with excessive sensualism to precipitate both Theron Ware and Vandover over the slope and into the nightmare chasm. Obeying their impulses and meditating obsessively upon their inadequate visions of the world, both men discard aspects of their conventional masculine behavior for something far more risky. They try, and fail, to integrate feminine sensibility into their lives, and they end by producing only their own degeneration. Nor are Theron Ware and Vandover the only ones to display symptoms. In their compulsion to examine their idée fixe lest "harm will follow," their philosophizing, their elaborate accretion of facts and vivid description of "real life," and their obsessive, detailed enumeration—of, among other things, money, clothes, houses, phrases—the naturalists recapitulate in lesser degree those very symptoms they sought to critique. Like their characters, they walked dangerously close "to the edge of the slope, at the bottom of which lie pessimism and the nightmare or suicide view of life," which constitute the real menace of degeneration.

CHAPTER FIVE

Dreiser, London, Crane, and the Iron Madonna

· I ·

In "Women as Superfluous Characters in American Realism and Naturalism," Jan Cohn contends that naturalistic novels relegate women to a specific and very limited role. Women such as Laura Jadwin are not viable characters in their own right; rather, they exist as adjuncts to the real focus of naturalistic novels, the worlds of finance and business. Cohn is one in a long line of writers who have argued that characters, especially female characters, in naturalistic novels are not carefully delineated figures but crude sketches drawn to demonstrate some portion of naturalistic philosophy. Both the local color writers and the naturalists tended to create characters as types, but in their use of stereotypes, the naturalists showed that they held differing assumptions from those of their local color predecessors about the relative positions of character, reader, and narrator. Characters in local color works display the qualities of a particular region, whereas naturalistic characters show the effect of impersonal forces on a representative person; that is, the characters are signs of something larger than, and different from, either individuals or their regions. Implicit in this view of characters as types is the idea that somehow these characters are "other" than the author, and, by extension, the reader, who presumably shares the author's quick perceptions, level of education, and attitudes. The alterity of local color characters is a donnée of the movement, creating the outsider's view as an implicit norm against which the actions of the characters are judged.

The same vision of "otherness" or alterity is present in many naturalistic novels. In naturalistic novels, otherness is typically marked more by differences in class (delineated through dialect, level of education, economic circumstances, and ancestry of the characters) than by differences in time and locale.[1] Whereas some local color works, notably those of Sarah Orne Jewett, suggest exclusion from the community as a source of anxiety, naturalistic works threaten to include readers in the uncertain and frequently miserable world they depict, deliberately undercutting the safe position traditionally enjoyed by the reader. The fragility of a position based on something as rigidly enforced yet tenuously defined as class, particularly when, as in America, class itself is defined by the presence or absence of something as fluid as money, forces readers into an anxious identification with characters they might otherwise disregard.

Another sort of otherness or alterity exists in naturalistic novels: the idea of women as "other," as objects of study in themselves rather than as the representatives of human nature they had frequently been in local color fiction. Underlying this approach was a statement of alienation, not from women, but from a culture rigid in its insistence on stratified class and gender roles and its elevation of a feminine mode of literature. If establishing class as a basis for alterity was one naturalistic response to increasing industrialization, economic upheaval, and social and political uncertainty, then establishing gender as another basis surely reflects the need to express a similar anxiety, since gender roles as social constructs depend on something as strong or as fragile as the holding of mutual beliefs by members of a society. The threat is not that one can change from male to female, but that one can, as we have seen in chapter 4, become effeminate. By first divorcing female experience from the mainstream of human experience—treating women as "other"—and then by encapsulating certain female characters within the limits of stereotyping, naturalistic writers could achieve several aims at once, among them objectivity in representation, control over the parameters of feminine discourse, and the supersession of local color's perceived dominance of the literary magazines.

As men tacitly committed to social justice, Frank Norris, Jack London, Stephen Crane, and David Graham Phillips sympathized with the powerlessness of women in an inequitable social system, and they inverted and reinvented the stereotypes of fallen women to expose the economic basis of the double standard. Yet striving to create a new literature under a system they saw as dominated by feminine discourse, they exaggerated the power of "respectable" women and railed against the entrenched forces allied against young male writers. Their principal strategy for voicing this resentment was the inversion of existing attitudes on fallen women and the rearticulation of these women's stories. By examining these women's lives, and by surrounding with ambiguity the hitherto clear-cut moral judgments about them, the naturalists sought to "rescue" these women, not merely as stereotyped or sensationalized subjects for fiction, but as representative human beings worthy of study. The relegation of women to the status of "other" is preserved by emphasizing their role as objects of mystery or inspiration for male characters. Surrounding prostitutes with an air of indeterminacy provides the necessary distance.

A second means of expressing rage and regaining control of the prevailing feminine discourse was to discredit their attackers, the female figures whom the naturalists suspected were responsible for suppressing naturalism's depictions of "real life." The fallen woman's reliance on but a single defense—silence—contrasts markedly with the good woman's array of verbal and psychological weapons, as novels by London and Crane make clear. If the use of prostitutes as subjects suggests that "bad women" are or can be good, the opposing corollary is that "good women" can be bad—that is, life denying and repressive. In contrast to the prostitutes' silence, language proves to be the redemptive force for the male characters in Jack London's *Martin Eden* and Stephen Crane's *George's Mother*, as the use of what Norris called "the crude, the raw, the vulgar" emancipates male characters such as Martin Eden and George Kelcey from the dominance of feminine discourse. Both Kelcey's and Eden's respective liberations through language function as symbolic representations of the naturalists' own struggles.

The third response to local color and its ideals is a broader examination of the masculine and feminine social systems involved. If *George's Mother* shows the failure of local color virtues in a naturalistic world, *The Monster* shows that these virtues cannot flourish even in their natural habitat, the local color story. Evoking the local color conventions of order, praiseworthy virtues, a panoply of character types including strong spinsters, and storytelling, Crane uses the language and themes of naturalism to undercut the earlier tradition. *The Monster* stands as the consummate "outsider" story. It is a parable of alienation, not only that of Henry Johnson and Dr. Trescott, but of naturalism from the local color world that it had to destroy.

· II ·

One of the naturalists' central premises was that the whole of life must be examined if one wished to present a truthful or, to use a favorite naturalistic term, "sincere" representation of reality. Frank Norris distinguished truth from accuracy by stating that the latter was merely a part of the truth, that in fact "it is not difficult to be accurate, but it is monstrously difficult to be True."[2] Representing the truth meant bridging the gap between two realities: to use Norris's metaphor, literature should not "stop in the front parlor and discuss medicated flannels and mineral waters with the ladies," but instead "be off upstairs with you, prying, peeping, peering into the closets of the bedroom, into the nursery, into the sitting room; yes, and into that little iron box screwed to the lower shelf of the closet in the library."[3] Sex and money, the two great unspoken forces of the Victorian age, were dragged out of the closet at last as legitimate, rather than covert, subjects for fiction.

The naturalists' fascination with fallen women, particularly prostitutes, has been well documented,[4] most recently in *Girls Who Went Wrong*, Laura Hapke's study of prostitution in turn-of-the-century literature. Hapke finds that, despite their commitment to truth, writers such as Crane, Frederic, and Phillips "revealed in their evasive attitude toward the prostitute both the genteel influence and their own ambivalence about the quintessential fallen woman."[5] The daring subject matter thereby masked the essentially conventional treatment of fallen women. Several of these tales end with retribution, the women either committing suicide, like Maggie Johnson, or being ravaged by disease, like Flossie in *Vandover and the Brute*. David Graham Phillips's Susan Lenox pays the price by being deprived both of all her illusions and of the man she loves. Even *Maggie: A Girl of the Streets* (1893, 1896), one of the earliest tales, can be seen as "essentially a tract, written by the son of a gentle Methodist."[6] Despite these limitations, for the naturalists the image of the prostitute forced to negotiate a hazardous existence with only her body and her wits as assets epitomized the struggle to survive in an indifferent universe. She therefore provided an appropriate proving ground for naturalism's deterministic theories. As a social outcast shunned by genteel society, she also gained a great deal of sympathy from the other (self-elected) outcasts, the naturalists.

The naturalists' investigations emphasized that the prostitutes' position as "merchandise" conflated commerce and sexuality, forcing the women, like their more fortunate peers, to objectify themselves as consumable commodities for the male gaze. For example, in *The House of Mirth*, Lily Bart views herself as "human merchandise," most obviously when, posing for the Wellington Brys' tableaux vivants, she markets not only her charm but her figure when she appears in the clinging robes of Joshua Reynolds's *Mrs. Lloyd*.[7] Within the rapt assembly of male admirers, each simultaneously admires publicly the ideal of womanhood that he projects onto Lily and assesses privately his ability to "buy" her. In the humbler world of *Sister Carrie*, *Maggie*, and *Susan Lenox*, the image of a woman posing for male purchasers pervades each work: Carrie Meeber trying on clothes for Drouet and appearing on stage in *Under the Gaslight*; Maggie Johnson parading the streets; Susan Lenox singing before rowdy riverboat crowds and trying on Paris fashions for her lover, Freddy Palmer. Possessing only themselves as a medium of exchange, they keep their market value inflated by infinitely deferring the process, implied by their promise of sexuality, of gratifying their purchasers' desires. The "successful" women, Susan Lenox and Carrie Meeber, accomplish this balancing act in two essential ways: by selling themselves sexually, they fulfill one half of the promise, but they deliberately maintain a distinction between the commercial self of sex-for-cash and the inchoate longings that comprise their personalities. Striving to maintain a cohesion between the commercial and the inner self, as Maggie and Lily do, drives down their value as commodities: Maggie, for example, gets few customers because when her identity becomes wholly bounded by her profession, she has nothing new to offer her customers; Lily, having gambled away her chances, cannot accept the distinction between commercial-sexual and inner self that her society demands, and her quest for maintaining herself as an integrated personality leads to her death. Obscured by the economic rather than sexual basis of human transactions, the whole issue of women's sexuality becomes distanced, as if of secondary importance.

Another form of distance arises from the novels' paradoxical figuration of exposure and concealment. The authors began, in fact, with the basic question posed by such autobiographical prostitute narratives as *Nell Kimball: Her Life as an American Madam* and *Madeleine: An Autobiography*.

Indeed, it is the question that these and other "fallen women" declare is the one most frequently asked of them by their patrons: "What circumstances drove you to sell yourself?"[8] In asking this question, the naturalists skirt the edges of the white-slave narrative, the sensationalistic genre that reached its height of popularity in the Progressive Era with novels such as Harold Wright Kauffmann's *House of Bondage* (1910), a host of thinly disguised tracts like Clifford Roe's *Great War on White Slavery; or, Fighting for the Protection of Our Girls* (1911), and reports like George Kneeland's *Commercialized Prostitution in New York City* (1913) and the Chicago Vice Commission's *Social Evil in Chicago* (1911).[9] Kimball and "Madeleine" dismissed the "white slave" scare from their perspective as retired madams, yet these women felt, with some justice, that in asking this question men sought to buy some essential part of themselves, not merely their bodies, and they lied accordingly. "Madeleine" comments:

> I had yet to learn that lying was a part of the profession. . . . and I had yet to learn that every man's vanity, regardless of how casual his intercourse with "one of the girls" may be, leads him to expect that she shall take *him* into her confidence, and tell *him* the truth about her family affairs . . . and why she is adventuring in the primrose way, though he is quite ready to concede her right to "conceal hersel', as weel's she can, frae critical dissection" on the part of others.[10]

In seeking to perform this dissection, writers like Crane, Phillips, and Dreiser place themselves simultaneously in two positions. As sympathetic interpreters, they function as social intermediaries, reaching an audience, in effect a market, otherwise inaccessible to the prostitute. But as questioners, they resemble the prostitute's customers, a role that the reader doubly reenacts by asking the question (why did this woman sell herself?) and by paying (buying the book) to have the question answered. In uncovering what the prostitute seeks to conceal, the transaction of storytelling recapitulates her exploitation via the fictional invasion of her privacy, even as the exposure of social evils (like the clients' money) in the short term benefits her.

By their sympathies, however, and above all in their position as human beings attempting to sell a commodity that represents some portion of themselves, naturalistic writers acknowledge their kinship to the fallen women they describe. Living close to the edge of starvation, Crane,

Dreiser, and London understood the factory worker's or shop girl's losing struggle to make ends meet on $5.00 a week. They generally viewed her fall into prostitution as a matter of economic necessity—and, in the case of kept women like Carrie Meeber, economic good sense. With almost obsessive repetition, they chronicle the minutiae of her existence: the sixty cents that Dulcie, of O. Henry's "Unfinished Story," must pay out for supper each week; the foolishness of Carrie Meeber for spending $1.25 on an umbrella; the eighty cents a day on which Susan Lenox calculates she must learn to live. The difference between these women and characters such as Martin Eden, Vandover, and Hurstwood, all of whom also agonize over pennies, is that the men's poverty results from an act of choice, either a refusal to take better-paying work, like Martin Eden, or a willingness to drift, like Vandover and Hurstwood. For women, the choice is really no choice. Prostitution places them at risk, but no more so, argue the naturalists, than the only other possibility open to them: monotonous jobs at inadequate wages. Turning out collars and cuffs like Maggie (and like Roberta Alden of *An American Tragedy*), punching out shoe uppers like Carrie, or pasting boxes and sewing hats like Susan Lenox (and Lily Bart) all offer physical and emotional debilitation similar to that of prostitution, but with less prospect of tangible reward.

Despite the naturalists' sympathy, presenting a portrait of fallen women that, in Norris's terms, could be both accurate and true proved to be difficult. Local color writers like Jewett, Freeman, and Cooke envision storytelling, especially women's storytelling, as a communal activity, one that by strengthening the community's bonds also helps to protect the community and its members from the incursions of a hostile world. The prostitute, however, lives a life of isolation, for, as becomes clear in *Susan Lenox*, the independence, better pay, and shorter hours she gains from her "immoral" life distinguish her from the virtuously downtrodden women who teach their daughters to shun her. She thus cannot participate in a community's storytelling rituals, and indeed her only defense is to "hoard" her story as a means of preserving a sense of self. Thus, like their real life counterparts, the fictional fallen women resist telling their own stories; for example, Susan Lenox, "[l]ike all the girls in that life with a real story to tell . . . never told about her past self."[11] Deprived of the female communities that comprise a legitimate market for circulating stories and entrapped into a one-way economy of male purchasers that can only consume their tales (and lives), the fallen women operate within a preservationist ethos that, like Trina McTeague's, isolates even as it sustains them.

This resistance to language can be seen in the most saintly of their number, the heroine of Dreiser's *Jennie Gerhardt* (1911). Jennie fears the consequences of having her story told, although she gives herself to men with the noblest of motives: to save her family. Her story in fact resembles the "usual lies men like to hear" of an innocent, unsuspecting girl ruined by an older man of superior class.[12] At the age of eighteen, Jennie is seduced by Senator Brander and subsequently bears his child. Later, she attracts the attention of Lester Kane, the son of a wealthy manufacturer. After two chapters filled with his family's and his social circle's badinage about his unmarried state, Lester's "mind wandered back to Jennie and her peculiar 'Oh, no, no!' *There* was someone who appealed to him. That was a type of womanhood worth while."[13] Expressing her objections in a nearly inarticulate form, Jennie appeals to Lester precisely because of her difference; her resistance both to language and to his sexual demands contrasts with the linguistic and social voracity of those at the Knowltons' coming-out party. Indeed, the incidents of Jennie's life revolve around the stories she fails to tell and the silences she maintains; she keeps her involvement with Senator Brander from her family; her involvement with Lester from her father; her supposed marriage from the neighbors; her child, Vesta, from Lester.

Jennie is nonetheless a "good girl" (344) and a "good woman" (410) as her father and Lester, the two most judgmental men in the book, tell her on their respective deathbeds. Part of her goodness is signaled by her lack of original language. As Carol Schwartz observes in "*Jennie Gerhardt*: Fairy Tale as Social Criticism," "Lester speaks the language of natural determinism, Jennie that of the nineteenth-century sentimental heroine."[14] Jennie "possesses a world of feeling and emotion" (338) and is "an ideal mother," although "[s]he isn't quick at repartee" and "can't join in any rapid-fire conversation" (339). Not being "quick at repartee" signals her essential difference from her rival, Letty Pace, for, having no social wiles, she achieves the greater naturalistic virtue of sincerity. Jennie is deficient in the kinds of speech commonly valued but eloquent in the language of feeling and gesture that allows Lester's imagination free play in envisioning her as his ideal woman. As a "good woman" who paradoxically chooses silence as her weapon, however, Jennie cannot capitalize on her strengths. Indeed, when Lester praises Jennie to Letty Pace as a "good woman" (339), Letty is quick to seize the linguistic advantage to reframe his definition: "Why, Lester, if I were in her position, . . . I would let you go. I would, truly. I think you know that I would. Any good woman would" (341). At Gerhardt's funeral shortly thereafter, Lester watches Jennie: "The woman's emotion was so deep, so real. 'There's no explaining a good woman,' he said to himself" (347). By objectifying Jennie in this manner, by encasing her within the narrowly defined parameters of womanly self-sacrifice, he comes a step closer to leaving her without, however, accepting Letty's judgment uncritically: "Was she as good as Jennie?" (369).[15] He chooses a woman with linguistic weapons whose fortune makes her a "weapon" in her own right, one who can help him to "repay an indifferent, chill, convention-ridden world with some sharp, bitter cuts of the power-whip" (361), whose fortune will be a "club to knock his enemies over the head" (369). By contrast, even the sexuality that paradoxically should mark Jennie as a "fallen," hence silent, woman is rendered harmless by her commonplace language and maternal, self-sacrificing emotions. In marrying Letty, Lester in effect forsakes the representative of the self-sacrificing goodness common to local color fiction for one epitomizing naturalistic force.

Like Jennie, Maggie Johnson of Crane's *Maggie: A Girl of the Streets* (1893) is passive and almost wholly reactive in her use of language. She early adopts a protective silence, first in sheltering her baby brother from their parents' violence, and later in distancing herself as much as possible from her environment. Her gestures of removing herself inevitably fail, as does her attempt at artistic expression, the creation of a lambrequin of "flowered cretonne." Maggie views it and "some faint attempts which she had made with blue ribbon" as an amelioration of the grim surroundings and the "dingy curtain" before which, metaphorically speaking, her life is being played out.[16] Decorating home rather than self marks Maggie as a good woman; however, Pete, her seducer, cannot read such fine distinctions. He gazes only at himself in the mirror when he comes to call, and he then vanishes "without having glanced at the lambrequin" (21), Maggie and mirror alike functioning merely as self-reflective panels for his narcissistic vision of himself as seducer. Similarly, Mrs. Johnson, a failed "good woman" and the symbolic first destroyer of her daughter's innocence, vents "some phase of drunken fury upon the lambrequin."[17] After her fury, the lambrequin is destroyed and "[t]he knots of blue ribbons appeared like violated flowers"(22)—not unlike Maggie herself, who "blossomed in a mud puddle" (17) before her final return, via suicide, to those other dirty waters, the oily surfaces of the river.[18]

Like Jennie, Maggie expresses herself through a combination of gestures, commonplace speech, and authorial descriptions of her feelings. With characteristic phrases like "dis is great" (23), she lacks the exaggeratedly correct grammar and diction of Nell, one of her rivals for Pete's affections: "Oh, it's not of the slightest consequence to me, my dear young man" (49). Her dilemma, like Jennie's, is that the inarticulateness that signifies her sincerity proves to be no match for the glib sophistry of her rival. In his linguistic analysis of *Maggie*, Alan Robert Slotkin comments that Nell's speech "displays an effort on her part to hide her background and to escape from it,"[19] an effort confirmed by Hapke's observation that many prostitutes saw their profession as a means of upward mobility.[20] Maggie's lack of volubility thus doubly condemns her, although for the most part her dialect can be attributed to Crane's representation of lower-class life; most of the characters in *Maggie* speak a language of dialect, oaths, and rampant clichés, over which Crane casts the irony that is his trademark. But the inarticulate quality of her exchanges, like that of Carrie Meeber's, serves also as a reminder of what she is and must be if she is to succeed at her profession: a receptive blank on which the fantasies of others can be played out.

Crane demonstrates this point in his description of "a girl of the painted cohorts" (52), presumably Maggie, walking the streets. After being cursed by her mother and cut off abruptly by Pete, her seducer, Maggie ends by being almost completely without words. Chapter 17 details her stroll through the streets, "giving smiling invitations to those of rural or untaught pattern and usually seeming sedately unconscious of the men with a metropolitan seal upon their faces" (52). During her walk, a polyglot assortment of men stare at her and answer her, though she does not speak: a "belated man in business clothes" tells her, "Brace up, old girl"; a young man with a "mocking smile" asks, "you don't mean to tell me that you sized me up for a farmer?"; a laborer wishes her "a fine evenin'"; a drunken man, more direct than the others, roars, "I ain' ga no money, dammit" (53); a "huge fat man" with "brown, disordered teeth gleaming under a grey, grizzled moustache from which the beer-drops dripped" chuckles and leers as he wordlessly follows her to the silence of the river (53). Each reads upon her face an invitation or a threat that he himself has inscribed there, for her profession operates in a semiotic system that has less to do with words than with the written language of the paint on her face. Quite literally, her body speaks for her. Only once does she actually speak to any of the men, hailing a "man with blotched features"(53). Their exchange—"Ah, there." . . . "I've got a date"—demonstrates that her words are not only neutral but irrelevant. Assuming the mantle of silence and blankness, she can express herself only within the constraints of her body and her status as a prostitute. Maggie, in retreating into silence, makes a fatal mistake. She has recreated not only her body but her personality as a surface for inscription and interpretation by others—Pete, her mother, men on the street—and as such her silence is not self-protective, but self-negating.

By contrast, when Carrie Meeber adapts to her surroundings and the men with whom she associates, her behavior is not self-negating but self-defining, as critics have noted. Although she does not sell herself on the streets as Maggie or Susan Lenox do, she operates on the same basic principle of presenting herself as a surface upon which Hurstwood and Drouet can inscribe their fantasies. This process is most evident in their response to her performance in *Under the Gaslight*, when each man invests the words she speaks with a significance that he alone can appreciate: "The manager suffered [her speech] as a personal appeal. It came to him as if they were alone. . . . Drouet also was beside himself. He was resolving that he would be to Carrie what he had never been before."[21] The part Carrie plays multiplies the layers of concealment. As Laura, a "lissome figure, draped in pearl gray" (190), she is a society woman hiding her past as a juvenile pickpocket; when her past is revealed, she exposes a spiritual nobility through her willingness to sacrifice her own happiness for the sake of others. Like Woolson's Madam Carroll in *For the Major*, Carrie, as the character Laura, enacts the local color virtues of self-denial and self-sacrifice beneath her disguise as a society woman. In her equally fictive incarnation as "Carrie Madenda," however, Carrie chooses self-interest over self-sacrifice, renouncing generations of local color heroines bound by duty to enfeebled older family members with her curt note to Hurstwood: "I'm going away. I'm not coming back any more" (439). Not surprisingly, Hurstwood fails to note that the "pale face" that charms him is made so by an artificial "touch of blue under the eyes," and that the pearls are "imitation" (190); instead, he and Drouet interpret Laura's story as an emotional gloss on Carrie's own, and they invest Carrie herself with romance. By contrast, Carrie's background, which she does not reveal, is decidedly prosaic. Philip Fisher comments perceptively on this scene and the potent connections it establishes between acting, sex, and commerce:

> The sexualized quality of acting, protected as it is by fantasy and the barrier of the stage that separates the beloved actress from the numerous fantasizing suitors in the audience repeats the paradox mentioned earlier that sheltered within the fiction of her role the actress sells precisely the vitality of her personality. . . . Acting involves primarily in Dreiser not deception but practice, not insincerity but installment payments on the world of possibility.[22]

Selling herself from a position of relative control, preserving the "fiction of her role," is exactly what the protective conventions implied by the open frame of the proscenium arch allow Carrie to do, thereby avoiding both extremes: the constraints of marriage and the limitless consumption of self implied by prostitution.[23]

A further instance of Carrie's self-protective instincts occurs in one of her later plays. Her wordless frown as the "little Quakeress" evokes a response much like that of Maggie's patrons or Lester Kane: "The portly gentlemen in the front rows began to feel that she was a delicious little morsel. It was the kind of frown they would have loved to force away with kisses" (447). Although this scene appears late in the novel, her appearance as the frowning Quakeress provides a key to her appeal. Her silence, in fact, echoes that of the prostitutes like Madeleine: as a sexualized woman enacting innocence, she projects resistance, not capitulation—the "usual lies men like to hear." "As the Quaker maid, demure and dainty" (459), Carrie is clad once again in gray, the neutral background color for her admirers' fantasies in *Under the Gaslight*, as she recapitulates the "parlor acting" of the prostitute. Further, her Quakeress garb recalls the standardized costumes of lost innocence in houses like Nell Kimball's, emphasizing as it does her status as an unwritten page of innocence upon which the male text of sexuality can be written "with kisses." Too, throughout most of her encounters with Drouet and Hurstwood she maintains a stance of resisting or denying their various claims, a stance that is at once self-protective for her and arousing for the men ("it was the kind of frown they would have loved to force away with kisses"). Like "Madeleine," Carrie allows the men in her life to make up their own version of what her story (and consequently her real self) must be while maintaining a separate version that she never tells. She resists interpretation and saves herself.[24]

Making a virtue of their heroines' verbal passivity, Crane and Dreiser draw their fallen women as figures of dimensions more complex than their utterances would suggest. Both men allow indeterminacy to help shape their characters, trusting to the reader's curiosity about the character, and especially about answering the "question" of her story, to help maintain his engagement with the work. On the other hand, pinning down a character to a few specific dimensions, as David Graham Phillips attempts to do in *Susan Lenox: Her Fall and Rise* (1911; published 1917), risks violating the prostitute's principle of refusing to tell her story. It helps to reduce her to a more simplistic figure, hence one more vulnerable to conventional moral judgments. Born out of wedlock and forced into an arranged marriage, Susan runs away from Cincinnati to New York, where she survives by alternating between what Phillips scornfully calls "honest toil"—making boxes, singing on a showboat and in cheap restaurants, modeling clothes— and prostitution. Like Carrie Meeber, she becomes a successful actress, a profession that translates into respectable terms the lessons in advantageous use of men's imaginations that each had learned as a fallen woman.

In some ways, Susan is a naturalistic test case, within whom heredity, early training, and present environment battle continually:

> One of the strongest factors in Susan's holding herself together . . . was the nearly seventeen years of early training her Aunt Fanny Warham had given her. . . . Susan Lenox had been trained to order and system, and they had become part of her being, beyond the power of drink and opium and prostitution to disintegrate them. [2:255]

Unlike Dreiser, who insisted that one's inner biological system of "chemisms" such as "catastases" and "metastases" inexorably determined outward behavior, Phillips believed strongly that preserving the outer man or woman through exercise, good food, and even, as in *Old Wives for New* (1908), plastic surgery could stave off both physical and moral decay. By keeping physically healthy, then, Susan demonstrates her steadfast commitment to a higher goal. Her ambitions, as Louis Filler describes them, are "provokingly plain: to do useful work, and to be free to do whatever she liked."[25] But Phillips, despite his seven years of earnest work on the novel, tries to reduce Susan's character to a few simple, and endlessly repeated, traits of behavior: she refuses to explain herself or tell her story; her greatest wish is to be both free and strong; she neither dissembles nor lies, speaking up frequently to her own detriment; like George du Maurier's Trilby, she has beautiful feet and is admired for them; her eyes turn grey when she is businesslike, violet when she is moved emotionally. In spelling out the expressions and interpreting them for the reader, Phillips fails to allow Susan to retain the indeterminate air of wistful melancholy that constitutes Carrie's appeal for her audience—the mouth that appears "about to cry," the "pathetic" shadow about her eyes (*Sister Carrie*, 484). As Ames tells Carrie, "You and I are but mediums, through which something is expressing itself. Now, our duty is to make ourselves ready mediums" (485). In reducing Susan's position as a "ready medium" through his "critical dissection" of her into discrete parts, Phillips breaks the code of her profession and damages the "truth" of his character in the process.

· III ·

If the naturalists proved sympathetic to fallen women, they heaped heavy scorn upon the convention-bound type of girl whom H. H. Boyesen had damned as the "Iron Madonna," a phrase suggesting both her intransigence and the iconlike status granted to her by worshipers and detractors alike. Cowardice separates this type from the New Women of London and Norris. In Norris's *Vandover and the Brute*, for example, Turner Ravis at first appears to be a courageous New Woman. As Don Graham notes, she is not straitlaced: on the contrary, she joins with Vandover, Ellis, and the others in drinking beer, eating tamales, and playing cards. But Turner shows her true colors when Vandover begins to disintegrate. Instead of attempting to save him, as Norris and his character Vandover believe good women should do, she deserts him after the Ida Wade affair. After Vandover is snubbed at a society dance, Geary explains the real problem: "It's that business with Ida Wade. . . . It got around somehow that she killed herself on your account."[26] Earlier, Vandover, Geary, and Haight had bemoaned society's unwillingness to chastise its erring members; in getting caught, however, Vandover has transgressed the most important law of all and suffers the consequences that he did not think existed.

Meeting him at the library one afternoon, Turner explains that he does not love her enough; girls "really love the man who loves them most" (458), and she believes Vandover incapable of this kind of regard. She ends with a pep talk, telling Vandover to "live up to the best that's in you" (459), and disappears from his life, taking up first with Dolly Haight and then finally, opportunistically, with the amoral but successful Charlie Geary. In other words, she has sold herself. From Norris's perspective, she has deserted Vandover and abnegated one of the highest and noblest functions of a "man's woman": the saving of a weak man through her good influence.

Jack London's *Martin Eden* (1909), a more sustained attack, resembles both Norris's *Blix* (1899) and *Vandover and the Brute* in its broad outlines, including the portrait of a young artist struggling both to find love and to remain true to his art. *Martin Eden* is also a novel of degeneration. Like Vandover, who destroys himself through an excessive love of civilization and its comforts, Martin demands more from his culture than it can possibly provide until, surfeited with its material pleasures and sickened by the absence of spiritual ones, he commits suicide. Through his spiritual malaise and his viewing suicide as an act of self-affirmation, Martin additionally resembles Dick Heldar, the hero of Kipling's artist novel, *The Light That Failed* (1891), as in some ways the conventional Ruth Morse recalls Maisie, Dick's talentless and restrictive foster sister–lover. Beyond these superficial parallels, in *Martin Eden* London launches a wholesale assault on the legend of good women current in his day. From the unlettered Martin's first awestruck visit to the Morse home to his final disdainful departure from it, the novel demonstrates the destructive influence of a feminine culture in which weak men like Arthur, Ruth's brother and pander, survive, while strong, stalwart men like Martin must perish.

The novel's origins are largely autobiographical, as London readily acknowledged. Writing to Anna Strunsky in 1901, London explained his attraction to Mabel Applegarth, his onetime fiancée and the prototype of Ruth Morse:

> It was a great love. But see! Time passed. I grew. I saw immortality fade from her. Saw her only woman. . . . She was pure, honest, true, sincere, everything. But she was small. . . . Her culture was a surface smear, her deepest depth a singing shallow. . . . I awoke, and judged, and my puppy love was over.[27]

The stages of London's disillusionment parallel the experiences of his protagonist, Martin Eden, and in creating Ruth, London initially seems to provide for his readers a conventional love interest for Martin and a wealthy, cultured, feminine figure to contrast with his rough, unlettered hero. Instead, the story pivots on Ruth, who carries within her statically conceived notion of culture the seeds for her own destruction. Martin's increasing discontent with her and with her view of culture parallels and informs that of the reader.

The first chapter of the book establishes the series of antitheses between Martin Eden and the middle-class culture that first ignores, then celebrates, and finally defeats him. The epitome of this culture is Ruth Morse, "a pale, ethereal creature, with wide, spiritual blue eyes and a wealth of golden hair."[28] Her spirituality and "Anglo-Saxon" beauty, so beloved by Norris and London, evoke for Martin visions of the other sorts of women he has known, women darker and more sexual, from "Eurasians . . . stamped with degeneracy" and "full-bodied South-Sea-Island women, flower-crowned and brown-skinned" to the "grotesque and terrible nightmare brood" of Whitechapel prostitutes (6–7).[29] Ruth and Martin become aware not only of the contrast that the other represents, but simultaneously of a lack within themselves. They busily invest each other with the missing admirable traits: Martin worships Ruth as "Iseult," heroine of romance and intellectual high priestess, and she speculates on the great strength and vitality (and forbidden sexuality) promised by the phallicism of his "muscular neck, heavy corded, almost bull-like, bronzed by the sun" (11). What each will come to realize, of course, is that the culture and sexuality that each seeks is no route to salvation. Martin's extreme response to Ruth, however, is consistent with his bipolar thinking, and he maintains both physical vigor and intellectual curiosity as long as he oscillates between two points of contrast.[30] Ironically, as long as he struggles to find a place of permanence for himself, his vitality is unimpaired, but, as his beloved Spencer and Darwin would suggest to him, in static "being" rather than in dynamic "becoming" he faces only entropy, disintegration, and death. When the reality and his visions of the ideal coincide near the end of the novel, he ceases to exist.

Throughout the novel, Martin's intellectual maturity can be gauged by the degree of divergence between his view of Ruth and ours. London employs a dual perspective in describing her: the unlettered Martin is initially dazzled by her, although London's narrator and the reader are considerably less easily impressed. When Martin's disdain for her limitations parallels that of the reader and narrator, we understand that he has grown up at last. During her very first meeting with Martin, Ruth disapproves of Swinburne, whom even Martin's unlettered eye can see is "great," because, she says, "he is, well, indelicate. There are many of his poems that should never be read" (10). Her system of social morality determines her standards of literary value. The doubt that London casts over Ruth's understanding of literature coincides with Martin's later judgment (akin to Norris's) that she and her brothers "had been studying about life from the books while he had been busy living life" (25). When Martin reads her his story "The Plot," a story of "the big thing out of life . . . not sentence-structure and semicolons" (104), she is "gripped" and "mastered" by it. Her only response is nevertheless wholly consistent with the stuffy views of one who had condemned Swinburne: "Oh! It is degrading! It is not nice! It is nasty! . . . Why didn't you select a nice subject? . . . We know there are nasty things in the world, but that is no reason—" (105). Ruth believes that art should be divorced from life; moreover, she dislikes literature that masters her, preferring instead to retain the mastery over literature granted by her role as feminine arbiter of culture.

The essence of the relationship between Ruth and Martin is, in fact, a struggle for control, a masochistic reversal of Pygmalion and Galatea in which the statue "kills" first his creator and then himself.[31] Willingly ceding the power of good influence to Ruth, Martin seeks to reestablish himself in her eyes and his own as an ideal man of her class. Her reading of Browning has not taught her that "it was an awkward thing to play with souls" (60), and she works with a vengeance at molding Martin's. Like Letty Pace of *Jennie Gerhardt* and Mrs. Kelcey of *George's Mother*, Ruth turns out to be a woman with weapons. When she plays the piano for him, "[h]er music was a club that swung brutally upon his head; and though it stunned him and crushed him down, it incited him" (20). Similarly, "[h]er purity smote him like a blow" (20). Once Martin is properly bludgeoned into submission, Ruth attempts "to re-thumb the clay of him into a likeness of her father's image, which image she believed to be the finest in the world" (59); her methods, and London's images, grow gentler. She "played to him—no longer at him—and probed him with music that sank to depths beyond her plumb-line" (59) much as Celia Madden, another cultured woman, seduces the ignorant Theron Ware. Here as elsewhere, London's narrator continually undercuts not only Ruth's mastery of culture but Martin's uncritical appreciation of her limited gifts. Though an imperfect interpreter of her culture, she remains a satisfactory vehicle for its transmission, in part because her obvious intellectual limitations render inevitable the moment of his disillusionment with her shallow standards.

Martin's disillusionment with genteel standards progresses through a tightening circle of denunciation scenes; his first occurs when he displaces his considerable wrath at genteel standards onto the magazine editors. Through his voracious reading, the naive Martin discovers early on that "the immense amount of printed stuff . . . was dead" (99) and begins "to doubt that editors were real men. They seemed cogs in a machine" (100). As Martin's passionately cynical friend Brissenden tells him, they favor "wish-wash and slush" (235), not guts, and the "magazine rhymesters" that they publish are effectively "a band of eunuchs" (235). London's worst insults vilify the "dead" literature itself and question the manhood of the editors. They are not rough, virile red-bloods with a taste for real life, like Martin, but pale mollycoddles upholding feminine standards. Discovering that editors match intellectual with fiscal dishonesty, Martin, in a scene reminiscent of one in *The Light That Failed*, tries unsuccessfully to collect payment for an article appearing in the *Transcontinental*. His editors resist until, like Dick Heldar, he threatens them with "red-blood" bodily harm. His friend Russ Brissenden, an intellectual whose cynicism and quest after sensual beauty identify him with the mood of fin de siècle decadence, refuses altogether to allow such riffraff to judge his work, preferring obscurity to their adulation. Fittingly, the worst moment for Martin thus occurs when the editors fawn with "cheapness and vulgarity" (289) over "Ephemera," Brissenden's exquisitely pessimistic poem, which Martin submits for publication after Brissenden commits suicide.

Moving closer to the source of meretricious values, at Ruth's dinner party Martin takes on the social system that allows such tyranny and shoddy dealings. Even though his fierce determination to be published leads him into writing formula fiction from his self-devised "story chart," Martin despises the editorial cabal that forces him into such expedients. The editors, he says, are backed up in their judgments by a man who (like Howells) is "the Dean of American criticism" and one of "the two foremost literary critics in the United States. . . . Yet I read his stuff, and it seems to me the perfection of the felicitous expression of the inane" (169). Having disposed of his Howells-substitute, Martin next excoriates the "English professors—little, microscopic-minded parrots!" (169). The old literature is dead, entombed and enshrined, and its unjust preservation by Vanderwater and his acolytes constitutes a crime against writers of "real life" like Martin Eden and Jack London.

London uses the image of the dinner party, and indeed food in general, as both a structural device within the novel and a metaphor for Martin's ravenous need for knowledge and approval from the culture that excludes him. Beyond money, Martin wishes to have his own judgment of his literary gift vindicated. He hungers for it, in fact. The dried apricots, rice, and beans that he cooks so excellently well in his room cannot nourish him, as his belief in himself cannot sustain him, without occasional infusions of food/praise from others. Although Martin does not realize it, he commits the same mistake as Mr. Butler, whose entrepreneurial drive Ruth has urged him to emulate: for the sake of a fanatically felt passion, he destroys his appetite for life through intensive privation. Dinner parties function as occasions for Martin to assimilate the ideas, particularly contrasting ideas, that strike him, whether he is gratefully receiving soup from Maria, his landlady, or sharing candy with her children; feeling out of place at a workers' picnic with Lizzie, his lower-class friend; feeding cherries to Ruth; or arguing ideas over a bottle with Brissenden. At his first dinner party at the Morses' residence, for example, he recognizes his own cultural deficiencies, whereas at his final dinner party at their house, he comes to understand that the deficiencies are theirs, not his: "To real literature, real painting, real music, the Morses and their kind, were dead" (213). Like the editors that print dead literature, the Morses are less alive than the soon-to-be suicide, Martin. Later in the novel, surfeited with fame, effort, and life generally, he will decline both adulation and food when he refuses an invitation to the captain's table on the ship, an action that signals his imminent suicide.

As Martin's language of food refers metonymically to spiritual nourishment, so Ruth's language figures economic exchange. Despising the expedients of pawnshops and gas ring cookery that he is driven to by his poverty, Ruth tries to turn Martin variously into a capitalist like Mr. Butler, a lawyer, and a clerk in her father's business. Her entire answer to the problems that Martin encounters in publishing his work is to hold up the popular magazines as correct judges of success: magazine writers, she tells Martin, "sell [their stories], and you—don't" (225). Later, becoming annoyed, she challenges his determination:

> "But why do you persist in writing such things when you know they won't sell?" she went on inexorably. "The reason for your writing is to make a living, isn't it?"
>
> "Yes, that's right; but the miserable story got away with me. I couldn't help writing it. It demanded to be written."
>
> "But that character, that Wiki-Wiki, why do you make him talk so roughly? Surely it will offend your readers, and surely that is why the editors are justified in refusing your work."
>
> "Because the real Wiki-Wiki would have talked that way."
>
> "But it is not good taste." [248]

Martin speaks of literary power, of passion felt and communicated; Ruth counters with "good taste," coded language for the ability to sell, in effect to prostitute, that literary passion. The connection between sex and money becomes explicit when Ruth learns that Martin has passed the Railway Mail civil service exam and still will not get a job. Hitherto she has expressed a healthy physical passion for him in a gesture evocative both of affection and of strangulation: "[S]he reached up and placed both hands upon Martin Eden's sunburnt neck. So exquisite was the pang of love and desire fulfilled that she uttered a low moan, relaxed her hands, and lay half-swooning in his arms" (149–50). Now, however, she proves "a passive sweetheart" when Martin kisses her; the erotic charge of Martin's neck, it seems, owes more to the testimony it provides about his ability to work, to function in the marketplace, than to his own sexual power.

The final chapters of the novel describe Martin's growing emancipation from Ruth and from the dominance of feminine discourse that she represents. The truly terrible corollary of the Iron Madonna's power, London implies, is not just that she deludes herself about the benefits of what she does, but that she creates such havoc under the guise of doing good. Although his determination to educate himself arises from within, Ruth gives Martin his first taste of culture, proffering the apple of the false Tree of Knowledge that ever after makes his old, lower-class existence impossible. Her sincerity does not mitigate the pernicious effects of her destructive influence, and the nihilism in Martin to which she has unwittingly contributed works against her at the last. His final renunciation scene occurs when, tired finally of fame, wealth, and all else he had sought, Martin refuses Ruth when she offers to renew their engagement, recognizing only now that he has never loved her. Ruth then volunteers to come to him "in free love if you will" (330). Martin, however, remains unmoved, for he realizes that the love she offers is anything but "free." Unlike the working-class Lizzie, whose unconditional love for the uncultured Martin critiques Ruth's mercenary ethos, Ruth craves his success and his royalties more than she wants the man himself. Yet as Martin himself realizes, his knowledge of the world of culture has rendered a relationship with Lizzie impossible. Recognizing that he had loved "an idealized Ruth . . . an ethereal creature of his own creating" (329), he now can appreciate neither the real lower-class woman whom Lizzie represents nor the real, if mercenary, woman that Ruth has become.

The price of Martin's emancipation from Ruth, then, is cultural anomie and a Pyrrhic victory. Too spiritually depleted to relish the irony in Ruth's humiliation, he nonetheless has exposed the Iron Madonna for what she really is, for Ruth, that bastion of purity who even when she propositions Martin tells him not to swear, has been reduced to a position lower than that of Lizzie and the other girls who equate sex with love. She has agreed, with her family's consent, to barter sex for money, just as Turner Ravis does. The Iron Madonna thus not only forfeits all credibility as a cultural arbiter but becomes in moral terms no better than Maggie Johnson, Susan Lenox, and the other street girls; indeed, in terms of the naturalists' morality, she offers to sell herself with far less excuse than the others, since she need not do so in order to survive. With her much vaunted critical judgment discredited and her claims to idealism and physical purity proven to be a sham, Ruth, and by implication the Iron Madonna, has nothing left. By revealing the shallowness and limitations of her values, by reducing, reinventing, and parodying her, London destroys the Iron Madonna's image of herself, and with that image her power.

· IV ·

Stephen Crane's short novel *George's Mother* (1896) explores further limitations of the "good woman" and her weapons. Like *Vandover and the Brute,* it is the story of a weak man's reaction, or lack of reaction, to the external and internal forces that cause his degeneration.[32] In his introduction to the Virginia edition, James B. Colvert speculates that *George's Mother* "was conceived as a response to Crane's 'literary fathers,'" since it is "a study in the psychology of moral deprivation, more subdued than *Maggie* and less conspicuously concentrated in execution. . . . in short, the kind of realistic novel Howells or Garland might write."[33] One might add that, with its emphasis on moral deprivation, its depiction of ordinary life for a mother and son only three years removed from a small town, and its unsparing look at the effects of an excess of unexamined virtues, the novel also indirectly recalls the local color tradition that Howells approved and Garland defended. In *George's Mother* Crane does not side with the meliorists of that tradition; he resembles rather those who, like Mary Wilkins Freeman and Rose Terry Cooke, cast a critical eye on either the motives or the good sense of those who represent traditional Christianity and conventional virtues. For the most part, however, the novel stands as Crane's ironic commentary on the destructive power of a good woman's saving influence. With unassailable virtue and the best of intentions, Mrs. Kelcey unwittingly drives George from comparative respectability into the pointless existence of a street drifter.

Within the first few chapters Crane presents the opposing choices open to George Kelcey: saloon and street corner, home and church. Also introduced is the repeated pattern of rejection and helpless entanglement that characterizes George's relationship with his mother. Hailed by the men at the "little smiling saloon," George stays past suppertime drinking beer; his mother, sensing a change in him, asks him to "come t'prayer-meetin'" with her.[34] George, annoyed by the request, uneasily excuses himself ("it wouldn't do me no good t'go if I didn't wanta go" [124]) and heads once again for the saloon. This pattern of mild misbehavior–confrontation–worse misbehavior recurs throughout the novel. The cycle establishes George's life as following the classic naturalistic downward spiral into degradation and thus forms a basic structural element.

Although Crane had originally entitled the novel "A Woman without Weapons," Mrs. Kelcey in fact has several in her arsenal: fanatical housekeeping, right beliefs, and a sharp tongue. Pointing her broom "lance-wise, at dust demons," she raises her voice "in a long cry, a strange war chant, a shout of battle and defiance" (120) as she cleans the house. Other weapons include Mrs. Kelcey's misplaced confidence in George and herself. She believes that "she must be a model mother to have such a son" (133), a son who "was going to become a white and looming king among men" (135). To control George, she tries various methods, including coaxing "him with caresses" (124), giving him a "martyr-like glance" (125), nagging at him about swearing and drinking (as Ruth Morse does with Martin Eden), and finally, on her deathbed when her mind regresses in time, failing to recognize him at all, presumably because he has fallen so far from the "Georgie" whom she tries to call in from the fields.

Weapons or no, Mrs. Kelcey begins to lose the battle right from the start, as George slips away from the feminine realm of stability and virtue to the masculine world of the saloon. If Mrs. Kelcey's weapons and beliefs allude to medieval romance, as Brennan suggests, surely George's thoughts refer equally strongly to classical epic, or rather mock-epic tradition. The saloon scenes, with their focus on drinking, stories, and the camaraderie of men, provide the most direct classical allusions. On his first visit, for example, George meets Bleecker, who, sensing the boy's admiration, extends himself: "Directly, then, he launched forth into a tale of by-gone days, when the world was better. He had known all the great men of that age. . . . He rejoiced at the glory of the world of dead spirits. He grieved at the youth and flippancy of the present one" (126-27). The tales of great men in a mythic golden age, the allusion to an (under)world of dead spirits, the *ubi sunt* tone of the whole—all these suggest epic tradition, even if, as here, the tradition is parodied through its association with a group of drunks in a Bowery saloon. The men seek consolation from a "grinding world filled with men who were harsh," and they find it in the "chorus of violent sympathy" (128) with which they greet each other's stories. Like George, they believe that "they were fitted for a tree-shaded land, where everything was peace" (129), recalling perhaps Odysseus's lotus-eaters on Circe's island. Such a belief conflicts directly with the aims of women like Mrs. Kelcey, whose creaking hymn and "war-chant" addresses the same rhetorical question:

"Should I be car-reed tew th' skies
   O-on flow'ry be-eds of ee-ease,
While others fought tew win th' prize
   An' sailed through blood-ee seas." [119]

Her answer, and the church's answer, is of course a resounding "no." Battling to win the prize of salvation, not "ease," is the purpose of life on earth.

George's initiation into the world of men occurs during the feast at Bleecker's lodgings. In analyzing initiation rites from what an 1897 *North American Review* article called "the Golden Age of Fraternity," Mark Carnes provides a framework for interpreting George's initiation. Carnes found the rituals' models of "liminality," "extended allegor[ies] involving personal development," and "emotionally charged psychodrama[s] centering on family relations" to have a specific function in their practitioners' re-creation of a primitive past:

> Restated in gender-role terms, the dilemma for boys in Victorian America was not simply that their fathers were absent . . . but that adult gender roles were invariant and narrowly defined, and that boys were mostly taught the sensibilities and moral values associated with the adult female role. . . . As young men, they were drawn to the male secret orders, where they repeatedly practiced rituals that effaced the religious values and emotional ties associated with women.[35]

George's initiation follows a similar pattern, and Crane again evokes the world of ancient epic as a means of heightening its ritualistic qualities. The "feast" of beer, whiskey, and pipes is carefully laid out upon a table resembling a "primitive bar" (142) so that the feast becomes an exalted version of their nightly rendezvous at the saloon. The audience listens raptly when, "in rapid singsong" like that of traditional bards (144), the symbolically named Zeusentell recites his ridiculous saga "Patrick Clancy's Pig." After the recitation, the members hurl the drunken George into a corner "and pile chairs and tables upon him" (149), suggesting the symbolic executions common to fraternal initiation rituals, after which the epic games commence with ritual wrestling, degraded here to a "great old mill" between Zeusentell and O'Connor (151). The religious quality of their meeting is reinforced by the image of "lazy cloud-banks" (143) of tobacco smoke "from which the laughter arose like incense. He knew that old sentiment of brotherly regard for those about him. . . . He was capable of heroisms" (146). Having undergone a ritual initiation into the world of men, George deludes himself that he has found a heroic brotherhood that will provide an escape from his mother's demands.

By contrast, the church meeting he attends with his mother offers ritual with no feeling of brotherhood. When Kelcey enters the comfortably dim saloon, he is greeted by a sympathetic brotherhood of men; but the "riot of lights" in the church highlight the judgmental "multitudinous pairs of eyes that turned toward him . . . implacable in their cool valuations" (156). The "indefinable presence" that pervades the altar makes him brood as the "portentous black figure" of the beer keg in the saloon never does, although the latter is more to blame for his downfall. The minister preaches a sermon, and the churchgoers, like the men at the saloon, tell stories, "little tales of religious faith" (157), but Kelcey, "not familiar with their types," chooses to understand only that he is damned. The saloon, by cementing brotherhood and fostering heroic action, replaces the church in George's mind. With his fallible judgment, George ironically never perceives his total inability to sustain this brotherhood or to act heroically.

His initiation into the saloon world of "heroic" men tips the balance of his descent into degeneration. When George loses his job and is thereby barred from the men's world of the saloon, he finds an acceptable substitute in the company of street toughs led by Fidsey Corcoran and his gang. The forms are less courtly, but the message is the same: drink and its ritual sharing, consisting of standing the others to rounds of drinks at the saloon, or taking turns ("smokes") at a pail of beer in the vacant lot, differentiates the men's world from the women's. The distinction between "real men" and "Willieboys" that so occupied Gelett Burgess, Theodore Roosevelt, and the naturalists is never more evident than in this slum setting. Passing the vacant lot, George refuses Fidsey's repeated offers to share a pail of beer:

> Kelcey turned dejectedly homeward. "Oh, I guess not, this roun'."
> "What's d' matter wi'che?" said Fidsey. "Yer gittin t' be a reg'lar willie. Come ahn, I tell ye!" [172]

When the others drink too much, Fidsey again condemns them with what is apparently a dreaded epithet: "'Look what yeh lef'us! Ah, say, youse was a dandy! What 'a yeh tink we ah? Willies?'" (173). Clearly, effeminate Willieboys don't drink the way real men do, and Fidsey repeats the term in its shortened form—"Willie"—as though it is a favored and deadly insult needing no explanation. Requiring no further impetus, Kelcey drinks his share. The boastful heroism of the saloon reasserts itself, and when Blue

Billie demands, "Did youse say yeh could do me?" Kelcey, newly rebaptized "Kel," growls, "Well, what if I did?" (174). The fight is postponed because George's mother calls for him on her deathbed, a temporary retreat into the woman's world of his mother's ordered flat. From the world of epic grandeur and brotherhood evoked by the saloon habitués, George has sunk to a narrowly averted fight with Blue Billie and the other street toughs. Only guilt remains of his mother's teachings, a legacy that leaves him singularly unfit to survive.

Crane's use of mock epic obscures but does not conceal a very real concern with the place of courage and right action in such a world. Mrs. Kelcey *is* courageous. She battles unceasingly for the welfare of herself and her son, calling into play those virtues—cleanliness, family loyalty, self-sacrifice—that should secure for her a degree of success in the small-town world from whence she moved to the city. Yet these virtues do not work for her in a naturalistic environment. Her cleanliness becomes a pointless exercise, her faith in George a delusion, her self-sacrifice a snare to prevent his leaving her and to delay the necessary process of his individuation. Local color virtues cannot save a woman who, like Wharton's Bunner sisters, fails to see the truth of the naturalistic world surrounding her.[36] Not only has her limited arsenal of virtues failed, but the environment conspires to deprive her of her ability to dominate George. In unfilial revolt, George blurts out the true state of affairs between them when Mrs. Kelcey admonishes him for swearing: "Whatter ye goin' t' do 'bout it?" (167). The fact of her economic dependence thus brought home, she "threw out her hands in the gesture of an impotent one . . . as if she had survived a massacre in which all that she loved had been torn from her by the brutality of savages" (167). George, whose brutishness, like Vandover's, results from his drinking, has thus "massacred" her illusion that virtue counts. Set adrift by a world of transience and inverted values, one physically as well as symbolically dominated by the "machine of mighty strength" (120) that is the brewery, George's mother learns that all along she has been a woman without weapons. Like her blowzy, drunken neighbor Mrs. Johnson of *Maggie: A Girl of the Streets*, she is helpless to control her child. Even Mrs. Kelcey's death does not ensure her victory, since the final vision is of George, staring at the wallpaper with his "nerveless arms [allowing] his fingers to sweep the floor" (177) in one of naturalism's characteristic trance scenes. Rather than attempting to integrate elements of the men's world with his mother's, George settles for the dichotomy of moral absolutes and ends up a failure both in his mother's terms (the church) and his own (the spurious heroism of the saloon). Attempting to be independent, he has degenerated into a street tough; attempting to save him and recognizing her defeat, she dies. In a world that values neither her efforts nor his, both are failures.

Nor does the irrelevance of a good woman's virtues render George's choices any easier. George faces a different problem from that of his mother: her impossible task was to impose a set of prescribed moral values on an actively hostile environment. George, on the other hand, confronts a shifting and uncertain world with few absolutes save those based on opposition to his mother. Following the code of the street and saloon, he becomes for his mother a bad provider and a "wild son"; yet he prefers those consequences to the far more dreadful fate of having the men on the street question his manhood and condemn him as a "Willie." Only one force can efface the "good woman's" moral apothegms: the swaggering linguistic fearlessness of the Jimmie Johnsons, Blue Billies, and, in the future, George Kelceys of Hester Street. As a gesture not of hopelessness but of nihilistic defiance, "Wot de hell!" infuses *Maggie* and *George's Mother* with a kind of anarchic energy. The phrase functions also as a charm, an incantation against the literary world's supercilious and too-proper ways. Crane uses it in his fiction as if he relished its power to deflate pretenses, as if the victory belongs not just to his characters but to himself. Through language, a self-described "frail boy" like Crane (or George) can escape the world of Willieboys and participate in the masculine pursuits of "real life."

· V ·

According to Eric Solomon, "In Stephen Crane's own judgment, *The Monster* was his best novel."[37] Solomon places it in the tradition of unsentimental small-town satires begun by Edward Eggleston's *Hoosier Schoolmaster* (1871), E. W. Howe's *Story of a Country Town* (1883), and Joseph Kirkland's *Zury: The Meanest Man in Spring County* (1887), a tradition continued by such writers as Edwin Arlington Robinson, Sherwood Anderson, and Sinclair Lewis (178–79). The story tells of two outcasts: Henry Johnson, an African-American hostler horribly disfigured when he rescues his employer's son from a fire; and Dr. Trescott, who, grateful for Henry's

action, undertakes to protect him against the town's outrage at his mutilated presence. In one sense, *The Monster* combines a broad message of
alienation and an attack on hypocrisy, for, as Thomas Gullason points out,
"the monster is society, and it becomes the anti-heroic central character
only after Henry's tragedy."[38]

Like *George's Mother*, *The Monster* demonstrates that "the prescribed
virtues of honesty, good intentions, and a sense of obligation"[39] are
insufficient protection against the fluctuating, violent, naturalistic world of
the New York slums, but Crane's readers would have anticipated the absence, not the presence, of virtues in such surroundings. Within the conventions of each genre, the slum literature of naturalism could present the
grotesque and horrifying because it promised its readers the safety of economic distance, just as local color fiction, through its use of village life and
a nostalgic recent past, assured its public that outrageous or violent human
behavior was beyond its geographic and symbolic scope of representation.
The Monster shocks precisely because Crane, by intermingling them, undercuts the safety implied by both genres. Two years before *The Monster* was
published, Frank Norris wrote of the essential element in naturalistic
fiction:

> Terrible things must happen to the characters of the naturalistic tale. They
> must be twisted from the ordinary, wrenched out from the quiet, un-
> eventful round of every-day life, and flung into the throes of a vast and
> terrible drama that works itself out in unleashed passions, in blood, and
> in sudden death . . . no teacup tragedies here.[40]

The mutilated Henry Johnson ("a thing, a dreadful thing") functions as a
destabilizing influence cast into the seemingly secure but actually fragile
social structure of the town.[41] His presence, together with Dr. Trescott's
obstinate and heroic defense of him, simultaneously wrenches the townspeople from their "quiet, uneventful round of everyday life" and reveals
the inadequacy of their moral systems. Like Henry Johnson, Crane out-
rages convention by dragging an alien form—naturalism—into the serenity
of the local color tale.

Until chapter 11, *The Monster* promotes the myth of the orderly, almost
idyllic small town. Local color elements abound, including the small-town
atmosphere, the ritual gatherings, the place of gossip and storytelling, and,

perhaps most importantly, the theme of the outsider. The sense of order is established in chapter 1. Critics have generally agreed that the first chapter, virtually a prologue, establishes the themes of the whole. As he will later figure in Henry's destruction, Jimmie Trescott, playing at being a mechanical "engine number 36," destroys part of the natural world, a peony. He tries to prop it upright but fails to do so. Just as Jimmie must accept punishment for being unable to fix what is broken, his father must suffer the town's punishment for the opposite reason: he transgresses natural law when he heals Henry Johnson, who in Judge Hagenthorpe's opinion "ought to die" (31), and he is ostracized as a result. Eric Solomon reads this passage as a warning unheeded: "Dr. Trescott 'could make nothing of it.' . . . The lesson is lost on him, and he will later challenge this law of nature."[42] Later the same day, the rituals continue undisturbed: amid "tremendous civilities" (16) Henry courts Miss Bella Farragut; the barbershop habitués, who function as a chorus for the perspective of the town's men, exchange gossip and stare at Henry; people wait for their out-of-town mail and stroll to the band concert.

The first intimations of disorder, provided by the "great hoarse roar of a factory whistle" (18) that signals a fire, reach all simultaneously. It is a measure of Whilomville cohesiveness that everyone, right down to the child Willie, who wants to see the fire, understands instantly its significance, for they are educated in interpreting what concerns their town. So confident of success and well versed in interpretation are the town's boys that, rather than fearing the fire, they wish for even more excitement, contrasting the new chief's slow style unfavorably with that of his predecessor, the dramatic "old Sykes Huntington [who] . . . used to bellow continually like a bull and gesticulate in a sort of delirium" (27). The last to hear of the calamity is the person most directly involved. Driving home from a case, Dr. Trescott enjoys the sense of control that he has over life because "this last case was now in complete obedience to him" (25). It is an instance of control that he will not enjoy again after the news of the fire reaches him.

The fire allows the town to do what it likes to do best: indulge its penchant for mythmaking. Henry plunges into the burning house, rescues Jimmie, and, stymied by the "delicate, trembling sapphire shape like a fairy lady" that blocks his path, falls prey to the "ruby-red snakelike thing" that destroys his face (24).[43] He enters the house "the biggest dude in town"

(15) and leaves it "a thing . . . laid on the grass" (26). The story of the fire travels through several versions as the townspeople refine it to fit their prejudices. The first version, that of "[t]he man who had information," blames Henry:

> "That was the kid's room—in the corner there. He had measles or somethin', and this coon—Johnson—was a settin' up with 'im, and Johnson got sleepy or somethin' and upset the lamp, and the doctor he was down in his office, and he came running up, and they all got burned together till they dragged 'em out." [28]

It is a story of duty neglected rather than heroism performed, wrong on every point. Wrong, too, is the man "preserved for the deliverance of the final judgment," who decrees abruptly that "they'll die sure. Burned to flinders. No chance. Hull lot of 'em. Anybody can see" (18).[44] In true local color fashion, the disturbing element has been rendered harmless by being placed in the recent past. Certain that Henry "could not live . . . [because] he now had no face" (29), the town congratulates itself on its tolerance; now that Henry will die, the customary social sanctions and color bar can briefly be suspended.

In one way or another, Henry has been a "thing" for the townspeople his whole life: as a second-class citizen in a white man's world, as a being whose realm is in the stable with the horses, as the parodic cynosure of the mocking eyes in Reifsnyder's Barber Shop, as the "thing" that had been a man. Now, however, he becomes a hero when the town's official voice, the morning paper, continues the mythmaking process by wrongly printing a laudatory obituary of Henry. To bask in the reflected glory of Henry's apotheosis, Bella Farragut also contributes to the misinformation with a false story of her own, namely "that she had been engaged to marry Mr. Henry Johnson" (30). Even the children sense Henry's change in stature. Because his name "became suddenly the title of a saint," they try to bury the "odious couplet" that ironically fulfills itself: "Nigger, nigger, never die, / Black face and shiny eye" (30). James Halfley suggests that the townspeople treat the veiled Henry as God;[45] further, like God, he keeps his "shiny eye" on the town's actions: watching Judge Hagenthorpe suggest uneasily that Henry be allowed to die, witnessing the cowardice of Bella and her mother, and peering into the real lives of the white ruling class as they are symbolized by Theresa Page's party. And like God, Henry disconcertingly refuses to go away. Although his madness prevents him from judging them, his gaze, the reproachful reflection of their racism, rests on a society indicting itself.

Confident of their ability as interpreters, the townspeople feel that they understand the conventions governing this local drama—first fire, then rescue, then death—well enough to know that Henry must die, an expectation that becomes for them an imperative. Having elevated him from object of gossip to subject of myth, they can relax as he becomes literally yesterday's news. They are in essence rewriting not only Henry's life but Henry's body, inscribing his race as a manageable discourse within the narrative they create. At least one part of their fury at Henry's survival is sheer frustration: like the characters of local color villages, the residents of Whilomville want to control their version of the story. Denied that possibility, they vent their hostility on those who, like Henry and Dr. Trescott, disrupt or otherwise transform the conventions of their genre. The story cannot have closure or any kind of satisfactory ending, and it is this quality of uncertainty that dominates the town's reactions to the situation. Deprived of a coherent myth to render him harmless, the group must destroy Henry.

The middle sections of the story describe this process of destruction, and along with it the deterioration of the town's moral certitude. In the first of three parallel discussions that exemplify the town's viewpoint, Alek Williams, the black man who boards Henry, complains to the judge that his family is disrupted and is gradually being ostracized, a foreshadowing of Dr. Trescott's fate. The embarrassingly facetious scene that follows his complaint ends with Alek's accepting six dollars a week rather than five, the extra dollar apparently compensating for the social inconvenience. The money alone is not enough, since Alek tries to compel the judge's respect: "'Well, if I bo'd Hennery Johnson fer six dollehs er week, I uhns it! I uhns it!' cried Williams, wildly" (39). However burlesqued the portrait of Alek may be, Crane does make a serious point, juxtaposing Alek's willingness to sell his principles against Dr. Trescott's refusal to do so. Further, just as Crane has Henry's exaggerated manners mimic those of the town's white society, Alek's exaggerated complaints and his frantic attempts at self-justification both parody and foreshadow those later made by the townspeople, thus undercutting any possible moral legitimacy of their claims.

The setting for the second scene of discussion is that perennial small-town men's club, the local barbershop. As they had earlier discussed Henry's lavender trousers, now the barbershop patrons discuss his mutilated face, taking opposing sides on the question of Dr. Trescott's action. The unusually garrulous barber, Reifsnyder, begins by defending Dr. Trescott, using virtually the doctor's own words to Judge Hagenthorpe: "How can you let a man die?" (40). But Bainbridge the engineer indirectly threatens Reifsnyder—"You'd better shave some people"—reminding Reifsnyder that, after all, his livelihood depends on his customers and not on defending Dr. Trescott. His opposition wavering, Reifsnyder significantly then joins the others in singing a bit of doggerel: "'He has no face in the front of his head, / In the place where his face ought to grow'" (40). Summing up the town's new attitude, this "story" fragment replaces both the "odious couplet" and the official myth of Henry as saint. Reifsnyder, who has been putting himself in Trescott's place, now projects himself imaginatively into Henry's: "'I wonder how it feels to be without any face?'" (41). The cycle begins anew as a man repeats Reifsnyder's initial argument that if a man had saved your son, "'you'd do anything on earth for him'" (41). Reifsnyder, meanwhile, can no longer attest to the rightness of the doctor's decision, saying that the doctor "may be sorry he made him live" (41). The chapter ends with the two alternating ideas being repeated. There is no answer or solution, Crane suggests: to delve, like Reifsnyder, into the ethics of the situation leads not to certainty but to moral ambiguity.

In contrast with the indecisive men at the barbershop, the women and their fixed prejudices emerge as the most important force in the final third of the story. Crane devotes much of chapter 19 to an extended character sketch of Martha Goodwin, whose secure position and immense power are unmistakable despite her being the "mausoleum of a dead passion" (51). Martha is, in fact, a sharp-tongued spinster of the New England local color school, dominating her meek married sister and bullying the other women until they ally themselves "in secret revolt" against her (50). While the men in the barbershop dither pointlessly over ethics, and Dr. Trescott's one overt antagonist, Jake Winter, yelps angrily after the doctor "like a little dog" (59), Martha fearlessly pronounces judgment like Atropos herself: "'Serves him right if he was to lose all his patients,' she said suddenly, in bloodthirsty tones. She nipped her words out as if her lips were scissors" (52). She functions as the town's voice of prophecy, and as its executioner.

Left as the vengeful Fury-Fate she is in chapter 19, Martha would be nothing more than an emblem of all that is wrong with the town, a straw woman for Crane to demolish. But Crane makes of Martha much more than a mere stereotype. She is vengeful, but she also has a moral sense similar to, but more developed than, that of her male counterpart, Reifsnyder, the voice of the town's men as she is of the women. By chapter 22 she has become one of Dr. Trescott's defenders—one of the last people, in fact, to defend him and his vision of truth against the distortions put forth by the town. Martha's instinct for gossip is matched by an equally keen desire to get at the facts. When her sister Kate and Carrie Dungen exaggerate gossip about the illness of Sadie Winter, the little girl Henry had frightened at Theresa Page's party, Martha, a good woman with weapons, sets the record straight: "Martha wheeled from the sink. She held an iron spoon, and it seemed as if she was going to attack them. 'Sadie Winter has passed here many a morning since then carrying her school-bag. Where was she going? To a wedding?'" (60). Told that "you can't go against the whole town" (60), Martha will still not be denied: "I'd like to know what you call 'the whole town.' Do you call these silly people who are scared of Henry Johnson 'the whole town'?" (60). In setting herself against the town, she resembles indomitable women like Mrs. Flint of Rose Terry Cooke's "Mrs. Flint's Married Experience" and such Mary E. Wilkins Freeman heroines as Hetty Fifield ("A Church Mouse"), Sarah Penn ("The Revolt of Mother"), and Candace Whitcomb ("A Village Singer"). For a brief moment, she lives up to the kind of courage and moral sense that local color literature tried to promote, virtues represented in Whilomville only by Dr. Trescott.

In addition to her respect for truth, Martha tries to live up to the inclusivity characteristic of local color communities. However grotesque Henry's appearance may be, however stiff-necked and peculiar Dr. Trescott's refusal to give Henry up may seem, Martha resists consigning them to the status of outcasts, arguing instead for their inclusion.[46] Like Mrs. Todd, who finds for poor Joanna a place in the human community after the legalistically minded minister gives her up, Martha recognizes that the town is a human community greater than the influence of one faction of "silly people." Ironically, this is apparently the only time when her opinion has no impact on the people of Whilomville. Recognizing that gossip is the source of her power as the barbershop is Reifsnyder's, she is

readily distracted by fresh news and leaves the outcasts to their fate. Like
the literary tradition from which she springs, she has been sheltered from
direct knowledge of the "real life" that naturalism describes and that Henry
Johnson symbolizes, and her failure to meet this test of inclusivity marks
equally the failure of the local color community.

The final chapters suggest initially the triumph of respectability and
the town's women. In the penultimate chapter, the rich grocer, John
Twelve, and his cohorts try one last time to persuade Dr. Trescott to give
Henry up. To justify their actions, some speak of concern for Trescott, but
one excuse reverberates throughout: "It's the women" (63).[47] And indeed
it is the women who administer the coup de grâce. Returning to his house
in the final chapter, Dr. Trescott sees his wife weeping among the un-
touched teacups and, recognizing that she shares his ostracism, distractedly
finds "himself occasionally trying to count the cups" (65). The monster-
town becomes, at least in the men's retelling, a female monster-town, one
that destroys both accidental victims like Henry and principled heroes like
Dr. Trescott. From the naturalists' point of view, the ending becomes
another ghastly triumph for the conventional good woman with weapons.
Yet naturalism has struck some telling blows of its own. Like Twain's
Hadleyville, the town and its perceptions of order, its virtue, and its storytelling abilities have been destroyed. Whilomville is no longer any place for
Dr. Trescott to be, but neither is it the cohesive social unit it was at the
beginning. It cannot regain the lost image of its own perfection.

The Monster in one sense combines the conventions of local color and
naturalism, most notably in its themes of exclusion and the outsider, a
local color staple. Central to stories by Mary E. Wilkins Freeman, Rose
Terry Cooke, Mary N. Murfree, Sarah Orne Jewett, and Constance
Fenimore Woolson, the problem of the outsider is typically one of inclusion: how to incorporate the outsider into the life of the community
without disrupting its rituals or its inhabitants. *The Monster*, however,
provides instead a story of the almost violent exclusion of two men who
should be firmly fixed within the structure of the community. A mirrored
pair encompassing the polarities of rich/poor, educated/superstitious,
black/white, socially entrenched/socially tolerated, the two men together
represent a form of otherness that the town fears even as it studies them.
The stories of two dissimilar outsiders are each so extreme that they help

to explode the form as Henry's and Dr. Trescott's inevitable ostracism from the town provides a frightening tale of virtue wronged. As Levenson remarks in his introduction to the University of Virginia edition, it is the story of "how Dr. Trescott, firmly set in the established order and prompted only by motives of which his society approved, acted to bring on himself a relentless process of exclusion and alienation."[48] The town thrusts him out ruthlessly because he is a turncoat. Talking with Judge Hagenthorpe midway through the novel, Dr. Trescott chooses right action over the town's storytelling when he declines any longer to interpret their language "correctly":

> "Well, I don't want you to think I would say anything to— It was only that I thought that I might be able to suggest to you that—perhaps—the affair was a little dubious."
>
> With an appearance of suddenly disclosing his real mental perturbation, the doctor said: "Well, what would you do? Would you kill him?" he asked, abruptly and sternly.
>
> "Trescott, you fool," said the old man, gently. [33]

Trescott is a fool because he cuts directly to the point of the Judge's evasive, hesitant language. He speaks the unspeakable—"Would you kill him?"—and ushers in the age of truth and discord. If, as Jewett's narrator claims, "tact is a kind of mind-reading" that facilitates community understanding, Trescott refuses to participate. When he removes himself from participation in the community's discourse, he inexorably removes himself from the community.

The tale of Henry Johnson is quite another kind of ultimate outsider story, so extreme that it reads as a kind of invasion myth. It is an invasion story of the most terrifying kind, for the "monster" comes from within the town's psyche, generated by its fears of social instability, its prejudices about appearance (including racism), and its all-consuming passion for gossip and drama. Dr. Trescott, the one man free from such illusions, ironically becomes in the town's eyes a captive to the "monster," first to "the monster" Henry Johnson, to whom he owes his son's life, and then to "the monster" of the town and its attitudes. None of the townspeople want to look at him, for to look "real life" in the face, so to speak, involves recognition that it can be unimaginably grotesque. In his preface to *The Picture of Dorian Gray*, Oscar Wilde writes, "The nineteenth-century dislike of Realism is the rage of Caliban seeing his own face in a glass."[49] Because of his Caliban-like qualities, which are actually projected onto him by the town's fantasies, the people initially see Henry as the monster. What Henry does, however, is within his own visage hold up that mirror to the Caliban-town, exposing fraudulent harmony and corrupt virtue.

Read symbolically, Henry represents both naturalism and the naturalists' idea of "real life." As he makes his way through the town, recognizing no social distinctions and following no decorum, Henry becomes a force sweeping "from high to low," much like the personified Romance (naturalism) of Norris's metaphor. Also, in his degenerated physical state, he resembles other naturalistic "things" that had been men, among them Wolf Larsen at the end of *The Sea-Wolf*, the gibbering Vandover at the end of *Vandover and the Brute*, and the crusader in Norris's "Lauth," who becomes a spineless puddle of protoplasm by the end of the story. The naturalistic version of "real life" has no neat story; "real life" does not adapt well to mythmaking, closure, or safety. Bereft of their first comfortable myths of Henry, the townspeople still cannot escape because Dr. Trescott, the principled man of science, like the "scientific" naturalists, refuses to allow them to look away, to return to their idealized town and forget about Henry and the unpleasant reality he represents. They create new, darker myths, this time not laudatory ones but tales of Henry-the-monster and, by association, Trescott-the-monster. "If you're sick and nervous, Doctor Trescott would scare the life out of you, wouldn't he?" says Carrie Dungen (52). By interweaving elements of local color and naturalism, Crane has also accomplished another seemingly impossible feat. In his discussions of Zola, of Howells, and of naturalism, Frank Norris had several times spoken contemptuously about "teacup tragedies" as if the term were an oxymoron. Blending the terrible with the ordinary, Crane ends *The Monster* with just such a seemingly conventional scene: Mrs. Trescott, realizing the finality of her ostracism by the town, cries among the unused teacups set out for her party as Dr. Trescott pointlessly begins to count them.[50] But the horror of Henry's plight, and the tragedy of Dr. Trescott's destruction for the sake of principle, renders the ordinary scene extraordinary. As if taking up the gauntlet that Norris had flung down, Crane makes *The Monster* a "teacup tragedy."

· VI ·

The conflict being waged in these works is clearly the one against what these authors perceived as the excessive feminine discourse controlling masculine literature in particular and male lives in general. The reader sees within the first chapter of *Martin Eden* that Ruth is an Iron Madonna, and that she is limited, shallow, and unworthy of Martin, yet the narrative voice hammers away at these points chapter after chapter, contrasting always Martin's eagerness for real life and fresh experience with Ruth's preference for the canned variety. Mrs. Kelcey, Ruth, and the other highly conventional good women wreak havoc despite the kindest of intentions. In one sense, the legends of good women here are all tales of resisting female influence and of monster creation: Ruth tries mightily to remake Martin into what London clearly sees as a mere effigy of a man; Mrs. Kelcey tries to recreate a dutiful son on her own terms and instead spawns Kel the street tough; and the woman-dominated society of Whilomville creates Henry and Dr. Trescott as monsters by its rigid insistence on conventional behavior. Small wonder that the naturalists identified themselves rather with those other persecuted victims of too much respectability, the fallen women.

Interestingly, by telling the prostitutes' stories, the naturalists achieve what George's mother and the other good women cannot: the naturalists "rescue" the fallen women as fit subjects for fiction, but George's mother, despite her virtues, cannot save George from the streets. The point is not merely that by joining the world of convention and professed virtue the men would be stifled. It is that they would be becoming adjunct women— "Willieboys." In *George's Mother*, Mrs. Kelcey perceives George as a mythic St. George fighting "green dragons," never realizing that the dragon he must fight is herself. As guilt is her weapon, so words become George's in his ongoing struggle to differentiate himself from his mother and her feminine values. Through language, Crane and the naturalists, like the street tough, can render her not only harmless but defenseless—a woman without weapons.

CHAPTER SIX

Edith Wharton and the "Authoresses"

· I ·

In her autobiography, *A Backward Glance* (1934), Edith Wharton tells of inviting William Dean Howells to the first night of *The House of Mirth* as dramatized by Clyde Fitch:

> The play had already been tried out on the road, and in spite of Fay Davis's exquisite representation of Lily Bart I knew that (owing to my refusal to let the heroine survive) it was foredoomed to failure. Howells doubtless knew it also, and not improbably accepted my invitation for that very reason; a fact worth recording as an instance of his friendliness to young authors, and also on account of the lapidary phrase in which, as we left the theatre, he summed up the reason of the play's failure. "Yes—what the American public always wants is a tragedy with a happy ending."[1]

Writing "a tragedy with a happy ending" was just what Wharton was determined to avoid. Themes of loss and renunciation pervade works such as *The House of Mirth* (1905), *The Reef* (1912), *The Age of Innocence* (1920), and *The Mother's Recompense* (1925), as does the grim spectacle of principled figures such as Lily Bart (*The House of Mirth*), Ethan Frome, or Ralph Marvell (*The Custom of the Country*) being destroyed by the predatory characters surrounding them. Marriage, that most traditional of happy endings, becomes in Wharton's fiction a kind of prison, even when, as in *Summer* (1917), it promises the only available form of sanctuary for the main character. Wharton's decidedly unsentimental approach occasioned a backlash, however, in Lionel Trilling's "Morality of Inertia." Trilling so resoundingly rejects Wharton's gratuitous "cruelty" and her "limitation of heart" in *Ethan Frome* that he denies the work's moral significance, attributing what he sees as the misguided acclaim for *Ethan Frome* (1911) to "the modern snobbishness about tragedy and pain."[2] In effect, he charges Wharton with heaping on the cruelty and horror to pander to sophisticated readers by writing tragedies with "sad" rather than "happy" endings.

Wharton's reputation has often been subjected to just such contradictory opinions, and even her seemingly safe choice of old New York as a subject met with some controversy. According to Wharton, "the novelist should deal only with what is in his reach" (*A Backward Glance*, 206). But because "the material nearest to hand" was "fashionable New York" (206), Wharton faced the criticism that her work was somehow not about "real life" (i.e., lower-class life). Wharton's own later comments in *A Backward Glance* and other nonfiction writings not only suggest an awareness of the charges that had been leveled against her; they also reveal a writer determined to pursue her own course, resisting the specious in literary fads while remaining attuned to the trends of the time. In writing "The Secret Garden," the chapter of her autobiography dealing with the process of creating fiction, the self-assured grande dame of literature that Wharton had become still betrays a certain defensiveness in discussing reactions to her work. She dismissed her detractors somewhat acerbically: "At present the demand is that only the man with the dinner pail shall be deemed worthy of attention, and fiction is classed according to its degree of conformity with this rule" (206). In a 1904 letter to William Crary Brownell, her editor at Scribner's, Wharton expressed the same exasperation more bluntly:

> I have never before been discouraged by criticism . . . but the continued cry that I am an echo of Mr. James (whose books of the last ten years I can't read, much as I delight in the man), and the assumption that the people I write about are not "real" because they are not navvies and char-women, makes me feel rather hopeless. I write about what I see, what I happen to be nearest to, which is surely better than doing cowboys *de chic*.[3]

The critical and popular success of *The House of Mirth* (1905), published the year after this letter, showed Wharton that she need not write about "navvies and char-women," although, perhaps with a tongue-in-cheek nod to literary fashion, she gives a small but pivotal role to the blackmailing charwoman in that novel. Yet even when Wharton tried to depict a class of people vastly different from her own, like the impoverished villagers of *Ethan Frome* and *Summer*, she was seen as condescending and artificial, creating what Bernard De Voto called "a version of village life by the great lady of a Lenox manor, a kindly and sympathetic but completely un-comprehending observer."[4] She sought distance from her subjects in order to treat them with objectivity (a naturalistic requisite), but her self-imposed spiritual and geographic exile rendered suspect the depth of her engagement with her subjects. Wharton's dilemma presented itself as a kind of Hobson's choice: to describe her own class was to invite the kind of withering rebukes offered by V. L. Parrington and Alfred Kazin,[5] yet to search out a different milieu and class left her vulnerable to charges of artificiality and condescension. Attempting to describe two very different fictional terrains while occupying neither, she risked becoming a woman without a literary country.

Resisting the placement of her fiction in such "movements and trends" throughout her career, Wharton nonetheless encouraged ambiguities by transgressing the usual demarcations of class and geography; a third area of her refusal to follow convention is that of gender and genre. Her determined efforts at exclusion themselves suggest at least one type of inclusion: Wharton, like her male contemporaries Frank Norris, Stephen Crane, Theodore Dreiser, and Jack London, may profitably be viewed within the context of the shift in literary dominance away from women's local color and toward naturalistic fiction.[6] As an ambitious woman writer responding to the 1890s transition between these two movements, she in fact provides a test case, an example of how the literary alliances of a strongly feminine, gender-linked tradition gave way before the imperatives of a predominantly masculine and generation-based rebellion against established forms.

Wharton was not the only woman writer to attempt this fusion of naturalism and local color. Frequently eschewing the urban surroundings of male naturalists like Norris, Crane, and Dreiser, Wharton's contemporaries Kate Chopin and Ellen Glasgow,[7] and, to a lesser extent, the Western writer Mary Austin, merged elements of naturalism into their predominantly regional fiction, incorporating biologically based theories of human behavior and themes of determinism, dehumanizing economic exchange, and degeneration into their studies of isolated locales. The fiction resulting from the convergence of these two movements differed from the bitter stories of earlier local color writers like Rose Terry Cooke or Mary E. Wilkins Freeman largely in its degree of stylistic sophistication and its philosophical underpinnings, but the naturalistic influences seem unmistakable, especially in the opposing themes of endurance and degradation. For example, in Chopin's *The Awakening*, Edna Pontellier follows a path of sensual self-indulgence similar to that of men like Vandover and Theron Ware, and the end of her naturalistic "degeneration" is the same as theirs: an excess of unexplored possibilities leads to an end of all possibilities, followed by actual or spiritual death. Glasgow's *Barren Ground* (1925) sums up the local color and naturalistic responses to misfortune in the characters of its heroine, Dorinda Oakley, and her lover Jason Greylock. Confronted with the loss of her lover and of the child she carries, Dorinda responds to the destruction of her dreams by cultivating the land and garnering qualities of stoic endurance that would put even a Freeman character to shame.[8] Wharton seemed determined, however, to distance herself both from the local colorists and from those other women authors who, like herself, were determined to correct their excesses.

In her own response to local color fiction, Wharton showed that her desire for literary independence contained more than the junior author's customary chafing for recognition. She seems to have recognized early the pitfalls that awaited her if she followed the conventional route to success as a female author. The first is the danger, which her talent and wealth narrowly enabled her to avoid, of being a woman so closely identified with a great male author—in her case, Henry James—that her work becomes perpetually overshadowed by his. In her introduction to *Patrons and Protegées*, Shirley Marchalonis describes this type of literary sponsorship as consisting of "the important male author and the aspiring lady writer, he using his talent and intelligence to create literature, she a 'sweet singer'— an empty vessel through which the winds, or perhaps breezes, of inspiration might blow."[9] The second and potentially more serious threat, as Amy Kaplan has shown, was to risk identification with the "the same tradition of women's fiction that her aunts and grandmother devoured" or with their successors, the "society" novelists:

> To become a woman novelist involved the further risk of being devoured as well as rejected, of being trivialized and absorbed into the category of the forbidden yet the consumable. If the upper-class lady was treated as a

conspicuous commodity—a unique objet d'art, the sentimental produced inconspicuous commodities—mass-produced novels.[10]

Further, Wharton's coming-of-age as an author, like that of her male naturalist contemporaries, coincided with the cultural shift in perceptions of local color fiction.

Wharton employed several strategies to combat these threats. The first, according to Kaplan, was to embrace an "ethos of professionalism" that opposes the domestic realm and "imagines a way of entering a cluttered literary marketplace while transcending its vagaries and dependence upon public taste."[11] Wharton also appropriated certain stylistic features for this purpose; as Katherine Joslin observes, "In order to tell the story of the individual within society and to tell it without the sentimentality of female domestic novelists, Wharton sought and borrowed the 'objective' tone and jargon of the male scientific discourse of her day."[12] Finally, Wharton's most central means of establishing her authority was to resist being judged as a "woman" author at all, as the following passage from *A Backward Glance* demonstrates:

> For years I had wanted to draw life as it really was in the derelict mountain villages of New England, a life even in my time, and a thousandfold more a generation earlier, utterly unlike that seen through the rose-coloured spectacles of my predecessors, Mary Wilkins and Sarah Orne Jewett. In those days the snow-bound villages were still grim places, morally and physically: insanity, incest and slow mental and moral starvation were hidden away behind the paintless wooden house-fronts of the long village street, or in the isolated farm-houses on the neighboring hills; and Emily Brontë would have found as savage tragedies in our remoter valleys as on her Yorkshire moors. [293–94]

Identifying local colorists Jewett and Freeman rather than the previous generation of sentimentalists as her "predecessors,"[13] Wharton defines herself as a rebel against the tradition of women's local color fiction rather than as a practitioner of it. Significantly, she refers to herself as an "author" in the introduction to *Ethan Frome*, but she damns the local colorists by their very femininity, attributing the uproar over her portrait of the outlaw Mountain folk in *Summer* to the New Englanders having "for years sought the reflection of local life in the rose-and-lavender pages of their favorite authoresses" (*A Backward Glance*, 294). In *Edith Wharton's Letters from the Underworld*, Candace Waid's thorough and insightful analysis leaves no doubt as to Wharton's unacknowledged debt to the local colorists, particularly Freeman's "Old Woman Magoun," and in this context Wharton's protestations appear almost disingenuous. Still, Wharton saw that, even if they hid their identity behind a masculine alias (as did Mary N. Murfree and Alice French), women writing in a female tradition like local color were obsolete. To survive in the increasingly professionalized world of fiction writing, as Josephine Donovan points out, "Wharton needed to distance herself from 'authoresses' in order to establish herself as an 'author,' to reject their view as feminine and 'unrealistic' in order to legitimate her masculine view as the serious, adult one" (48).

As an ambitious woman writer responding to the 1890s transition between local color and naturalism, Wharton effected this repudiation very early in her career, well before challenging the tradition in regional novels such as *Ethan Frome* and *Summer*. In both "Mrs. Manstey's View," her first published story (1891), and *Bunner Sisters* (written circa 1891; published 1916 in *Xingu*), Wharton interfuses the city landscapes of naturalism with the potent iconography and themes of local color, providing a devastating commentary on the limitations of local color fiction in a naturalistic world that encroaches on and threatens its ideals. *Ethan Frome* (1911), which with *Summer* marks Wharton's most determined attempt to rewrite local color fiction, employs naturalistic conventions of narrative detachment and thematic determinism to comment on, and ultimately to transform, such staple local color elements as the narrative conventions, the assumptions underlying its use of the sympathetic narrator, storytelling, preserving, and healing, and its insistence on the value of self-denial.[14]

· II ·

Edith Wharton began publishing fiction when the local color movement was in its ascendancy and naturalistic rumblings of discontent were just beginning to be heard. "Mrs. Manstey's View," her first published story, appeared in *Scribner's Magazine* in July 1891; Sarah Orne Jewett's "A Captive Maid," Octave Thanet's "A Recognition," and Thomas Nelson Page's "Run to Seed" appeared in the same volume. The story suggests Wharton's conscious effort not only to test herself in the genres current at the time, but to test those genres against her own standards of what fiction should be. In an undated fragment from her unpublished papers, Wharton articulated a surprisingly naturalistic view of the value of poverty as a subject: "[T]o the student of human nature, poverty is a powerful lens, revealing minute particles of character imperceptible to the prosperous eye. Wealth keeps us at arm's length from life, poverty thrusts us into stifling propinquity with it."[15] More significant than her study of poverty, however, is the attempt to explore the possibilities and dangers of genre art for the woman artist who, like Wharton herself during this period, is caught in the historical shift between local color and naturalism.

"Mrs. Manstey's View" tells of an elderly widow, bereft of her family by death and distance, whose sole pleasures in life are tending her diminished window garden of "an ivy and a succession of unwholesome-looking bulbs" and watching the limited landscape that can be seen from the window of her room.[16] Wharton uses the window garden and other vegetation effectively in the story: the magnolia is the story's emblem of the view's fragility and beauty, and a "neglected syringa, which persisted in growing in spite of the countless obstacles opposed to its welfare" (118) suggests Mrs. Manstey. Within the safe confines of her room, she lives her life vicariously, walled off by the glass of her window from the people and gardens she watches with such delight. When her view is threatened by the building of an addition, Mrs. Manstey tries and fails to defend her territory, at first peacefully, by paying to have the project stopped, and ultimately violently, by setting fire to the addition. Ironically, her one act of real force in the story leads to pneumonia and her subsequent death. Although she dies triumphant, believing that she has stopped the addition, on the day of her death "the building of the extension was resumed" (122), certifying the futility of her efforts.

In contrast to earlier critics such as R. W. B. Lewis, who describes the story as "a nice little tale about an elderly widow," Barbara A. White sees Mrs. Manstey as "a stand-in for Jewett and Freeman at a loss in the new world" and reads it as "the story of a female artist" who struggles with the "impossibility" of her role.[17] Qualifiers flank Wharton's description of Mrs. Manstey as an artist—she is "perhaps" one "at heart"—but in attitude, sensibility, and domestic subject matter, she is indeed a local color artist, knitting away as she "creates" her vision of life. As a local colorist, she works within specific limitations and is "sensible of many changes of color unnoticed by the average eye" (118). She also practices rigid selectivity in the pictures she both composes and views from the frame of her bow window, in part because "hers was the happy faculty of dwelling on the pleasanter side of the prospect before her" (118). After all, "the view surrounded and shaped her life as the sea does a lonely island" (118), much as it shapes Joanna Todd's life in *The Country of the Pointed Firs*. Further, the enclosed gardens she watches are what Gwen Nagel describes as the characteristic New England garden in Jewett's fiction: "small tidy plots, confined by fences, associated with the past and not the future, and lovingly cultivated by women."[18]

To read "Mrs. Manstey's View" as simply a local color parable about the artist's role, however, would be to ignore Wharton's pointed critique of the genre's limitations and the distance she creates between its conventions and her own narrator.[19] For one thing, the tone here is tentative, the prose and authorial stance distanced from the feelings of the character whose deficiencies of vision Wharton's narrator does not share. The narrator sees, as Mrs. Manstey will not until forced to do so, the landscape of naturalism that threatens her view: "[the] street where the ash-barrels lingered late on the sidewalk and the gaps in the pavement would have staggered a Quintus Curtius" (117).[20] As if to reinforce this clash of genres, Wharton introduces a "coarse fellow with a bloated face," reminiscent of Frank Norris's naturalistic story "Brute," who picks Mrs. Manstey's beloved magnolia blossom and throws it to the ground (121).[21] Nor in composing her work of art does the narrator ignore, as does Mrs. Manstey, the "untidiness" and "disorder" of broken barrels and empty bottles that litter the yards. Describing the restricted life of her elderly female character, Wharton employs both the sympathy and the respect of a Sarah Orne Jewett; but, unlike Jewett's, her classical allusions here are ironic, and her language is studded with uncertain phrases and halfheartedly presented alternatives that distance the narrator from her character: "Mrs. Manstey, perhaps, might have joined her daughter" (117); "It was, perhaps, this tenderness . . ." (117); "Perhaps at heart Mrs. Manstey was an artist . . ." (118); "She might move . . ." (119). The self-conscious tentativeness of the repeated "perhaps" suggests the narrator's consideration, if not endorsement, of other possibilities for Mrs. Manstey, an open acceptance of change that distinguishes narrator from character. It is fitting that Mrs. Manstey's failure of vision parallels her final failure to communicate: she cannot express her dying wish to have the bow window—her frame on the world—opened. Taking the local colorists' interest in quotidian detail to a mistaken extreme, Mrs. Manstey has sealed herself into the self-consuming and self-absorbed frame of her art.[22]

Its skeptical look at triumph through persistence, satisfaction through endurance, and strength in limitation marks "Mrs. Manstey's View" as a veiled critique of those local colorists whose "view" is as selective, enclosed, and circumscribed as that of the artist Mrs. Manstey. The rigid restrictions that give Mrs. Manstey's art its beauty also constrain her life and negate her ability to accept change. Because the subject of her art is both dynamic and evanescent, she can neither control nor preserve it, only maintain the illusion of control provided by the frame of the window and the barrier of the glass. Her room thus becomes simultaneously the "room of one's own" necessary for women artists and a self-created prison where she must, like so many local color characters, make the best life she can from the materials available to her. As a spectator, she loses the capacity for meaningful intervention in the world she sees but will not join. More ominously, the voyeuristic overtones of her art suggest what has in fact become the case: ordinary people, except as a subject of her art, strike her as annoying and grotesque. By treating others solely as objects of her art, she loses her connection with humanity. She becomes a symbol of the sort of artist that Wharton was determined not to be.

· III ·

Bunner Sisters, according to Edmund Wilson an "undeservedly neglected" short novel, explores the same fictional terrain between local color and naturalism as "Mrs. Manstey's View." Written in 1891 and 1892, *Bunner Sisters* remained unpublished until its inclusion in *Xingu* (1916), although the story was reportedly a favorite of Wharton's.[23] Like *The Age of Innocence*, the story is set in the 1870s, "when society applauded Christine Nilsson at the Academy of Music," but the New York of Ann Eliza and Evelina Bunner is worlds away from the fashionable purviews of Newland Archer and May Welland.[24] *Bunner Sisters* is the name of the sisters' "very small shop, in a shabby basement, in a side-street already doomed to decline" (187), a street of rooming houses (like Mrs. Manstey's) and small businesses not unlike the Polk Street of *McTeague*. In a description that anticipates Sinclair Lewis's representation of Gopher Prairie in *Main Street*, Wharton provides the traditional naturalistic catalogue of squalor in describing the street:

> The middle of the street was full of irregular depressions, well adapted to retain the long swirls of dust and straw and twisted paper that the wind drove up and down its sad untended length; and toward the end of the day, when traffic had been active, the fissured pavement formed a mosaic of coloured hand-bills, lids of tomato-cans, old shoes, cigar-stumps and banana skins, cemented together by a layer of mud, or veiled in a powdering dust, as the state of the weather determined. [188]

In the midst of this "depressing waste," the storefront of Bunner Sisters stands out as an oasis of order, although, ominously, the evident care and cleanliness with which the store has been kept cannot save it from the general decline of the street.

Despite the urban landscape, the Bunner sisters initially live a life straight out of local color fiction. In contrast to the lavish, chaotic profusion of discarded objects outside, their window display is almost excessively ordered and unchanging, having "the undefinable greyish tinge of objects long preserved in the show-case of a museum" (188), perhaps suggesting the place of the literary tradition that the sisters represent. Other local color elements abound: the interior of the store is also neat, sparsely furnished, and orderly even to the "two tea-cups, two plates, a sugar-bowl and a piece of pie" (189) that constitute the frugal birthday feast Ann Eliza prepares for Evelina. Although both women are presumably under forty, Ann Eliza and Evelina Bunner display prematurely elderly habits, including a fussiness over trifles and a preference for the "monastic quiet of the shop" over the "tumult of the streets" (193), traits that recall Freeman's Louisa Ellis of "A New England Nun." In addition, both sisters speak a kind of generalized country dialect, complete with dropped syllables ("s'posin'") and rural pronunciations ("You hadn't oughter say that. . . . Set down"). In defiance of the current fashion shown by the "lady with the puffed sleeves," Ann Eliza wears as her best dress the same sort of respectable but rusty "double-dyed and triple-turned . . . sacramental black silk"

(189) that Freeman celebrates in "A Gala Dress."[25] Their attitude, too, reflects the sort of resignation common to local color figures. Like the two sisters in Freeman's "A Mistaken Charity," who were "happy and contented, with [a] negative kind of happiness and contentment," the Bunner sisters live a life of muted satisfaction.[26]

The closeness of their companionship within this tiny local color community also manifests itself in the traditional activities of sewing and storytelling. Ann Eliza's experiences in the city only become real or relevant to her when they are transformed into a means of cementing her relationship with Evelina:

> [C]ertain sights and sounds would detach themselves from the torrent along which she had been swept, and she would devote the rest of the day to a mental reconstruction of the different episodes of her walk, till finally it took shape in her thought as a consecutive and highly-coloured experience, from which, for weeks afterwards, she would detach some fragmentary recollection in the course of her long dialogues with her sister. [194]

The "mental reconstruction," the shaping and polishing of mundane events into a suitable narrative, and the telling of the story in the process of "long dialogues" recall, for example, the narrative structure of Jewett's *Country of the Pointed Firs*, "On the Walpole Road," and "Miss Tempy's Watchers." These small, carefully selected true episodes from which Ann Eliza creates her stories are a far cry from those of the histrionic dressmaker Miss Mellins. Miss Mellins derives "her chief mental nourishment from the *Police Gazette* and *Fireside Weekly*" (205), and thus her tales, full of prophecy, poisonings, and sudden madness, supply a necessary element of excitement to the circumscribed lives of the sisters. Within such demonstrably safe surroundings, Miss Mellins's lurid tales appear to have a comfortable air of unreality; yet one tale she tells, that of a bride whose husband "took to drink" and who "never was the same woman after her fust baby" (205), foretells chillingly the fate of Evelina when she leaves the enclosed world of the shop. Surrounded by the small, supportive community of women who live in the neighborhood, supported by their few regular customers, including a mysterious and fashionable stand-in for Wharton, a "lady with the puffed sleeves,"[27] the Bunner sisters contrive to make of their life together a thing perfect of its kind.

The major portion of the story chronicles the destruction of this peaceful local color existence, a process that provides the sisters with a bitter initiation into the naturalistic "real life" beyond the threshold of their shop, and, for the more self-aware Ann Eliza, a harsh reassessment of the values she holds dear.[28] It is Ann Eliza who unwittingly initiates the process of destruction. With characteristic self-denial, she goes without a new pair of shoes in order to get Evelina a birthday present; the "loud staccato tick" of the clock (195) she buys signals not only the intrusion of Herman Ramy, the clock repairman for whose attentions they compete, but of present time itself, thus ending their existence as characters in the undifferentiated time of local color fiction. Mr. Ramy's appearance also marks Ann Eliza's growing discontent with the modest satisfactions she has previously enjoyed: "All the small daily happenings which had once sufficed to fill the hours now appeared to her in their deadly insignificance; and for the first time in her long years of drudgery she rebelled at the dullness of her life" (197). When her self-centered younger sister Evelina—she of the "elaborately crinkled hair" (197)—meets and unofficially claims Mr. Ramy as her own, Ann Eliza, "well-trained in the arts of renunciation" (199), removes herself from the competition, but a rift has opened between the sisters. Just as their harmony is disturbed by the thoughts that they no longer feel free to articulate, the stability of their synergistic roles of storyteller and audience is disrupted by the tales Mr. Ramy tells and the poems he reads. A German immigrant who has lived in St. Louis, Mr. Ramy strikes the sheltered pair as a man of the world. After all, he reads Longfellow to them and "his culture soared beyond the newspapers" (215). Indeed, he introduces the Bunner sisters to the larger world. Traveling on an endless series of jolting streetcars and crowded ferryboats, they experience as marvelous the ordinary places he shows them: Central Park, a stereopticon show, the dingy rural suburbs of Hoboken. The sisters' community and its rituals have been breached by this representative from the threatening world beyond their shop.

The communication between the sisters is further strained when Mr. Ramy proposes to the "wrong sister," Ann Eliza—a situation that parodies "Howells's subplot in *The Rise of Silas Lapham*."[29] Having already consecrated herself to her sister's happiness and embraced "the chill joy of renunciation" (207) much as Freeman's Eunice Fairweather does in "A Moral Exigency," Ann Eliza of course refuses him, but her withdrawal from romance allows her to see more clearly Evelina's vanity and selfishness. Ann Eliza begins to withhold her true self but continues to display an overpowering maternal protectiveness that expresses itself through self-denying acts, such as giving Evelina, at Mr. Ramy's request, all of the sisters' savings. Cash, not affectionate explanation, is now the medium of communication between the sisters; naturalistic economic exchange has replaced local color talk. After Evelina's wedding, the strained communication between the sisters comes to a virtual halt as Ann Eliza's storytelling ability, and consequently her ability to stay connected with the community, deserts her: "the 'talking over' on which [the neighbors] had evidently counted was Dead Sea fruit on her lips" (232). She receives an inscrutably vague letter from Evelina, one whose cliché-riddled, comically ornate public discourse is but a poor substitute for the homely clarity of the natural, private talk that the sisters share.[30] The physical distance between them is cemented by obfuscatory language that is worse than silence.

From the comic misunderstandings of romance, *Bunner Sisters* descends into melodrama and, finally, into the naturalistic world of the streets. Stories of unpleasant reality replace the pleasantly melodramatic stories of Miss Mellins: surrounded at Tiffany's by ticking clocks suggestive of her time-dominated postlapsarian state, Ann Eliza learns of Mr. Ramy's drug problem; returning to the shop after her marriage, Evelina "pile[s] up, detail by detail, her dreary narrative" (251) of her child's birth and death, of Ramy's abuse and abandonment, and of begging in the streets, a tale quite unlike the uneventful happenings she used to report. Like the naturalistic brute that crushes Mrs. Manstey's magnolia blossom underfoot, Mr. Ramy is thus identified as a disruptive, threatening emissary from the world of naturalism, and Evelina has moved from her sister's local color world to a naturalistic one. This dose of unpleasant reality ironically turns Ann Eliza back into a storyteller, this time as a creator of false rather than true stories. Miss Mellins had invented lurid stories of the city and brought some (controlled) excitement into their safe environment; now Ann Eliza must invent stories of safety to conceal the terrifying reality of their plight. Knowing at last the "truth" of life as it is lived outside the shop, she must use her fictive arts to conceal Evelina's situation, just as she had once used similar arts to conceal the breach between her feelings and her actions when Evelina fell in love with Mr. Ramy.

The concluding sections of *Bunner Sisters* emphasize the completeness of the sisters' assimilation into the naturalistic world of "real life" and the utter hopelessness of their plight. As Evelina reveals her final betrayal—conversion to Roman Catholicism—Ann Eliza barely protests, for the faith that had early caused her to kneel in fervent prayer has given way to the belief that "if he was not good he was not God, and there was only a black abyss above the roof of Bunner Sisters" (254). The dissociation of time from faith that had begun when Ann Eliza gauged time by the nickel clock instead of the church tower is completed when she denies that either time or faith has a place in her life: "[She saw] the church tower with the dial that had marked the hours for the sisters before [she] had bought the nickel clock. She looked at it all as though it had been the scene of some unknown life" (262). Her refusal is ironic, however, for she has moved into the clock-metered biological time of naturalistic fiction, where the natural processes of decay chip away at the advantages of youth and strength. Having lost her savings, her shop, her faith, and her sister, she plunges into the indifferent "great thoroughfare" of the city and asks about a position as a saleslady, only to be told that the stores "want a bright girl . . . not over thirty, anyhow; and nice-looking" (263). Like Mrs. Manstey, whose movement beyond the "frame" of her bow window costs her her life, Ann Eliza, bereft of the safe "frame" of her shop window, faces the dangers of the city alone. She looks for a replacement refuge—"another shop window with a sign in it"—in much the same way that Carrie Meeber and Susan Lenox were to do. But unlike Carrie and Susan, she is neither eighteen years old nor beautiful; in a world that favors those who are young, male, prosperous, and well-connected, she remains a local color heroine—old, female, poor, and alone. Her story reverses the happy ending of the heroine starting fresh, marking instead, as Edmund Wilson comments, "the grimmest moment of Edith Wharton's darkest years."[31]

Bunner Sisters, like "Mrs. Manstey's View," calls into question some of the most seriously held beliefs of local color fiction: the critique of limited perspective and subject matter in "Mrs. Manstey's View" gives way here to a persistent attempt to refute the power of renunciation. Ann Eliza sacrifices everything for her sister, and her reward is Evelina's self-pity, selfishness, simpering vanity, and peevish demands for yet more sacrifice, as Blake Nevius comments, for Ann Eliza, like Ethan Frome, is "tied to an inferior partner."[32] In addition, she must face the possibility that she is, as Evelina hints, somehow to blame; after all, she did bring the clock home and help the courtship along. Part of Ann Eliza's education is learning to confront, as she now does, that Howellsian dilemma, "the awful problem of the inutility of self-sacrifice":

> Hitherto she had never thought of questioning the inherited principles which had guided her life. Self-effacement for the good of others had always seemed to her both natural and necessary; but then she had taken it for granted that it implied the securing of that good. Now she perceived that to refuse the gifts of life does not ensure their transmission to those for whom they have been surrendered; and her familiar heaven was unpeopled. [254]

Ammons objects that "there have been no 'gifts of life' to surrender, much less transmit," but if one can accept the local color notion that the "silvery twilight hue which sometimes ends a day of storm" (188) or, less poetically, the small daily pleasures of the sisters represent a satisfying life, then Ann Eliza's turn of phrase must be accepted as legitimate.[33] Both Mrs. Manstey and Ann Eliza make tremendous sacrifices to preserve something they value, and in neither case does the action have any meaning. Both risk everything they have, and lose.

· IV ·

Begun in Paris as an exercise in idiomatic French, *Ethan Frome* initially seems an imaginative projection in distance and time; Wharton wrote to Bernard Berenson that it amused her to "do that decor [Starkfield, Massachusetts] in the rue de Varenne."[34] Criticism of the novel focused on two problematic areas of distance: the structure, with its frame story and educated narrator; and Wharton's own abilities as an interpreter of the lives of rural villagers. The presence of her 1922 introduction—"the first I have ever published of any of my books"—bespeaks her great concern about being misread.[35] In particular, she addresses those writers who have criticized both her choice of subject matter and what they considered to be her unnecessary reliance on an objective narrator. Wharton defends her qualifications as a New England author in "The Writing of *Ethan Frome*," a 1932 article for the *Colophon* that appeared in abbreviated form in *A Backward Glance*:

> Not long since I read a thoughtful article . . . in which the author advanced the theory that . . . one might conceivably write a better book about Main Street if one lived as far away from it as Paris or Palermo; in proof of which *Ethan Frome* was cited as an instance of a successful New England story written by some one who knew nothing of New England. I have no desire to contest the theory, with which, in a certain measure, I am disposed to agree; but the fact is that *Ethan Frome* was written after a ten years' residence in the New England hill country where Ethan's tragedy was enacted, and that during those years I had become very familiar with the aspect, the dialect, and the general mental attitude of the Ethans, Zeenas and Mattie Silvers of the neighbouring villages. [72–73]

Wharton was concerned about establishing her reliability as a reporter for several reasons, one of which is, obviously, that she did not want her veracity in reporting details questioned. Further, after refusing to write about popular subjects like navvies, cowboys, and charwomen because they were beyond her circle of experience, Wharton must have been stung by the injustice of having her accusers hint that she had violated her own literary code.

Another reason for Wharton's concern with accuracy reveals itself in her 1922 introduction to *Ethan Frome*:

> I had had an uneasy sense that the New England of fiction bore little— except a vague botanical and dialectical—resemblance to the harsh and beautiful land as I had seen it. Even the abundant enumeration of the sweet-fern, asters and mountain-laurel, and the conscientious reproduction of the vernacular, left me with the feeling that the outcropping granite had in both cases been overlooked. [v]

The "abundant enumeration of the sweet-fern, asters and mountain laurel" and "conscientious reproduction of the vernacular" belong stylistically, of course, to local color fiction, and Wharton charges the local colorists with at best a refusal to look at the region's dark underside and its "foundation" in general, at worst a willful superficiality in treating the "flowers" and not the substance beneath. Using language reminiscent of that used by Rose

Terry Cooke to describe Amasa Flint ("Mrs. Flint's Married Experience") and by Mary E. Wilkins Freeman to describe Barnabas Thayer (*Pembroke*), Wharton uses a natural metaphor: her characters are "*granite outcroppings*; but half-emerged from the soil, and scarcely more articulate" (vi; italics Wharton's). In other words, her characters do not, like Jewett's, change and grow in harmony with their land, but resist it and wear away in the process. The task Wharton sets for herself in writing *Ethan Frome* is, quite simply, to confront the genre of local color fiction on its own terms, and, using the same local color settings and characters as her predecessors, particularly those of Sarah Orne Jewett's *Country of the Pointed Firs*, to disrupt and transform its narrative conventions, the assumptions underlying its iconographic and symbolic structures such as storytelling, preserving, and healing, and its insistence on the value of self-denial.[36]

The structure of *Ethan Frome* actually comprises two stories, both involving the initiation of the main character into a kind of truth: the frame story, which involves the narrator's quest to solve the puzzle of Ethan's life and his initiation into the community of suffering that is Starkfield; and the inner story, the tragedy of Ethan, Zeena, and Mattie as the narrator imaginatively reconstructs it. Wharton further divides the frame story into two parts, a device that fulfills several functions in the novel. The distancing of the main story, suggestive perhaps of the "doubly distanced" narratives common to local color fiction, reinforces the thematic significance of the novel's threshold scenes; as Cynthia Griffin Wolff explains, narrator and character alike spend a "timeless eternity of hesitation on the threshold" that signifies opportunities lost and discarded.[37] Extending this observation, Candace Waid suggests that the threshold is another in a series of symbolic barriers as the narrator makes his way through the screen of snow and "the obstacles of snow drifts, just as he tries to penetrate and pass the barriers and obstacles that blind and block his desire to know the story of Ethan Frome." The flow of narrative is additionally disrupted by Wharton's use of a series of witnesses from whom the narrator must glean the story. Besides increasing the suspense, the fragmentation of reality into a series of half-interpreted snippets demonstrates forcefully Wharton's stated unwillingness to resort to the artifice of having a know-all, tell-all village gossip give a single version of the events. To interpret such a purposefully refracted vision is the task of her much-maligned narrator.

Although he has frequently been treated as an impediment to the "real" story of the Zeena-Ethan-Mattie triangle, the seemingly ordinary narrator exists as the frame story's most powerful and irreducibly ambiguous character. As Wharton's introduction makes clear, he is to be the traditional local color "sophisticated" onlooker who will act as the "sympathizing intermediary between his rudimentary characters and the more complicated minds to whom he is trying to present them" (introduction, viii). In this way he becomes, like his counterpart in *The Country of the Pointed Firs*, the outside observer or reader's representative whose initiation into the community depends on his ability to reconstruct and relate the story he hears. He is the sort of man who, as Wharton's reference to Emily Brontë suggests, will visit an isolated spot, experience some puzzling phenomena, receive some facts from a longtime resident (Nellie Dean/Mrs. Hale), and present to a sophisticated audience a sympathetic version of the tragic story he hears. The literary reference, however, scarcely hints at the complexities surrounding the narrator's position. For one thing, Wharton chooses a male rather than a female narrator to construct the story from the "small incidental effects" supplied by Mrs. Hale, a choice that reflects her own composing processes: "I conceive my subjects like a man—that is, rather more architectonically and dramatically than most women—& then execute them like a woman; or rather, I sacrifice, to my desire for construction & breadth, the small incidental effects that women have always excelled in" (*Letters*, 124). Blake Nevius defends her use of the male narrator on grounds of practicality and consistency: a male engineer might more plausibly linger at Starkfield and be invited into Ethan's house; also, "[T]he narrators employed in the framework of Edith Wharton's early stories are *always* men."[38] Equally important in Wharton's choice of this male narrator, however, is her determination to contrast her own modern (masculine) perspective with that of the local color "authoresses" who used female interpreters. Toward that end she gives him a hardheaded masculine profession—engineering—and creates an observer whose forte is objectivity rather than sympathy.

Wharton further distances herself from the local color use of the female narrator by emphatically rejecting a convention common to local color fiction and forming a good portion of *Wuthering Heights*: "I might have sat him down before a village gossip who would have poured out the whole affair to him in a breath" (ix). The engineer thus exists in a peculiarly temporary sort of powerlessness: because he must become a supplicant, dependent on the villagers for scraps of knowledge, he seems at first to exist as a village parasite. The also unnamed narrator in *The Country of the Pointed Firs*, for example, spends her time with Mrs. Todd in a kind of Wordsworthian wise passiveness. Hearing the tale of Poor Joanna, itself a tale of pride, lost love, and self-imposed isolation not unlike that of Ethan Frome, she forms her own opinions but "did not like to interrupt" the flow of narrative between Mrs. Todd and Mrs. Fosdick (*The Country of the Pointed Firs*, 64). Her rare questions are sympathetic and tactful, for "[t]act is after all a kind of mind-reading" (46). Far more frequent are the occasions when she is able to comment, as she does of her relationship with Mrs. Todd's mother, Mrs. Blackett, that "we understood each other without speaking" (54). But as the existence of the frame story itself makes clear, the narrator of *Ethan Frome* is not a parasite or even a recorder, but a creator; it is his "vision," after all, that grants unity, stability, and decipherability to the fragmentary mutterings of his informants. He controls the vision imaginatively in two important senses, formulating it from the scraps of what he learns and presenting it to an audience that it would otherwise never reach. He is thus responsible for its unity, for he rivets the disparate elements that he hears and experiences into the form of classic tragedy, rendering the substance of Ethan's tale intelligible by enclosing it in a coherent form. As Waid observes, "frustrated in his attempts to become a reader of Frome's inner story, the narrator will have to become an author" (66). Since Wharton implicitly forswears the traditional companionship of local color author–eager outside auditor in her introduction, the narrator also opens out the story to a variety of interpretive communities potentially scornful as well as sympathetic.

From the beginning the narrator does not wait and watch like Jewett's female narrators; a modern man of action, he begins immediately and directly to investigate his characters.[39] After sensing a mystery surrounding Ethan, one of the strange folk of Starkfield from whom he feels himself distanced, the narrator pursues his quarry relentlessly, well past the bounds of simple politeness he might offer to one of his own class. Even the mail is not sacrosanct: he watches Ethan openly, noticing that Ethan "seldom received anything but a copy of the *Bettsbridge Eagle*" (4); nor does he scruple to read the return addresses on Zeena's mail from the patent medicine manufacturers. After failing to glean information first from Harmon Gow, he hesitates with Mrs. Hale: "So marked was the change in her manner, such depths of sad initiation did it imply, that, with some doubts as to my delicacy, I put the case anew to my village oracle, Harmon Gow; but got for my pains only an uncomprehending grunt" (11). Presumably his "doubts" are meant to assure us of his sensitivity, but he immediately puts any delicacy aside, along with the memory of Mrs. Hale's "sad depths of initiation," in favor of renewed pursuit. The "uncomprehending grunt" turns out to be a paragraph of explanation about Mrs. Hale, including the useful information that she was "the first one to see 'em after they was picked up" and an admonitory hint that "she just can't bear to talk about it" (11). Despite sensing that "the deeper meaning of the stories was in the gaps" (6), the impatient narrator does not as yet realize how much information is contained in such laconic utterances.

Ironically, for he does not yet recognize the power of this local color method for getting at the story, the narrator gains the most information when he ceases to seek it. For a while he learns to keep still and accept information as a kind of community currency of exchange rather than as an ore to be extracted from the "granite outcroppings" of the villagers; his one-sided prying and interrogation give way to reciprocal social exchanges, as when he acknowledges his social indebtedness for Ethan's offer to drive him through heavy snow to the train station at the Junction. Like Jewett's narrator, who travels with Mrs. Todd to the secret pennyroyal field and "felt that we were friends now since she had brought me to this place" (*The Country of the Pointed Firs*, 49), Wharton's narrator believes that "the mere sight of the house had let me too deeply into his confidence for any farther pretence of reserve" (21). Indeed, Ethan does subsequently reveal himself obliquely, describing the isolation that caused his mother's slow decline and the reasons for the house's missing "L." Slowly learning to interpret the villagers' language metaphorically, the narrator, knowing that the L is "the center, the actual hearth-stone of the New England farm" (21), understands that Ethan is hinting at both the absence of life and love at the house and the demolition of his own dreams of romance with Mattie. The narrator further gains Ethan's trust when he symbolically descends to the older man's level, getting out of the sleigh "to walk along through the snow at the bay's side" (23) in order to "struggle on for another mile or two" beside, rather than above, his subject.

This lulling sense of communion does not last, however, for while Jewett's narrator, preferring companionship, turns back to her writing like a "reluctant child" (114), Wharton's narrator breaks off the story of growing friendship abruptly and, with a dramatic flourish and three rows of ellipses points, announces, "It was that night that I found the clue to Ethan Frome, and began to put together this vision of his story . . ." (25).[40] Unlike the pleasurable sharing of deferred experience common to local color fiction, the narrator's refusal to reveal the solution until a proper time teases his audience with heightened suspense as it reinforces his own control over the story. He relinquishes this control only reluctantly and clearly values his fictional art above humanity, Ethan's story over Ethan himself. At this point he still insists on maintaining the (masculine) linear mode of storytelling over the circular, digressive (feminine) one, unable as yet to reconcile twentieth-century technique with nineteenth-century sympathy.

The second part of the frame story, occurring after the "vision" of Ethan's life, marks a change in the narrator, since he has become initiated into Ethan's community of suffering. Understanding now that his modern, masculine, detective-style questioning served rather to exclude than include him in the life of Starkfield, he embarks on a new strategy for eliciting information from his uncommunicative sources: "Beneath [the townspeople's] wondering exclamations I felt a secret curiosity to know what impressions I had received from my night in the Frome household, and *divined that the best way of breaking down their reserve was to let them try to penetrate mine*" (176; italics mine). He has, in fact, learned their language—or, more correctly, to trust his perception that their language consists not in speech but in gaps and indeterminacies. More significantly, he has accepted the advantages of the feminine passivity he had hitherto ignored; as his language suggests, he will stop trying to invade their privacy and will instead allow his defenses to be "penetrated." Seeking confirmation from Mrs. Hale that the voice behind the "querulous drone" is Mattie's, not Zeena's, he comments, "I waited to let her trust in me gather strength" before his own understated observation that "it's pretty bad, seeing all three of them there together" (177), again employing passivity as a tactic. Mrs. Hale then pours forth the story of the day after the accident, of the village's response, and of the actions of Zeena, Mattie, and Ethan. Thus rewarded, the narrator learns at first hand the development of emotions in human relationships, the detached study of which began his quest into Ethan's past. He also becomes increasingly aware of the inverse relation between the strength of feelings and their ability to be articulated.

By the end of the frame story, the narrator is able not only to understand Ethan's story but to accept its gaps. He initially looks to Mrs. Hale to provide a final answer, but as she scrupulously reports the aftermath of the sledding accident, she can add only, "I never knew myself what Zeena thought—I don't to this day. Nobody knows Zeena's thoughts" (178). If "nobody knows Zeena's thoughts," and Ethan remains uncommunicative, then only Mattie's perspective can grant the narrator the closure that he seeks; yet even here his quest is frustrated. Mrs. Hale, Mattie's childhood friend, tells the narrator about the events of the next day: "'[Mattie] woke up just like herself, and looked straight at me out of her big eyes, and said . . . Oh, I don't know why I'm telling you all this,' Mrs. Hale broke off, crying" (178; ellipsis Wharton's). Like the unspoken word that passes between Lawrence Selden and Lily Bart at the end of *The House of Mirth*, the word here is never made concrete but remains a mystery to reader and narrator alike. The narrator has sought the word that would make his story perfect, confirming his vision and ending his search, but he is never to find it, for the situation remains finally unknowable. What he has learned is that he must, in effect, resign his quest, relinquishing his modern interest in facts and the "real story" in favor of a more fluid, emotion-based method of discerning truth. In contrast to his earlier probing, the narrator now cedes control over the story to Mrs. Hale. Occurring several paragraphs before the end of the story, his final words in the novel—"It's horrible for them all" (179)—confirm and intensify his allegiance to the language of sympathy, a language to which Mrs. Hale responds reciprocally by echoing his words: "Yes, it's pretty bad" (179). Now that he feels himself a part of Starkfield, an initiate of the villagers' inner lives as well as of their customs, the narrator completes the tale by recording Mrs. Hale's version, bridging indeterminacies by means of the emotional rightness of his vision. The feminine passivity and sympathy he has learned complement the objectivity with which he relates the tale, rendering both his "vision" and his initiation into the world of emotion complete.

· V ·

The inner story, the tale of Ethan's life, remains tragic whether one accepts the traditional view that the narrator's "vision" is a true one, or believes instead with Cynthia Griffin Wolff and John Crowe Ransom that "we are forced to conclude that he did not gather it really; that, mostly, he made it up" (Ransom, 89). The inner story is one of the most extensively analyzed pieces in all of Wharton's fiction; its imagery, symbolism, structure, and presentation of ethical choices have received a great deal of attention. What needs to be explored further is the way in which the modern perspective of Wharton's narrator interrogates and implicitly condemns such standard local color myths as those of cohesive community, of healing, and of preserving and self-denial.

The myth of cohesive community is the first element exposed by the narrator's gaze. Despite Michael Eady's prosperous store and its railway station, Starkfield is one of the impoverished dying villages common to local color fiction. In analyzing the isolation of Ethan's mother, Marlene Springer cites the motif of the railroad as an example of Wharton's "brilliant irony," since she "turns the coming of the railroad, historically the advent of mobility and expansion, into a catalyst for isolation and despair." As Wharton was doubtless aware, however, the irony really resides within the conventions of local color fiction, where the coming of railroads often signals a town's increasing isolation. By facilitating escape for the "smart ones" that "get away," as Harmon Gow tells the narrator, and by providing a conduit for outside ideas that threaten to destroy the village's integrity as a community, the railroad drains vitality from the local color village.[41] The dances and sledding parties Mattie attends show that even Starkfield inhabitants do not lack for social life; but the community life of the village takes place offstage, whereas the drama of its three self-willed isolates unfolds before the reader. Ironically, in refusing to join the community, all three become crystallized images of its people, frozen in time as virtual caricatures of New England types. For example, Ethan, who consistently refuses to interact with his fellow villagers, leans toward caricature in his taciturnity, which after the accident exceeds even that of legendarily close-lipped New Englanders like the self-willed isolate Nicholas Gunn of Mary Wilkins Freeman's "A Solitary." Trapped by Starkfield, all three main characters are nonetheless outsiders literally and figuratively. Zeena, whose "native village was slightly larger and nearer to the railway than Starkfield" (71), insulates herself from the town with a fierce pride that allows her to express a longing for human companionship only in her "sickly spells."[42] Set apart even in his youth by a superior intellect and a vision of other worlds, Ethan shares her pride, answering his neighbors in monosyllables and allowing few visitors to visit his bare house. Mattie Silver comes from Stamford, Connecticut, but after her father dies, she has nowhere to go except Starkfield. The compensations of the local color village, Wharton implies, fail to outweigh its limitations for characters such as these, particularly when their dearth of choices is compounded by "the hard compulsions of the poor" (179).

The motif of illness and healers also becomes transformed in the inner story. Although the characters' ailments have a physical basis, Ethan's deformed spine and Mattie's diseased one suggest Freeman's metaphor of spinal disease to indicate excessive Puritan will and frustrated lives in *Pembroke*, a disease of self-willed isolation curable only through a reintegration into the community.[43] Zeena's psychogenic illness, which "had since made her notable even in a community rich in pathological instances" (72), together with her constant "doctoring" of herself with patent medicines, recalls the many female healers and herb women in local color fiction. As embodied in Zeena, however, the concept of women as healers and servers has been warped into a monstrous parody of itself. Her ineffective patent medicines, unlike herbs, are as unnatural as her clicking upper plate of false teeth.[44] Further, Zeena acts as both healer and patient, collapsing the distinction between the two roles and negating the possibility of human sharing in the process. Her illnesses provide a sort of homeopathic remedy for the boredom of her life, an antidote or *pharmakon*, by way of small repeated doses of "complications," to the death-in-life that she shares with Ethan, who, in another role reversal, is the one who "always . . . done the caring" (7).

Wharton also borrows from local color tradition in her choice of situation and themes. Ethan's story is more than a classic love triangle; it recalls the tales of self-sacrifice and renunciation, of elderly lovers and unspoken, inchoate longings that pervade the works of Freeman and Jewett. Ethan's situation with Zeena is also a nightmare version of the crotchety mother–patient child theme prevalent in local color fiction. Wharton even alludes to the tradition when, in the second part of the frame story, Mrs. Hale relaxes once her exacting elderly mother Mrs. Varnum goes up to bed. Indeed, Mrs. Hale serves as more than a witness here. She represents the unspoken alternative story to Ethan's: the traditional local color tale *not* told of a middle-aged woman's domestic troubles and forbearance with an elderly parent. Generations of readers, culturally conditioned to praise self-denial and stoic endurance in local color heroines, have been frustrated when a man like Ethan chooses to exercise these same virtues, seeing his self-sacrifice as evidence of a wasted, tragic life. By telling instead the man's story, as the local colorists seldom did, Wharton simultaneously breaks with her "predecessors" and uses this change in gender to demonstrate not the nobility of self-denial but the dreadful consequences of a life ruled by what Wharton calls in *Bunner Sisters* "the inutility of self-sacrifice."

Like Rose Terry Cooke's and Mary Wilkins Freeman's characters, Ethan ultimately chooses resignation, despite his awareness that, as Elizabeth Shepley Sergeant puts it, "[t]he real New England tragedy . . . is not that something happens but that nothing does" (85).[45] Only once does he make an attempt to break out of his imprisonment: in making the suicide attempt, he chooses the ultimate renunciation—of life itself—and the ultimate extravagant gesture, to die with his beloved.[46] However, the earlier episode of Zeena's pickle dish has warned us that Ethan's self-denial will yield no satisfaction. Sent from Philadelphia as a wedding present, the red glass pickle dish is Zeena's pride and joy, so precious to her that she keeps it on the top shelf of the china closet and never uses it. On the night when Zeena is away, Mattie puts it on the supper table, but when Ethan's and Mattie's hands meet over the milk jug, Zeena's cat backs into the dish and knocks it off the table. Joseph X. Brennan sees the wedding gift, unused by Zeena but taken up and destroyed by Mattie, as a symbolic representation of "the pleasure and passion that Ethan had sought and Zeena had thwarted in their marriage"; when Zeena carries out the pickle dish "as if she carried a dead body" (128), it is, as Kenneth Bernard comments, the "corpse of her marriage" that she carries.[47] (112). Another significance, though, can be attached to the incident. The seldom-used pickle dish, like the medicine jar that, Zeena tells Mattie, will "do for pickles" if she can "get the taste out" (66), refers obliquely to local color fiction's preserving of food and stories, of the continual urge to postpone the savoring of experience. But preserving here is futile: all of Zeena's careful saving comes to naught when her precious possession is smashed by a chance occurrence, just as Ethan's constancy in the face of adversity fails to gain him happiness or to protect him against the accident of living through his suicide attempt. In presenting the utter bleakness of Ethan's life, the futility of his self-denial, and the impossibility of any change for the better, Wharton forges local color virtues into instruments of terror that sustain and prolong the torturous process of Ethan's life. It is a terror that, combined with the pity, transforms the elements of local color into New England tragedy.

· VI ·

The evidence of Wharton's repudiation of, and by extension her deep engagement with, local color and naturalism can be found in many of her writings. It underlies the irritated references to naturalism in her correspondence, and it exists in the earnest and atypical explanations of her work that she offers in the introduction to *Ethan Frome* and in *A Backward Glance*. Even more convincing is the fictional representation of this struggle for autonomy. "Mrs. Manstey's View" offers a picture of a woman artist so hampered by the limitations of her art, and so dependent on others for preserving its conditions, that she can ultimately maintain her sense of artistic integrity only through a violent action that leads to her death. The story suggests both Wharton's fear of entrapment within an unnecessarily limited tradition and her apprehension that a radical break could destroy her promising career; as Wharton probably recognized, the familiar local color elements of "Mrs. Manstey's View" may have helped this first story of hers to be published.

Bunner Sisters, Wharton's most overt exploration of naturalism and local color fiction, deserves to be better known than it is, not only because of its considerable literary merit, but because it provides in miniature an account of the literary shift from local color to naturalism from the standpoint of a woman writer who foresaw the changes and prepared herself to meet them. Versed in the self-sacrificing ethos of local color fiction, Ann Eliza Bunner interpreted the world with a deadly innocence and a willful insistence on what Wharton saw as its rosy light of romance, and she paid for her misreading in her naturalistically conceived fate. Determined not to emulate her hapless creature Ann Eliza Bunner, Wharton took care not to be stuck in what she saw as the airless, timeless, self-sacrificing confines of local color fiction until changing literary fashions should figuratively throw her out onto the littered naturalistic streets.

Viewed in this context, Wharton's much-maligned device of the male narrator in *Ethan Frome* becomes not only comprehensible but essential, for through her (re)vision of the local color world through his fact-obsessed masculine sensibility, Wharton seeks to reclaim for her own mainstream fiction the marginal territories occupied by the local colorists. Like Jewett and other local color writers, Wharton employs a sympathetic, well-educated outsider-observer as her narrator; like Jewett's, her narrator undergoes an initiation of sorts into the secrets of the village, but his aggressive seeking after facts, his horror at the self-denial that freezes Ethan's life, and even his choice of Ethan's story over that of Mrs. Hale mark him as an alien—modern, masculine—sensibility in this local color community. Yet he does learn to decode the villagers' digressive, fragmentary attempts at storytelling, and, in effect, he does resign his quest, relinquishing his modern interest in facts and the "real story" in favor of a more fluid, emotion-based method of discerning truth.

As the end of the story indicates, however, only the narrator, the modern man, escapes this frozen vision of wasted lives. Maintaining his objectivity allows him to sympathize with the Starkfield villagers without becoming enraptured by their world as Jewett's narrator is in Dunnet Landing in *The Country of the Pointed Firs*. Considered as the corrective rewriting of what Wharton saw as the bleak rural landscapes, grotesquely extended love affairs, excessive preserving, and incredible renunciations and self-denial of local color fiction, *Ethan Frome* almost becomes Wharton's blackly comic joke, a vision of the genre so extreme as to border on private parody. *Ethan Frome* argues that the kind of local color renunciation practiced by Ethan and his kind suggests not spiritual nobility but spiritual impoverishment; their habitual denial of healthy appetite for emotion recalls not the *anorexia mirabilis* of the saints but the *anorexia nervosa* of the cultural victim.

Hence although Wharton clearly encouraged the image of herself as a self-created artist, the evidence of her fiction suggests that, far from remaining aloof from literary trends, she developed into the kind of writer she became in part *because* of the complicated influences and pressures that women's local color fiction exerted on her. She tried to reinvent herself as a writer free from the constraints of local color, and critics have generally followed her wishes by downplaying her literary antecedents. As an upper-class woman vacationing genteelly in the impoverished communities of New England, she might have followed Jewett and represented herself as an eager postulant and sympathetic feminine recorder of the rituals of community life—Jewett's stance in *Deephaven* and *The Country of the Pointed Firs*. However, Wharton realized that to be taken seriously in the "man's game" that American literature was becoming, she would have to repudiate the local colorists thoroughly and unmistakably. In *Ethan Frome* she achieves this victory over "the authoresses," and the literary power of its bleak vision has until recently all but obliterated their "rose and lavender pages."

Afterword

The naturalists were heirs to a large and complicated tradition in which men critiqued and resisted women's influence, and partly because of that tradition, female local color fiction acquired a salient power for them. Although it would not be fair to say that the naturalists wrote solely in response to the female local color tradition, they clearly were not quite as indifferent to it as their nonfiction writings might suggest. The very diversity of their efforts bespeaks their eagerness to counteract, to demythologize, and sometimes to destroy what they considered a pernicious influence on the literary scene. Further, the use of such local color staples as storytelling, conventional virtues such as self-denial, and strong, crotchety women suggests at least an acquaintance with the form, as well as an enthusiasm for participating in its overthrow. The works of Norris, Crane, and Wharton additionally mingle local color conventions with naturalistic ones, as if the battle for supremacy between forms could be fought within the fiction itself. In a posthumously published essay, Norris summed up not only the passing of local color but the passing of "genteel" literature:

> The New England school for too long dominated the entire range of American fiction—limiting it, specializing it, polishing, refining and embellishing it, narrowing it down to a veritable cult, a thing to be safeguarded by the elect, the few, the aristocracy. It is small wonder that the reaction came when and as it did; small wonder that the wearied public, roused at length, smashed its idols with such vehemence; small wonder that, declaring its independence and finding itself suddenly untrammeled and unguided, it flew off "mobishly" toward false gods, good only because they were new.[1]

The reaction against and fragmentation of local color did not end critics' preoccupation with literature's domination by women. Elaine Showalter describes similar attitudes existing between the world wars:

In 1921, for example, the novelist Joseph Hergesheimer wrote the essay "The Feminine Nuisance in American Literature" for the *Yale Review*, in which he claimed that American literature was "being strangled with a petticoat." A similar essay in 1929 by Robert Herrick attacked women writers for their "feminization" of American literature. As the critic Paul Lauter has pointed out, these attacks reflected the concern of the age "that a truly American art [should] embody the values of masculine culture."[2]

Literature had progressed since Boyesen wrote of the Iron Madonna, but apparently metaphors, like attitudes toward women's influence in literature, had scarcely moved. Hergesheimer and company seemed to have picked up on the antifeminine attitudes of their predecessors, but, twenty to thirty years after local color had effectively ceased as a literary movement, they did so with far less provocation than their predecessors the naturalists. The writers of the 1890s who attacked feminine influence did so from the firm conviction that it was time to shift the balance. That the idols they "smashed" would remain so for much of the twentieth century attests to the success of their project and that of their twentieth-century heirs such as Sinclair Lewis and Ernest Hemingway. As Norris's emphasis on "reaction" implies, however, recalibrating a new balance demands reconstruction from what he would call a "true" perspective, one that neither ignores nor overstates the position of women's local color fiction in American literature. To find this balance is the task that remains as scholars in the past two decades have moved past the excitement of rediscovering local color texts and toward a criticism that invites synthesis, a criticism that allows consideration of those who in some ways are the local colorists' ostensible enemies—and logical heirs: the naturalists.

NOTES

1 Introduction: Local Color, Naturalism, and Gender

1. "Why Women Should Write the Best Novels: And Why They Don't," *Boston Evening Transcript*, 13 November 1901; reprinted in *The Literary Criticism of Frank Norris*, ed. Donald Pizer (Austin: University of Texas Press, 1964), 34–35. Subsequent page references to Norris's essays refer to this edition unless otherwise noted.

2. *Men's Ideas/Women's Realities: Popular Science, 1870–1915*, ed. Louise Michele Newman (New York: Pergamon Press, 1985). Among several studies that address this issue see especially Tom Lutz's *American Nervousness, 1903: An Anecdotal History* (Ithaca: Cornell University Press, 1991), Diane Price Herndl's *Invalid Women: Figuring Feminine Illness in American Fiction and Culture, 1840–1940* (Chapel Hill: University of North Carolina Press, 1993), and John S. Haller and Robin M. Haller, *The Physician and Sexuality in Victorian America* (New York: Norton, 1974).

3. William Dean Howells, "Editor's Study," *Harper's Monthly* 74 (1887): 485. *Harper's New Monthly Magazine* dropped the "New" from its title after 1900; for the sake of consistency, the later title has been used throughout this volume.

4. Michael Davitt Bell, *The Problem of American Realism: Studies in the Cultural History of a Literary Idea* (Chicago: University Chicago Press, 1993), 18.

5. Clara Marburg Kirk and Rudolf Kirk, the editors of *Criticism and Fiction and Other Essays* (New York: New York University Press, 1959), report that, according to Mildred Howells, her father "continued to do all that he could to help launch Crane, himself taking *Maggie* from publisher to publisher" (268). They add, "On one occasion Howells read Emily Dickinson's poetry aloud to his visitor" (269).

6. Jay Martin lists the writers influenced by Howells in *Harvests of Change: American Literature 1865–1914* (Englewood Cliffs, N.J.: Prentice-Hall, 1967), 50; letter to Fuller quoted on p. 249.

7. Howells praises Crane's *Maggie* as containing "perhaps the best tough dialect which has yet found its way into print" (40) in his brief *Harper's Weekly* review of 8 June 1895. He further singles out its "quality of fatal necessity" (47) in "New York Low Life in Fiction" (New York *World*, 26 July 1896) and calls *Maggie* "the best thing he did" (62) after Crane's death. The reviews have been collected in *Stephen Crane: The Critical Heritage*, ed. Richard M. Weatherford (London: Routledge and Kegan Paul, 1973), to which the page numbers above refer.

8. Howells's review of *McTeague* appeared as "A Case in Point" in *Literature* on March 24, 1899, collected in *Criticism and Fiction and Other Essays*, 279–82.

9. Lars Ahnebrink, *The Beginnings of Naturalism in American Fiction: A Study of the Works of Hamlin Garland, Stephen Crane, and Frank Norris with Special Reference to Some European Influences, 1891–1903* (Cambridge, Mass.: Harvard University Press, 1950; reprint, New York: Russell and Russell, 1961), 69; Hamlin Garland, *Roadside Meetings* (New York: Macmillan, 1930), 121.

10. *The Correspondence of Stephen Crane*, ed. Stanley Wertheim and Paul Sorrentino (New York: Columbia University Press, 1988), 1:63.

11. According to Richard Lingeman, Dreiser had referred to Howells as a "literary Columbus" in his September 1896 review of Abraham Cahan's *Yekl* for *Ev'ry Month*; Lingeman characterizes the tone of Dreiser's interview with Howells as "full of allusions to death, as if he were prematurely writing Howells's obituary" (*Theodore Dreiser: At the Gates of the City, 1871-1907* [New York: Putnam, 1986], 235-36). The letter is quoted in Ellen Moers, *Two Dreisers* (New York: Viking, 1969), 176.

12. Frank Norris, "A Plea for Romantic Fiction," *Boston Evening Transcript*, 18 December 1901; reprinted in *Literary Criticism of Frank Norris*, 76.

13. Quoted in Martin, *Harvests of Change*, 253.

14. Sinclair Lewis, "The American Fear of Literature" (Nobel Prize Address, 12 December 1930); reprinted in *The Man from Main Street: Selected Essays and Other Writings 1904-1950*, ed. Harry E. Maule and Melville H. Cane (New York: Random House, 1953), 15.

15. Ann Douglas Wood, "The Literature of Impoverishment: The Women Local Colorists in America 1865-1914," *Women's Studies* 1 (1972): 14.

16. Women's local color fiction has also undergone increasing attention since the early 1980s: the revised edition of Perry Westbrook's history of the movement, *Acres of Flint*, appeared in 1981 (Metuchen, N.J.: Scarecrow Press), a time when feminist critics Marjorie Pryse and Josephine Donovan were producing interpretive accounts of women's regional fiction such as the latter's *New England Local Color Literature: A Women's Tradition* (New York: Ungar, 1983) and *After the Fall* (University Park: Pennsylvania State University Press, 1989). Perceptive studies of individual authors such as Sarah Way Sherman's *Sarah Orne Jewett, an American Persephone* (Hanover, N.H.: University Press of New England, 1989) and a host of articles have contributed to a critical discourse on local color. In "'Distilling Essences': Regionalism and 'Women's Culture,'" Pryse, rejecting the limiting "essentialist" notion of a woman's natural sphere, distinguishes as "regionalists" those writers who consciously use region as a rhetorical device to express their opposition to some larger hierarchy of race, class, and gender (*American Literary Realism* 25.2 [Winter 1993]: 9). Defending the central position of regionalism in "'Not in the Least American': Nineteenth-Century Literary Regionalism," Judith Fetterley further defines the movement through its "efforts to dismantle and deconstruct hierarchies," its "commitment to empathy," and its "different model of storytelling" (*College English* 56 [December 1994]: 888, 889, 891). June Howard's *New Essays on* The Country of the Pointed Firs (Cambridge: Cambridge University Press, 1994) provides revisionist readings both of Jewett's text and of the premises of much feminist criticism on local color fiction. In "Material Culture, Empire, and Jewett's *Country of the Pointed Firs*," for example, Elizabeth Ammons reads the Bowden reunion in Jewett's *Country of the Pointed Firs* to be a celebration not only of female community but, more disturbingly, of "racial purity and white cultural dominance" (96).

17. The classic definition of naturalism is George Becker's "pessimistic materialistic determinism" in his introduction to *Documents of Modern Literary Realism*

(Princeton: Princeton University Press, 1963), 35. Other tenets of the movement include a preoccupation with action, struggle, growth, and the resistance of man to the clash of "forces," whether natural (heredity, for example, or Norris's "the Wheat") or man-made (the railroad, strictures of class and economics). In "Naturalism in American Fiction: A Status Report," *Studies in American Fiction* 10.1 (Spring 1982): 1-16, Don Graham defends the continuing use of the term to describe modern fiction, finding the naturalistic novel to be "a romance in which the adventurers never achieve clarity of illumination or even the comforts of irony" (8).

The significance of this transition from realism to naturalism and the radical dislocations that it occasioned have been amply documented in earlier critical studies and literary histories whose titles themselves often suggest the nature of the struggle: Maxwell Geismar's *Rebels and Ancestors: The American Novel 1890-1915* (Boston: Houghton Mifflin, 1953), Charles Child Walcutt's *American Literary Naturalism: A Divided Stream* (Minneapolis: University of Minnesota Press, 1956), and Jay Martin's *Harvests of Change* (1967). Other significant accounts of naturalism during this time include Werner Berthoff's *The Ferment of Realism: American Literature, 1884-1919* (New York: Free Press, 1965), Larzer Ziff's *The American 1890s: Life and Times of a Lost Generation* (New York: Viking, 1966), and Harold H. Kolb Jr.'s *The Illusion of Life: American Realism as a Literary Form* (Charlottesville: University of Virginia Press, 1969). Beginning with Eric Sundquist's *American Realism: New Essays* (Baltimore: Johns Hopkins University Press, 1982), more recent critical assessments have ranged beyond questions of genre to exploration of the cultural intersections of naturalism and realism. In a revised edition of his influential *Realism and Naturalism in Nineteenth-Century American Literature* (Carbondale: Southern Illinois University Press, 1984), Donald Pizer showed that the implications of evolutionary theory were threefold: a sense that literature was dynamic, that it grew and changed, like life, according to natural law; an emphasis on milieu rather than the individual (or individual writer) as a determining force in the production of literature; and a metaphor that conveniently equated the novelist and scientist as analytical observers (*Realism and Naturalism*, 88). Naturalism's basis in philosophy informed three studies that appeared at about the same time. Harold Kaplan's *Power and Order: Henry Adams and the Naturalist Tradition in American Fiction* (Chicago: University of Chicago Press, 1981) examines the "harsh virtues" (9) of the naturalist ethos, particularly the ways in which "the literature influenced by it submits to the thematic rule of conflict and power" (12). In *American Literature and the Universe of Force* (Durham, N.C.: Duke University Press, 1981), Ronald E. Martin traces Spencer's influence on American literature and concludes that intellectuals such as John Fiske and Joseph Le Conte interpreted Spencer optimistically, seeing in his system the inevitability of a social conflict resulting in progress—and even, for Le Conte, a reconciling of science and religion. It is this fascination with force, argues Richard Lehan in "American Literary Naturalism: The French Connection" (*Nineteenth-Century Fiction* 38 [1984]: 529-57), that ultimately drives naturalists like London toward writing novels of utopia and dystopia. John J. Conder's *Naturalism in American Fiction: The Classic Phase* (Lexington: University Press of Kentucky, 1984) finds philosophical coherence in naturalism's materialistic determinism.

Several recent historical approaches to the genre attempt to reveal the opposi-tions beneath the deceptively simple surface of a naturalistic novel, often by focus-ing on what Jane Tompkins has called the text's "cultural work." June Howard, in *Form and History in American Literary Naturalism* (Chapel Hill: University of North Carolina Press, 1985) views class anxieties and the "threat of proletarianiza-tion" as central to naturalistic works. Walter Benn Michaels's approach to the subject in *The Gold Standard and the Logic of Naturalism* (Berkeley: University of California Press, 1987) examines naturalistic novels' destabilizing and contradictory patterns of production and consumption, whereas Amy Kaplan's *Social Construction of American Realism* (Chicago: University of Chicago Press, 1988), situates realism historically "as a strategy for imagining and managing the threats of social change—not just to assert a dominant power but often to assuage fears of powerlessness" (10). A further historical approach to the relationship between realism, naturalism, and journalism informs the discussions of authorship, audience, and the construc-tion of authority in Christopher Wilson's *Labor of Words: Literary Professionalism in the Progressive Era* (Athens: University of Georgia Press, 1985) and Daniel Borus's *Writing Realism: Howells, James, and Norris in the Mass Market* (Chapel Hill: Uni-versity of North Carolina Press, 1989). Questioning standard assumptions about the naturalists' inattention to problems of style and form, Lee Clark Mitchell's *Determined Fictions: American Literary Naturalism* (New York: Columbia Univer-sity Press, 1989) reads naturalistic style as a means of "undermining narrative as-sumptions that realist authors invoked in their fiction" (xvi).

18. For an account of the emergence of these dichotomies, see Lawrence W. Levine's *Highbrow/Lowbrow: The Emergence of Cultural Hierarchy in America* (Cam-bridge, Mass.: Harvard University Press, 1988).

19. Eric Sundquist, "Realism and Regionalism," in *Columbia Literary History of the United States*, ed. Emory Elliott (New York: Columbia University Press, 1988), 503.

20. See Elizabeth Ammons's introduction to *Conflicting Stories: American Women Writers at the Turn into the Twentieth Century* (New York: Oxford Univer-sity Press, 1992). Ammons makes this point not about local color writers specifically but about women writers at the turn of the century. Richard Brodhead's *Cultures of Letters: Scenes of Reading and Writing in Nineteenth-Century America* (Chicago: University of Chicago Press, 1993) discusses the egalitarian promise of regional writing.

Marjorie Pryse uses the term *inclusivity* in "Distilling Essences," 11. In the introduction to their anthology *American Women Regionalists, 1850–1910* (New York: Norton, 1992), Pryse and Judith Fetterley distinguish between "local color" and "regionalist" writers, arguing that the former in effect condescend to their readers whereas the latter differentiate themselves "primarily in their desire not to hold up regional characters to potential ridicule by eastern urban readers but rather to present regional experience from within, so as to engage the reader's sympathy and identification" (xii). Fetterley and Pryse consider Constance Fenimore Woolson, Alice Brown, and George Washington Cable, for example, practitioners of "local color," whereas Jewett, Freeman, Murfree, and Chesnutt would exemplify region-alist writers. Although their thesis is provocative, even persuasive, I have chosen not to make this distinction, preferring instead to use *local color* and *regionalism* interchangeably. For a dissenting view of Fetterley and Pryse's theory, see June Howard's introduction to *New Essays on* The Country of the Pointed Firs.

21. Sundquist, "Realism and Regionalism," 509.

22. Alice Hall Petry, "Universal and Particular: The Local-Color Phenomenon Reconsidered," *American Literary Realism* 12 (1979): 119.

23. Brodhead, *Cultures of Letters*, 120.

24. In a curious way, being elderly is itself a virtue in local color writing. Even the young heroines seem ageless: Nan Prince of Jewett's *A Country Doctor*, for example, patterns herself as closely as possible on her elderly benefactor, Dr. Leslie, and his equally venerable friend Mrs. Graham.

25. As Lee Clark Mitchell notes in *Determined Fictions: American Literary Naturalism* (New York: Columbia University Press, 1989), Stephen Crane and Jack London never "accept[ed] the naturalist label" (viii), although their works are commonly seen as at least partly "naturalistic." *Naturalist* is used here in the sense of identifying the members of this loose generational cohort rather than as a descriptor of each writer's professed philosophical alignment.

26. Eric Sundquist, "The Country of the Blue," introduction to *American Realism: New Essays* (Baltimore: Johns Hopkins University Press, 1982), 13.

27. George Becker, introduction to *Documents of Modern Literary Realism*, 25.

28. David Graham Phillips, quoted by Larzer Ziff in *The American 1890s: Life and Times of a Lost Generation* (New York: Viking, 1966), 150.

29. Philip Fisher, *Hard Facts: Setting and Form in the American Novel* (New York: Oxford University Press, 1985), 132–33.

30. Malcolm Cowley, "A Natural History of American Naturalism," *Kenyon Review* (1947); reprinted in Becker, *Documents of Modern Literary Realism*, 432; Fisher, *Hard Facts*, 132.

31. Mitchell, *Determined Fictions*, 32.

32. In Norris's *McTeague*, McTeague's alcoholism, Zerkow's greed, Maria Macapa's madness, and Trina's miserliness all result from the environmentally induced emergence of latent inherited "racial" characteristics that marked their deviance from a hypothetically desirable Anglo-Saxon norm.

33. Sarah Orne Jewett, *A Country Doctor* (Boston: Houghton Mifflin, 1884; reprint, New York: New American Library, 1986), 77.

34. Westbrook, *Acres of Flint*, 88.

35. Rebecca Harding Davis, "In the Grey Cabins of New England," *Century* 49 (1895): 621, 620.

36. Westbrook's argument in *Acres of Flint* implies this connection.

37. June Howard, *Form and History in American Literary Naturalism* (Chapel Hill: University of North Carolina Press, 1985), 104. Rachel Bowlby, in *"Just Looking": Consumer Culture in Dreiser, Gissing and Zola* (New York: Methuen, 1985), calls the naturalists "spectators of spectatorship" (15), noting that in an emerging consumer society, people become spectators and human relationships are restructured as consumer goods take center stage. In *Writing Realism: Howells, James, and Norris in the Mass Market* (Chapel Hill: University of North Carolina Press, 1989),

Daniel Borus locates spectatorship in the distancing of author from audience, aris-
ing from the failure of "a language of shared assumptions" that rendered readers'
"interpretive space constricted and their role at times akin to that of a dazed
spectator" (101). According to Borus, "By concentrating on what readers knew (or
what realist authors believed readers knew), the realists hoped to restore a kind of
equality of function between author and audience" (102).

38. Brodhead, *Cultures of Letters*, 137.

39. In noting the devices of the "interloper" and "reverse interloper," Alice Hall
Petry indirectly supports this point of a figurative safety within tolerable contrasts.
The "interloper," an educated representative of life outside the region, enters the
region and observes it; the "reverse interloper," an inhabitant of the region, travels
to the city and observes it; but the fundamental purpose, according to Petry, is the
same: to contrast the two worlds (114-18) as Rose Terry Cooke does in "A Town
Mouse and a Country Mouse" (*Huckleberries from New England Hills* [1891]).

2   Necessary Limits: Women's Local Color Fiction

1. Fred Lewis Pattee, *The Development of the American Short Story: An Historical
Survey* (New York: Harper and Brothers, 1923), 268.

2. Claude Simpson, introduction to *The Local Colorists: American Short Stories,
1857-1900* (New York: Harper and Brothers, 1960), 7.

3. Donald A. Dike, "Notes on Local Color and Its Relation to Realism,"
College English 14.2 (1952): 86.

4. For an account of the connections between Southwestern humor and local
color fiction, see Arlin Turner's "Comedy and Reality in Local Color Fiction,
1865-1900" in Louis Rubin's *Comic Imagination in American Literature* (Washington, D. C.: Voice of America Forum Series, 1974), 167-74; Turner's is one of several
essays in this volume that address the topic. M. Thomas Inge's *Frontier Humorists*
(Hamden, Conn.: Archon Books, 1975) is focused more specifically on Southwestern humor.

5. "A Washoe Joke" was published in the *Virginia City Territorial Enterprise*, 28
October 1863; "Jim Smiley and His Jumping Frog" appeared in the *New York
Saturday Press*, 18 November 1865. For information on these and other publications,
an essential reference is Frank Luther Mott, *A History of American Magazines*, 5 vols.
(Cambridge, Mass.: Harvard University Press, 1930-1968). Mott calls *The Spirit of
the Times* "the first all-around sporting journal in the United States" (1:480).

6. After this volume, buoyed—or as Twain implied, corrupted—by a trium-
phal tour of the East and a $10,000 contract from the *Atlantic Monthly*, Harte was
unable to sustain the quality of his early work, and his lapses into sentimentality and
romance anticipate by only a few years the similar fates of later local colorists.

7. Bret Harte, "The Rise of the 'Short Story,'" *Cornhill Magazine*, n.s., 7.37
(July 1899): 3.

8. The first quotation is from Josephine Donovan's *New England Local Color
Literature*, 56; the second from her *Sarah Orne Jewett* (New York: Ungar, 1980), 8.
James M. Cox, Perry Westbrook, and Ann Douglas also identify Stowe and her

regionalist counterparts as originating a local color tradition, though Douglas sees the tradition as a dying offshoot of earlier, more vigorous women's fiction. Josephine Donovan vehemently disagrees with Douglas, finding not only Stowe but the local colorists who followed her to be part of a "coherent, feminine literary tradition," antiromantic and antipicaresque in form, that dates back to the eighteenth century (*New England Local Color Literature*, 3).

9. James Cox, "Regionalism: A Diminished Thing," in Elliott, *Columbia Literary History*, 767.

10. Henry May, introduction to *Oldtown Folks*, by Harriet Beecher Stowe (Cambridge, Mass.: Belknap Press of Harvard University Press, 1966), 30, 34.

11. Pattee, *American Short Story*, 248; Westbrook, *Acres of Flint*, 22.

12. Martin, *Harvests of Change*, 140. In her introduction to *"How Celia Changed Her Mind" and Selected Stories* (New Brunswick, N.J.: Rutgers University Press, 1986), Elizabeth Ammons comments on the "abundance of women eager to pose as the popular New England realist" (ix).

13. Howells, *Criticism and Fiction*, 105, 108.

14. Both quotations are from James Lane Allen, "Local Color," *Critic* 8.106 (9 January 1886): 13; italics are Allen's.

15. Howells, *Criticism and Fiction*, 193-94.

16. In addition to Pattee, Turner, Simpson, and Fetterley and Pryse (mentioned above), sources for information on regional writers include Bell, *Problem of American Realism*; Brodhead, *Cultures of Letters*; Cox, "Regionalism," 761-84; Sundquist, "Realism and Regionalism," 501-24; and Amy Kaplan, "Nation, Region, and Empire," in Elliott, *Columbia History of the American Novel*, 240-66.

17. As Millicent Bell comments in "Female Regional Writing: An American Tradition," *Revue française d'études americaines* 1.30 (November 1986): 469-80, local color writers "turned to a closer study of the lately warring regions in post–Civil War America. With the realization of the country's deep and ineradicable divisions, its precarious unity, they embraced the depiction of the still-distinguished sections" (469-70).

18. In noting that the local color movement is "the antithesis of realism" if realism is defined as "the world of men's activities," Michael Davitt Bell characterizes its world as being "distinguished above all by the absence of men and of masculine activity. The young and fit have fled this world for a reality which is always elsewhere, in the West or in the city, while those who remain, mostly women, maintain old proprieties and rituals whose function, like the men, seems long since to have vanished" (*Problem of American Realism*, 176-77).

19. Alvan F. Sanborn, "The Future of Rural New England," *Atlantic Monthly* 80 (July 1897): 74-83; Philip Morgan, "The Problems of Rural New England," *Atlantic Monthly* 79 (May 1897): 583.

20. Rollin Lynde Hartt, "A New England Hill Town," *Atlantic Monthly* 83 (1899): 569, 572.

21. Hartt, "New England Hill Town," 569. Thompson's comment on *Pembroke* reveals his perspective: "Such is Miss Wilkins's village, and it is a true picture; but it wholly represents New England life no more than the dying apple orchard wholly

represents New England scenery" ("Miss Wilkins: An Idealist in Masquerade," *Atlantic* 83 [1899]: 666).

22. Sarah Orne Jewett, *The Country of the Pointed Firs and Other Stories* (New York: Norton, 1981), 132. Subsequent references are to this edition and will be cited parenthetically in the text.

23. Douglas [Wood], "Literature of Impoverishment," 16.

24. Judith Fryer makes this observation in *Felicitous Space: The Imaginative Structures of Edith Wharton and Willa Cather* (Chapel Hill: University of North Carolina Press, 1986), 179.

25. Among those who have taken this approach are Fryer, Josephine Donovan, Marjorie Pryse, and Elizabeth Ammons, in her earlier work such as "Going in Circles: The Female Geography of Jewett's *The Country of the Pointed Firs*," *Studies in the Literary Imagination* 16.2 (Fall 1983): 83–92. Several critics treat female communities and domestic activities as important features of women's local color fiction, among them Marcia McClintock Folsom in "'Tact is a Kind of Mind-Reading': Empathic Style in Sarah Orne Jewett's *The Country of the Pointed Firs*," *Colby Library Quarterly* 18 (March 1982): 66–78. In *A Web of Relationship: Women in the Short Stories of Mary Wilkins Freeman* (Jackson: University Press of Mississippi, 1992), Mary Reichardt discusses similar patterns of community in Freeman's work. Helen Fiddyment Levy finds tropes of female creativity and the search for "a female-created pastoral setting" (6) in her chapter on Jewett in *Fiction of the Home Place: Jewett, Cather, Glasgow, Porter, Welty, and Naylor* (Jackson: University Press of Mississippi, 1992), and Ann Romines provides a sensitive and subtle reading of housekeeping and its variations as a central figure in Freeman and Jewett in *The Home Plot: Women, Writing and Domestic Ritual* (Amherst: University of Massachusetts Press, 1992). See also the revisionist readings in *New Essays on* The Country of the Pointed Firs, in which Susan Gillman, Michael Davitt Bell, Elizabeth Ammons, and Susan Zagarell historicize Jewett's work as part of a late-nineteenth-century recentralizing of national identity through the creation of a myth of common origins. For example, in revising their earlier work on Jewett, Ammons and Zagarell here focus on the politics of hierarchy, imperialist ideology, nativism, and exclusion implied by the work and its racial overtones.

26. In "Universal and Particular," Alice Hall Petry proposes that local color concentrates simultaneously on the otherwise trivial, providing picturesque details that pique curiosity but avoid controversy, and the universal. Petry identifies this avoidance as a means by "which the local colorists were able to universalize their works by refusing to give information which would particularize them in time" (121).

27. A notable exception is some of the fiction of Rose Terry Cooke. Both "Freedom Wheeler's Controversy with Providence" and "The Ring Fetter" include some horrifying infant murders, and the latter story includes beatings and a suicide.

28. "The Light Literature of Travel," review of *Country By-Ways*, by Sarah Orne Jewett, *Atlantic Monthly* 49 (1882): 421.

29. In addition to Donovan, Petry, Folsom, and others mentioned previously, several critics have read local color conventions sympathetically. See, for example,

Helen Westra's reading of Jewett's positive view of the elderly in "Age and Life's Great Prospects in Sarah Orne Jewett's *The Country of the Pointed Firs*," *Colby Quarterly* 26.3 (September 1990): 161–70.

30. Millicent Bell, "Female Regional Writing," 474, 470.

31. Elizabeth Ammons, introduction to Rose Terry Cooke's *"How Celia Changed Her Mind" and Selected Stories* (New Brunswick, N.J.: Rutgers University Press, 1986), xxii.

32. Thompson, "Miss Wilkins: An Idealist in Masquerade," 671–72.

33. Douglas, "Literature of Impoverishment," 16. In "Local Color and the Rise of the American Magazine" (*Essays Mostly on Periodical Publishing in America* [Durham, N.C.: Duke University Press, 1973]), Kimball King suggests that local color arose largely as a result of a paternalistic editors' cabal bent on moral improvement:

> Within the local color movement there were dramatically opposed philosophies, but these individual philosophies tended to be translated, altered, or absorbed into a bland mixture of platitudes acceptable to purposes of an editorial campaign intended to "shape" the thinking of the American middle class. The magazine was the proper medium for reaching the masses, and local color was felt to be the literary movement best suited to an audience inexperienced but eager to learn. . . . [124]

34. Sarah Orne Jewett, *Deephaven* (Portsmouth, N.H.: Peter Randall, 1993), 235. Subsequent references will be cited in the text. The dichotomy exists in the form itself: both local color and realism grew, according to Bernard Bowron, when the heavily symbolic literary forms necessitated by a doctrine of salvation by faith gave way to the realism favored by the here-and-now approach of salvation by works, a shift that Bowron sees Stowe as exemplifying ("Realism in America," *Comparative Literature* 3.3 [Summer 1951]: 268–85).

35. Sarah Orne Jewett, "Miss Tempy's Watchers," in *The Country of the Pointed Firs and Other Stories,* ed. Marjorie Pryse (New York: Norton, 1981), 247. Subsequent references to stories in this collection will be cited parenthetically within the text.

36. Rose Terry Cooke, *"How Celia Changed Her Mind" and Selected Stories,* ed. Elizabeth Ammons (New Brunswick, N.J.: Rutgers University Press, 1986), 123. Subsequent references to stories by Cooke are from this edition and will be cited parenthetically in the text.

37. Julia Bader, "The 'Rooted' Landscape and the Woman Writer," in *Teaching Women's Literature from a Regional Perspective*, ed. Leonore Hoffman and Deborah Rosenfelt (New York: Modern Language Association of America, 1982), 26.

38. As Nina Baym identifies them in *Woman's Fiction: A Guide to Novels by and about Women in America, 1820–1870* (Ithaca: Cornell University Press, 1978), the conventions of the genre variously termed "sentimental," "domestic," or "woman's" fiction focus on a young (often orphaned) heroine's struggle for self-mastery, confronting "the pain of learning to conquer her own passions" (Tompkins, 172) as she attempts to balance society's demands for self-denial with her own

desire for autonomy. The heroine often endures injustices at the hands of an "[abuser] of power," often a cruel aunt, before establishing a "network of surrogate kin" to provide solace and right guidance (Baym, 37–38); the "kin" often consists of an older brother or father figure who marries the heroine once she has successfully completed her "education." See also Susan K. Harris's *Nineteenth-Century American Women's Novels: Interpretive Strategies* (Cambridge: Cambridge University Press, 1990), Jane Tompkins's *Sensational Designs: The Cultural Work of American Fiction 1790–1860* (New York: Oxford University Press, 1985), and Gillian Brown's *Domestic Individualism: Imagining Self in Nineteenth-Century America* (Berkeley: University of California Press, 1990).

39. *Selected Stories of Mary E. Wilkins Freeman*, ed. Marjorie Pryse (New York: Norton, 1983), 310. Except as noted, subsequent references to Freeman's stories are to this edition and will be cited parenthetically within the text.

40. Marjorie Pryse, afterword to *Selected Stories of Mary E. Wilkins Freeman*, 328.

41. As Mary Reichardt describes the situation, Candace and Betsey Dole are both artists who "struggle to transcend the dead rituals of the community's hypocritical religiosity to attain a deeper truth based on a common humanity" (*Web of Relationship*, 143).

42. Although not a comment on community, Woolson's "Miss Grief" is a more sophisticated treatment of the same theme. The aesthetically sophisticated but disinterested male narrator attempts to edit the passionate and untidy fictional outpourings of Aaronna Moncrief; he finds, to his surprise, that they have a coherence and power beyond his conventional editing abilities. The "want of one grain" of his masculine qualities of distance and technique, however, causes her work to go unread, even as his lesser gift succeeds.

In analyzing several such stories of women characters' resistance to a dominant culture, Josephine Donovan uses Foucault's concept of "subjugated knowledges" to show how female local color writers resisted "the colonization of local traditions" through such "translocal homogenizing disciplines" as federalism, modern science, Calvinism, and sexology ("Breaking the Sentence: Local-Color Literature and Subjugated Knowledges" in *The (Other) American Traditions: Nineteenth-Century Women Writers*, ed. Joyce Warren [New Brunswick, N.J.: Rutgers University Press, 1993], 239–40). The "objective" aesthetic standards to which the works of Betsey Dole and Aaronna Moncrief are subjected fall into this category.

43. In her discussion of private communal and public associational language in *Fiction of the Home Place*, Helen Fiddyment Levy makes the point that "the mother's language banishes the intellectual constructions of Captain Littlepage and the chilly 'theoretical love,' as Fike characterizes it, of the ministers. The male language recedes as the woman narrator comes home to the local language" (55).

44. The phrase is Sharon O'Brien's, quoted by Ann Romines in *The Home Plot*. Romines goes on to comment that "the twig of bay [with which the pin is wrapped] eloquently links language, housekeeping, and endurance" (73).

45. Constance Fenimore Woolson, "The Lady of Little Fishing," in *For the Major, and Selected Short Stories*, ed. Rayburn S. Moore (New Haven: College and

University Press, 1967), 43. Subsequent references to Woolson's works are from this edition and will be cited parenthetically in the text.

46. Mary N. Murfree (Charles Egbert Craddock), *In the Tennessee Mountains* (1884; reprint, Ridgewood, N.J.: Gregg Press, 1968).

47. Jewett, *Deephaven*, 260.

48. The theme recurs also in works such as the title story of Alice French's [Octave Thanet, pseud.] *Slave to Duty and Other Women* (Chicago: Herbert S. Stone, 1898), Mary N. Murfree's [Charles Egbert Craddock, pseud.] "Drifting Down Lost Creek" from *In the Tennessee Mountains* (1884; reprint, Ridgewood, N.J.: Gregg Press, 1968), and Mary Austin's "The House of Offence," reprinted in *Stories from the Country of Lost Borders*, ed. Marjorie Pryse (New Brunswick, N.J.: Rutgers University Press, 1987).

49. Thompson, "Miss Wilkins," 671.

50. The connections between housekeeping and the minutiae of daily life and local color fiction have long been noted by critics. For example, in "The Dissolving Vision: Realism in Jewett, Freeman, and Gilman" (in *American Realism*, ed. Eric Sundquist), Julia Bader connects realism and an emphasis on the quotidian specifically with a woman's perspective that "asserts itself in the quiet dignity of everyday tasks and simple household objects seen as signposts in a fully lived life, rather than as trivial details that distract from achievement" (178).

51. Thompson, "Miss Wilkins," 665.

52. Mary E. Wilkins Freeman, *Pembroke*, ed. Perry Westbrook (New Haven: College and University Press, 1971), 71. Subsequent references are to this edition and will be cited parenthetically in the text.

53. According to Shirley Marchalonis's introduction to *Critical Essays on Mary Wilkins Freeman* (Boston: G. K. Hall, 1991), Freeman wrote to Fred Lewis Pattee saying that she would like "more symbolism, more mysticism" (6) but that it doesn't pay. Marchalonis observes that the warped curvature of Barney's back, "symbolic of the distortion of his mind" (6), is one such clear example.

54. Both "Louisa" and "A Taste of Honey" appear in Mary E. Wilkins Freeman, *The Revolt of Mother and Other Stories* (Old Westbury, N.Y.: Feminist Press, 1974).

55. Granville Hicks, *The Great Tradition* (New York: Macmillan, 1933), 56.

56. Freeman, *Revolt of Mother*, 35.

57. Mary E. Wilkins Freeman, *A New England Nun and Other Stories* (1891; reprint, New York: Harper and Brothers, 1919), 17.

58. Romines, *Home Plot*, 111, 126; Romines's italics.

59. Seeing Marion Carroll as one of Woolson's artist-heroines who adopts the "sentimental facade" and "physical fiction of a doll's face and curls" of a domestic heroine, Cheryl Torsney calls her "a fiction whose layered text has kept her safe and warm" (*Constance Fenimore Woolson: The Grief of Artistry* [Athens: University of Georgia Press, 1989], 139).

60. For an interesting reading of this motif of consumption, see Elise Miller, "Jewett's *The Country of the Pointed Firs*: The Realism of the Local Colorists," *American Literary Realism* 20.2 (Winter 1988): 3–20. Miller finds local color to be "a

distinctly feminine and, in some ways, purer version of realism" (11) that in its oral traditions (storytelling, eating) does not flinch from "images of cannibalism, parasites, and empty orifices" that describe "the ways in which the inhabitants—and in turn the artist—of the local have sucked the life out of their environment" (15).

61. As Philip G. Terrie comments in "Local Color and a Mythologized Past: The Rituals of Memory in *The Country of the Pointed Firs,*" *Colby Library Quarterly* 23 (March 1987): 16-25, "What distinguishes Mrs. Todd from Littlepage in the use of story-telling is that she recognizes the importance of the listener and the present-time union between teller and hearer, while Littlepage's story and the way he tells it reflect his egocentrism" (20).

62. Patricia Meyer Spacks, *Gossip* (Chicago: University of Chicago Press, 1985), 9.

63. Many readings stress the initiatory progress of the narrator, and some link this progress to mythic themes as well. See, for example, Richard G. Carson's "Nature and the Circles of Initiation in *The Country of the Pointed Firs,*" *Colby Library Quarterly* 21 (September 1985): 154-60, in which the narrator's progress through characters who are literally "eccentric" is a "quest romance of the circle of the pointed firs" (157).

64. These two stories are not included in the original volume of *The Country of the Pointed Firs,* and, as Sarah Way Sherman points out in *Sarah Orne Jewett, an American Persephone,* critics such as Warner Berthoff, Mary Ellen Chase, and Marjorie Pryse have argued for the integrity of the original 1896 version (235). I have followed Sherman's practice and included them in the discussion.

65. As one example of this analogy, Michael Holstein, in "Art and Archetype: Jewett's Pointed Firs and the Dunnet Landing Stories," *Nineteenth-Century Literature* 42 (September 1987): 188-202, finds that among the lessons she learns from Mrs. Todd are the ability to create and identify types and to "look for the best instance or the essence of a thing" (195).

66. Jewett, quoted in Charles Miner Thompson, "The Art of Miss Jewett," *Atlantic Monthly* 94 (1904): 490.

3   Opening the Door to the "Masculine Principle"

1. *Theodore Dreiser: A Selection of Uncollected Prose,* ed. Donald Pizer (Detroit: Wayne State University Press, 1977), 188.

2. In his introduction to *Critical Essays on Hamlin Garland* (Boston: G. K. Hall, 1982), James Nagel cites reviews in the *New York Daily Tribune,* the *Literary World,* and the *Dial* that would support this contention (5).

3. Hamlin Garland, *Crumbling Idols: Twelve Essays on Art Dealing Chiefly with Literature, Painting, and the Drama,* ed. Jane Johnson (Cambridge, Mass: Belknap Press of Harvard University Press, 1960), 59, 53-54; italics are Garland's. Subsequent references will be cited parenthetically in the text.

4. Charles Miner Thompson, "New Figures in Literature and Art: Hamlin Garland," *Atlantic Monthly* 76 (December 1895): 840. In the *Atlantic Monthly,* this feature is unsigned. Charles L. P. Silet, Robert E. Welch, and Richard Boudreau,

the editors of *The Critical Reception of Hamlin Garland 1891–1978* (Troy, N.Y.: Whitston, 1985), identify Thompson as the author. Subsequent references will be cited parenthetically in the text.

5. Paul Shorey, "Present Conditions of Literary Production," *Atlantic Monthly* 78 (1896): 164.

6. Johnson, introduction to *Crumbling Idols*, xii.

7. Edward Eggleston, preface (1892) to the Library Edition of *The Hoosier Schoolmaster: A Story of Backwoods Life in Indiana* (New York: Grosset and Dunlap, 1913), 6.

8. Charles Dudley Warner, "Editor's Study," *Harper's Monthly* 92 (May 1896): 961.

9. With his customary venom, Ambrose Bierce described James Whitcomb Riley, Mary Murfree, and Mary Wilkins Freeman, among others, as "the pignoramous crew of malinguists, cacophonologists and apostrophographers who think they can get close to nature by depicting the sterile lives and limited emotions of the gowks and sodhoppers that speak only to tangle their own tongues, and move only to fall over their own feet" (*San Francisco Examiner*, 18 December 1892). Quoted in Paul Fatout, *Ambrose Bierce: The Devil's Lexicographer* (Norman: University of Oklahoma Press, 1951), 194.

10. H. H. Boyesen, *Literary and Social Silhouettes* (New York: Harper and Brothers, 1894), 49.

11. Howells, *Criticism and Fiction*, 73, 75.

12. Gertrude Atherton, "Why Is American Literature Bourgeois?" *North American Review* 178 (May 1904): 779.

13. Quoted in Fatout, *Ambrose Bierce*, 138, 146.

14. Thomas Beer, *The Mauve Decade: American Life at the End of the Nineteenth Century* (Garden City, N.Y.: Garden City Publishing, 1926), 23.

15. Frank Norris, "The Decline of the Magazine Short Story," *Wave* 16 (30 January 1897); reprinted in *Literary Criticism of Frank Norris*, 28.

16. According to Paula Blanchard's *Sarah Orne Jewett: Her World and Her Work* (Reading, Mass.: Addison-Wesley, 1994), "The Contributors' Club" featured "anonymous, untitled short essays by regular contributors to the magazine" (136).

17. Quoted in Christopher Wilson, *The Labor of Words: Literary Professionalism in the Progressive Era* (Athens: University of Georgia Press, 1985), 46.

18. Stephen Crane, "Fears Realists Must Wait: An Interesting Talk with William Dean Howells," *New York Times*, 28 October 1894; reprinted in *Stephen Crane: Uncollected Writings*, ed. Olov W. Fryckstedt (Uppsala: Uppsala University Press, 1963), 81–82.

19. In the May 1896 *Harper's Monthly*, Charles Dudley Warner uses the term "lurid realism" to describe Crane's *Red Badge of Courage*, though he does not identify the book by name.

20. Frank Norris, "A Plea for Romantic Fiction," *Boston Evening Transcript*, 18 December 1901; reprinted in *Literary Criticism of Frank Norris*, 76.

21. Howells, *Criticism and Fiction*, 282.

22. William Dean Howells, "The Editor's Easy Chair," *Harper's Monthly* (April 1901); reprinted in *W. D. Howells as Critic*, ed. Edwin H. Cady (London: Routledge and Kegan Paul, 1973), 352–60.

23. Amy Kaplan, "Romancing the Empire: The Embodiment of American Masculinity in the Popular Historical Novel of the 1890s," *American Literary History* 2.4 (Winter 1990): 660, 671.

24. For example, Mary Hartwell Catherwood, whose 1870s local color stories of the Great Lakes were later collected in *The Queen of the Swamp and Other Plain Americans* (1899), had long since turned to historical fiction set in eighteenth-century Québec by the time the volume appeared. A frequent contributor to the *Atlantic* during the 1890s, her works published there include a novel, *The Lady of Fort St. John* (July-November 1891), and fifteen other pieces published between 1893 and 1899.

25. *Letters of Henry James*, ed. Leon Edel (Cambridge, Mass.: Belknap Press of Harvard University Press, 1984), 4:222–23. The "other Mary" may be Mary N. Murfree, who had written a series of Southern historical romances, including one called *The Story of Old Fort Loudon* (1899).

26. *Letters of Henry James*, 4:209; italics are James's.

27. Garland, *Crumbling Idols*, 65, 62. Everett Carter in *Howells and the Age of Realism* (Philadelphia: Lippincott, 1954) notes that impressionism was "a key word in Howells' critical vocabulary from the very beginning" (136), a preoccupation Howells shared with Garland and, in practice, with Crane. Though Norris's style is rarely impressionistic, Norris approved of impressionism in theory, referring to it as one technique in the quest for truth: "It is truth that matters, and the point is whether the daubs of pea-green will look like horseflesh and the mouth-filling words create the impression of actual battle" ("A Problem in Fiction: Truth Versus Accuracy," *Boston Evening Transcript*, 6 November 1901; reprinted in *Literary Criticism of Frank Norris*, 58).

28. Eggleston, preface to *Hoosier Schoolmaster*, 6.

29. Frank Norris, "The Great American Novelist," syndicated 19 January 1903; reprinted in *Literary Criticism of Frank Norris*, 123.

30. Warner, "Editor's Study," *Harper's Monthly* 86 (December 1892): 150.

31. William Dean Howells, "The Future of the American Novel," *Harper's Monthly* (March 1912); reprinted in *Criticism and Fiction*, 348, 347.

32. In his Editor's Study column for November 1891, Howells had similarly identified "two tendencies, apparently opposite, but probably parallel: one a tendency toward an elegance refined and polished, both in thought and phrase, almost to tenuity; the other a tendency to grotesqueness, wild and extravagant, to the point of anarchy"; Longfellow exemplified the first and Whitman the second (*W. D. Howells as Critic*, 210).

33. According to Allen, the Masculine Principle "is bent upon treating its subjects rather in the rough natural mass . . . instead of stretching each particular atom on a graceful rack of psychological confession, and bending the ear close to catch the last faint whispers of its excruciating and moribund self-consciousness" (440).

34. In *The Literary Criticism of Frank Norris*, Donald Pizer explains that Norris believed "that the conquest of the West was the most recent forward thrust of the 'long march'" or triumphant westward expansion of the Anglo-Saxon race (100). One of Norris's more alarming ideas, the racial chauvinism that accepted Anglo-Saxon superiority as biological and historical destiny was shared by many at this time, including Jack London.

35. For an account of Norris's work for the *Wave* and a complete listing of his pieces for that periodical, see Joseph R. McElrath Jr.'s introduction to his definitive *Frank Norris and "The Wave": A Bibliography* (New York: Garland, 1988).

36. In the introduction to the Virginia edition of *Maggie*, James B. Colvert says that Crane "apparently took over, point by point, the artistic credo of the hero of the novel [*The Light That Failed*], Dick Heldar" (xlvii). Crane himself later renounced his "clever, Rudyard-Kipling style" (*Stephen Crane: Letters*, 32) but not necessarily the ideas. Donald Pizer makes a similar point about Norris in his introduction to *The Literary Criticism of Frank Norris* (20–23). In his essays, Norris consistently uses Kipling as an exemplary model of style and vigor. London's letters are filled with admiring references to Kipling's work; for London, Kipling "touches the soul of things. 'He draws that Thing as he sees it for the God of Things as they Are,'" a line from Kipling's "When Earth's Last Picture Is Painted" (1892) (*The Letters of Jack London*, ed. Earle Labor, Robert C. Leitz III, and I. Milo Shepard [Stanford, California: Stanford University Press, 1988], 1:52).

37. The same matter-of-fact tone occurs in Alexander Harvey's book *William Dean Howells: A Study of the Achievement of a Literary Artist* (1917; reprint, New York: Haskell House, 1972): "Unless we perceive clearly the reasons which have raised Howells to sovereignty over the sissy school of literature, the dominant American one, we shall miss the point of his distinction between the romanticist and the realist" (184). The "sissy school" of realism reflects a feminine "attitude of receptivity" that reflects things as they are, whereas "[t]he novelist whose genius happens to be masculine will never submit to the trammels of such a female conception of his function. He will inevitably stamp himself upon the wax of life in patterns of his own temperament . . ." (184–85). Harvey's explanation of the difference between realism and romance sounds much like Norris's.

38. Atherton, "Why Is American Literature Bourgeois?" 781.

39. Matthews, "In Search of Local Color," *Harper's Monthly* 89:33–40. References have been cited parenthetically in the text. Riis, *How the Other Half Lives* (New York: Scribner's, 1890), xxx; London, "Local Color," in *Moon-Face, and Other Stories* (New York: Grosset and Dunlap, 1906), 41, 55. In addition to criticism and plays, Matthews wrote three collections of stories set in New York City: *Vignettes of Manhattan* (1894), *Outlines in Local Color* (1898), and *Vistas of New York* (1912).

40. Allen, "Two Principles in Recent American Fiction," 438; Atherton, "Why Is American Literature Bourgeois?" 781. A variation on this metaphoric usage is S. Weir Mitchell's 1887 complaint that "the monthly magazines are getting so lady-like that they will soon menstruate," quoted by Elaine Showalter in *Sexual Anarchy: Gender and Culture at the Fin de Siècle* (New York: Penguin Books, 1990), 77.

41. London, *Letters of Jack London*, 2:675.

42. Norris, "An Opening for Novelists: Great Opportunities for Fiction Writers in San Francisco," *Wave* 16 (22 May 1897); reprinted in *Literary Criticism of Frank Norris*, 30.

43. London, *Letters of Jack London*, 1:52, 60.

44. R. W. Stallman and Lillian Gilkes suggest that Crane later revised *Maggie* under the influence of Howells's and Garland's "literary creed" (*Stephen Crane: Letters*, ed. R. W. Stallman and Lillian Gilkes [New York: New York University Press, 1960], 16). According to Stanley Wertheim and Paul Sorrentino in *The Crane Log: A Documentary Life of Stephen Crane 1871–1900* (New York: G. K. Hall, 1994), "Crane [brought] the manuscript of *Maggie* with [Hamlin] Garland's letter of recommendation to Richard Watson Gilder, who reject[ed] it for publication in the *Century*" (82). In Thomas Beer's lively if probably apocryphal report of Crane's account, "Gilder sat pointing out excessive adjectives and slaughtered infinitives to the shy boy [Crane], who finally cut him short with an untactful question: 'You mean that the story's too honest?'" (*Stephen Crane: A Study in American Letters* [New York: Knopf, 1926], 86). For an account of the strengths and weaknesses of all four Crane biographers, see Wertheim and Sorrentino's introduction to *The Crane Log* and also John Clendenning's "Stephen Crane and His Biographers: Beer, Berryman, Schoberlin, and Stallman" (*American Literary Realism* 28.1 [Fall 1995]: 23–57).

45. Quoted in Wertheim and Sorrentino, *Stephen Crane Log*, 215. A fuller explanation of Gilder and his editorial policies appears in Arthur John's *Best Years of the Century: Richard Watson Gilder, Scribner's Monthly, and Century Magazine, 1870–1909* (Urbana: University of Illinois Press, 1981).

46. Crane, *Correspondence of Stephen Crane*, 1:63.

47. John, *Best Years of the* Century, 236, 253.

48. At the Lantern Club dinner for Crane on 7 April 1896, Howells was the principal speaker. According to the account of the dinner in the next day's *New York Sun*, "Mr. Howells spoke of the future of American literature, which he thought was bright. He said that he had critically compared the works of Miss Jewett and Miss Wilkins with the productions of the famous authors of other countries, and that the American Stories did not suffer by the comparison. Mr. Crane had taken the right course in looking at and describing men and things as they are" (Wertheim and Sorrentino, *Stephen Crane Log*, 178).

49. *Ev'ry Month* (September 1896): 23. In *Two Dreisers*, Ellen Moers says that "Dreiser went out of his way to compare Crane unfavorably to the New England local colorist Mary Wilkins Freeman" (36). It is difficult to say why Freeman was discussed by these writers when Jewett, for example, receives no mention at all. Freeman may have maintained a more public profile, as publicity stunts like her participation in the writing contest would suggest (see note 54, below). An interesting sidelight is that Freeman was one of the artists who supported Dreiser in his fight to keep *The Genius* from being suppressed in 1915.

50. Dreiser, *Letters of Theodore Dreiser: A Selection*, ed. Robert H. Elias (Philadelphia: University of Pennsylvania Press, 1959), 1:95, 185–86.

51. In a letter to Cloudsley Johns dated 16 February 1900, London writes, "You remember Edith Wharton's 'Tragedy of the Muse'? It is the first of a collection of

eight stories under the title *The Greater Inclination*. And they are all as good" (*Letters*, 1:157). For an account of London's reading later in life, see David Hamilton, *"The Tools of My Trade": The Annotated Books in Jack London's Library* (Seattle: University of Washington Press, 1986).

52. Norris, *The Letters of Frank Norris*, ed. Franklin Walker (San Francisco: Book Club of California, 1956), 77.

53. Norris, "An American School of Fiction? A Denial," *Boston Evening Transcript*, 22 January 1902; reprinted in *Literary Criticism of Frank Norris*, 109–10.

54. In *Mary Wilkins Freeman* (Boston: Twayne, 1988), Perry Westbrook confirms Freeman's chronic need of money. He also tells of a contest that would have interested Norris (who died in 1902): In 1907 the New York *Herald* promoted a writing contest in which Freeman was to write a "realistic tale of New England" and her competitor, the English author Max Pemberton, was to write a "swashbuckling romance of Old England" (118). According to Westbrook, "The readers were invited to vote each week on their preference, using ballots printed in the newspaper." Spurred on by the $5,000 prize, which she badly needed, Freeman won for *The Shoulders of Atlas*, which Westbrook describes as having a genuinely realistic tone, a final chapter with "multiple weddings," and a melodramatic plot (118).

55. Norris, "The Great American Novelist," syndicated 19 January 1903; reprinted in *Literary Criticism of Frank Norris*, 124; "A Plea for Romantic Fiction," 76.

56. Norris, *Letters of Frank Norris*, 30, 23, 48. Norris here uses *romanticism* in its conventional sense, though he customarily finds naturalism to be a part of romanticism. According to Donald Pizer in *The Literary Criticism of Frank Norris*, Norris posits realism and romanticism as antitheses, with naturalism as the synthesis.

57. Ernest Marchand, *Frank Norris: A Study* (New York: Octagon Books, 1971), 205–6; Howells, *Criticism and Fiction*, 282.

58. Donald Pizer, *The Novels of Frank Norris* (New York: Haskell House, 1973), 74; Charles Child Walcutt, *American Literary Naturalism: A Divided Stream* (Minneapolis: University of Minnesota Press, 1956), 129. In "The Old Folks of *McTeague*," William B. Dillingham summarizes these views as follows: "Ernest Marchand . . . feels that Norris's 'pattern' of naturalism is somewhat broken by the sentimental love story of old Grannis and Miss Baker. . . .' Grant C. Knight writes that 'the story of Old Grannis and Miss Baker is pure Dickens,' and . . . concludes that it is probably 'intended to be comic relief,' . . . Richard Chase dismisses the old lovers as 'absurd,' and their story is a 'romantic flaw' in the novel according to [Robert Spiller's] *Literary History of the United States*" (in Frank Norris, *McTeague: A Story of San Francisco*, ed. Donald Pizer [New York: Norton, 1977], 345, 347). Joseph R. McElrath Jr. carries this concept a step further in "The Comedy of Frank Norris's *McTeague*" (*Studies in American Humor* 2 [October 1975]: 88–95), arguing that Grannis and Baker are part of a larger comic pattern, one of the "comical-sentimental episodes" (95) which help to establish the first half of *McTeague* as "vaudevillian in spirit" (93) and "an extended joke" (94).

59. George Spangler, "The Structure of *McTeague*," *English Studies* 59 (February 1978): 48–56; reprinted in Graham, *Critical Essays on Frank Norris*, 88–98. In "Frank

Norris's *McTeague*: A Possible Source in H. C. Bunner," *Nineteenth-Century Fiction* 25 (March 1971): 474–78, James B. Stronks notes parallels between this plot and H. C. Bunner's 1890 story "The Love-Letters of Smith," although he does not claim that Norris read that work.

60. In "'Keeping Company' with the Old Folks: Unravelling the Edges of *McTeague*'s Deterministic Fabric," *American Literary Realism* 25.2 (Winter 1993): 46–55, Leonard Cassuto argues that the story provides "another voice, one of romance, individuality, self-assertion, possibility" (51) with which to counter the prevailing determinism of the work.

61. McElrath notes the Freeman-Norris connection in passing, commenting that "Grannis and Baker step from a Mary E. Wilkins Freeman tale into *McTeague* to flutter timidly through an unlikely courtship" ("Comedy of Frank Norris's *McTeague*," 92). Because of his focus on the novel's overall comic elements, McElrath understandably does not develop this connection.

62. Mary E. Wilkins Freeman, "Two Old Lovers," in *Selected Stories*, 7. Subsequent references will be cited parenthetically in the text.

63. Norris, *McTeague*, in *Frank Norris: Novels and Essays*, ed. Donald Pizer (New York: Library Classics of the United States, 1986), 273. Subsequent references will be cited parenthetically in the text.

64. Barbara Hochman, *The Art of Frank Norris, Storyteller* (Columbia: University of Missouri Press, 1988), 21.

65. Don Graham, *The Fiction of Frank Norris: The Aesthetic Context* (Columbia: University of Missouri Press, 1978), 50.

66. Hochman, *Art of Frank Norris*, 68.

67. William Cain, "Presence and Power in *McTeague*," in Sundquist, *American Realism*, 202.

68. Though Miss Baker nurses Trina through the fever that follows her discovery of Maria Macapa's body, the old people have no further substantive role in the novel.

69. Donald Pizer makes this identification, calling it one of Norris's jokes within the novel (*McTeague* [New York: Norton, 1977], 215n).

4   Frederic, Norris, and the Fear of Effeminacy

1. James Lane Allen, "Two Principles in Recent American Fiction," *Atlantic Monthly* 80 (October 1897): 440.

2. With the sinuous black-and-white drawings of its art editor, Aubrey Beardsley, John Lane's Bodley Head journal the *Yellow Book* (1894–1897) exemplified the artistic sensibility of the Decadents, although it also printed stories by more mainstream (realistic) writers like Henry James, Arnold Bennett, and Edmund Gosse. When Les Jeunes, a group of San Francisco writers led by Gelett Burgess, began publishing the *Lark* in the mid-1890s, the magazine was regarded as an irreverent American answer to the occasionally precious pieces in the *Yellow Book*. For an examination of Norris's connection with this movement, see Sherwood

Williams, "The Rise of a New Degeneration: Decadence and Atavism in *Vandover and the Brute*," *ELH* 57 (1990): 709–36.

3. For the social and historical construction of the masculinity crisis, see Peter Filene, *Him/Her/Self: Sex Roles in Modern America*, 2d ed. (Baltimore: Johns Hopkins University Press, 1986); Mark C. Carnes and Clyde Griffen, eds., *Meanings for Manhood: Constructions of Masculinity in Victorian America* (Chicago: University of Chicago Press, 1990); T. J. Jackson Lears, *No Place of Grace: Antimodernism and the Transformation of American Culture, 1880–1920* (1981; reprint, Chicago: University of Chicago Press, 1994); and Lutz, *American Nervousness, 1903*.

For the effects of this crisis on writers of the time, see especially David Leverenz, "The Last Real Man in America: From Natty Bumppo to Batman," *American Literary History* 3 (Winter 1991): 753–81; Ziff, *American 1890s*; and Kaplan, "Romancing the Empire." Daniel Borus's *Writing Realism* and Christopher Wilson's *Labor of Words* address the implications of the construction of masculinity and the profession of authorship.

4. *Theodore Roosevelt Cyclopedia*, s.v. "Mollycoddles" (New York: Theodore Roosevelt Memorial Association, 1941), 346.

5. Lutz, *American Nervousness, 1903*, 81–82.

6. Philip Rahv, "Paleface and Redskin," in *Image and Idea: Fourteen Essays on Literary Themes* (1949; reprint, Westport, Conn.: Greenwood Press, 1978), 2.

7. Rahv, "Paleface and Redskin," 3.

8. Gelett Burgess, "The Ballad of the Effeminates," *Lark* (November 1896): n.p.

9. Allen, "Two Principles in Recent American Fiction," 438.

10. Frank Norris, "An Opening for Novelists: Great Opportunities for Fiction Writers in San Francisco," *Wave* 16 (22 May 1897); reprinted in *Literary Criticism of Frank Norris*, 30.

11. "We have divided men into Red-bloods and Mollycoddles" (180). From G. Lowes Dickinson, "Red-bloods and Mollycoddles," in *Appearances: Notes of Travel, East and West* (Garden City, N.Y.: Doubleday, Page, 1914).

12. Quoted in Ziff, *American 1890s*, 220.

13. Ibid.

14. James R. Giles, "Beneficial Atavism in Frank Norris and Jack London," *Western American Literature* 4 (Spring 1969): 15.

15. Kaplan, "Romancing the Empire," 664.

16. As Kaplan notes, "Writers such as Frank Norris represented a historically changing construction of masculinity as no change at all but the return to a mythical [Anglo-Saxon] origin" ("Romancing the Empire," 664). For Kaplan, the redemptive process exists less in the remasculinizing activities of empire than in the spectacle that such activities engender, notably in audiences such as the New Woman and the "domestic audience—the jingo" (678).

17. London, *Letters of Jack London*, 1:337–38; punctuation is London's.

18. The connection between "excessive" civilization and the degeneracy of not merely individual men but of "native" (i.e., Caucasian) American stock was an early concern of the eugenics movement. As Newman notes in *Men's Ideas/Women's*

Realities, writers in *Popular Science Monthly* and other periodicals in the 1890s and early 1900s blamed the overcivilized (overeducated) woman for the declining birth rate and its threats of "race suicide." In "Plain Words on the Woman Question" (1889), Grant Allen, popular and controversial author of *The Woman Who Did*, writes, "there is a danger that many of the most cultivated and able families of the English-speaking race will have become extinct, through the prime error of supposing that an education which is good for men must also be good for women" (in Newman, 131).

19. According to Austin Briggs, "It is common in speaking of Theron Ware's illumination to say that he is exposed to the new, to the new science of Dr. Ledsmar, the new theology of Father Forbes, and the new hedonism of Celia Madden, the New Woman" (*The Novels of Harold Frederic* [Ithaca: Cornell University Press, 1969], 128).

20. In "Fakes and Good Frauds: Pragmatic Religion in *The Damnation of Theron Ware*," *American Literary Realism* 15 (Spring 1982): 74–85, Patrick K. Dooley argues that Frederic explores William James's pragmatism. Because "the truth of religion and religious belief is its beneficial consequences and valuable effects" (75), Frederic presents Theron and the Soulsbys as characters who "go on believing a lie" (82).

21. See, for example, Samuel Coale, "Frederic and Hawthorne: The Romantic Roots of Naturalism," *American Literature* 48.1 (March 1976): 29–45; George W. Johnson, "Harold Frederic's Young Goodman Ware: The Ambiguities of a Realistic Romance," *Modern Fiction Studies* 8 (Winter 1962): 361–74; and Joan Zlotnick, "*The Damnation of Theron Ware*, with a Backward Glance at Hawthorne," *Markham Review* 2 (February 1971): 90–92.

22. Ann Douglas, *The Feminization of American Culture* (New York: Knopf, 1977), 114–15.

23. Lisa MacFarlane, "Resurrecting Man: Desire and *The Damnation of Theron Ware*," *Studies in American Fiction* 20 (1992): 129. For a further discussion of gender roles, see Fritz Oehlschlaeger, "Passion, Authority, and Faith in *The Damnation of Theron Ware*," *American Literature* 58 (May 1986): 238–55; and Steven Carter, "'The Field Is the Only Reality': *The Damnation of Theron Ware* and a Physics of Interpretation," *American Literary Realism* 20.2 (Winter 1988): 43–64. Carter argues that, in keeping with the physics of relativism operating in the novel, Theron does not become progressively effeminized but rather "vacillat[es] between feminine and masculine stances" (56), becoming on occasion "hard and masculine" (56) with Alice after he has been yielding with Father Forbes. Whereas Carter believes that Theron wavers between masculinity and femininity, Oehlschlaeger goes further, stating that "Theron becomes progressively effeminized throughout the novel" (244).

24. Harold Frederic, *The Damnation of Theron Ware* (1896; reprint, New York: Riverside, 1960), 11. Subsequent references are to this edition and will be cited parenthetically within the text.

25. Lutz, *American Nervousness, 1903*, 22.

26. Eugene Taylor, *William James on Exceptional Mental States: The 1896 Lowell Lectures* (New York: Scribner's, 1983), 133; Lutz, *American Nervousness, 1903*, 31.

27. Bowlby, *Just Looking*, 20.

28. George Spangler, "Theron Ware and the Perils of Relativism," *Canadian Review of American Studies* 5 (Spring 1974): 38.

29. MacFarlane, "Resurrecting Man," 135.

30. Cooke, *How Celia Changed Her Mind*, 146.

31. In "The Nude and the Madonna in *The Damnation of Theron Ware*," *American Literature* 45 (November 1973): 379-89, John W. Crowley argues that Theron experiences an "overt, childish attachment to the madonna" (Alice) and a "covert, guilty attraction to the nude" (Celia); here, Theron's reaction to Celia's arms illustrates Crowley's point (379).

32. John Henry Raleigh summarizes these ideas in the introduction to *The Damnation of Theron Ware*. See also Robert Myers, *Reluctant Expatriate: The Life of Harold Frederic* (Westport, Conn.: Greenwood Press, 1994), which provides useful information on Frederic's sources.

33. Glenn Hendler's comment on sentimental narratives sheds light on this aspect of the novel: "sentimental narratives do not just describe or display sympathetic identification; they attempt to produce it in their audience, to perform it" ("The Limits of Sympathy: Louisa May Alcott and the Sentimental Novel," *American Literary History* 3 [1991]: 686).

34. Sydney Krause remarks "that an American should . . . have to resign himself to salesmanship, politics, the human void, is more than deprivation of his faculty for renewal. For him to throw away his Emersonian birthright of an original relationship to life is to accept a failure of historical magnitude" ("Harold Frederic and the Failure Motif," *Studies in American Fiction* 15 [Spring 1987]: 66).

35. In his account of the novel's creation, Stanton Garner identifies this as Frederic's original plan. For this and other details see Garner's "History of the Text" in *The Damnation of Theron Ware, or, Illumination*, vol. 3 of the Harold Frederic Edition (Lincoln: University of Nebraska Press, 1985), 353-415.

36. Luther S. Luedtke, for example, claims that "Sister Soulsby doomed Theron to a future of venery without love and opportunism without hope" ("Harold Frederic's Satanic Soulsby: Interpretation and Sources," *Nineteenth-Century Fiction* 30 [June 1975]: 98).

37. Frank Norris, *Vandover and the Brute*, 1914; reprinted in *A Novelist in the Making: A Collection of Student Themes and the Novels* Blix *and* Vandover and the Brute, ed. James D. Hart (Cambridge, Mass.: Belknap Press of Harvard University Press, 1970), 437, 471. Subsequent references are to this edition and will be cited parenthetically in the text. Don Graham identifies the opera as *Faust* (*Fiction of Frank Norris*, 18).

38. Donald Pizer identifies this as paresis, a stage of the syphilis Vandover has contracted from Flossie. He suggests that Norris uses the symptoms of paresis, or general paralysis, because "[i]n the late nineteenth century . . . though syphilis was often mentioned as a possible cause, it was more commonly

believed that intemperate sexual and drinking habits were the primary causes" (*Novels of Frank Norris*, 36).

39. The possibility exists that Norris, who studied writing at Harvard under Lewis Gates during the 1894–1895 school year, might either have heard James lecture or have heard his theories discussed, since, according to Eugene Taylor, James taught courses in mental pathology every year from 1893–1894 to 1898 (Taylor, *William James on Exceptional Mental States*, 3).

40. The *Boston Evening Transcript:* "And *The Lark*! You will wonder how you lived without it. It's the most excellent fooling for many years. And it's better than fooling, as all truly excellent fooling must be." Cited in the promotional insert "A Transcontinental Criticism: The Geography of Appreciation" included with the *Lark* (n.p., n.d.).

41. Norris, "An Opening for Novelists," 30.

42. Ibid. In *Frank Norris Revisited* (New York: Twayne, 1992), Joseph R. McElrath Jr. suggests that "Norris is likely to have suffered something akin to a nervous breakdown during the early spring of 1897" just before this attack on Les Jeunes (14).

43. Joseph McElrath Jr., "Frank Norris's *Vandover and the Brute*: Narrative Technique and the Socio-Critical Viewpoint," *Studies in American Fiction* 4 (Spring 1976): 27–43; reprinted in Graham, *Critical Essays on Frank Norris*. Charles Child Walcutt argues this viewpoint in *American Literary Naturalism*, and Donald Pizer comes to nearly the same conclusion when he finds fault with the naturalistic "constant analysis of the struggle in Vandover between his better and his brute nature" (*Novels of Frank Norris*, 48).

44. Mitchell, *Determined Fictions*, 85.

45. Pizer, *Novels of Frank Norris*, 43.

46. Graham, *Fiction of Frank Norris*, 27.

47. In Stanley Cooperman's terms, his lycanthropy is his "werewolf of guilt" ("Frank Norris and the Werewolf of Guilt," *Modern Language Quarterly* 20 [1959]: 252–58).

48. McElrath, "Frank Norris's *Vandover and the Brute*," 190.

49. Pizer, *Novels of Frank Norris*, 43. In analyzing the decor of these rooms for *The Fiction of Frank Norris*, Don Graham exposes Vandover's imitative tastes in art, finding additionally that the shrinking space of the novel's "declension of houses" serves as a metaphor for Vandover's diminishing possibilities until he is literally stuck in a cupboard under the sink in Geary's cottage (41).

50. Hochman, *Art of Frank Norris*, 46.

51. Taylor, *William James on Exceptional Mental States*, 133, 136, 134, 145.

52. Ibid., 135.

53. Walter Benn Michaels, *The Gold Standard and the Logic of Naturalism: American Literature at the Turn of the Century* (Berkeley: University of California Press, 1987), 168.

54. Ibid., 168.

55. Both quotations are from Taylor, *William James on Exceptional Mental States*, 154, 155.

56. William Dillingham, in *Frank Norris: Instinct and Art* (Lincoln: University of Nebraska Press, 1969), has shown that this work derives from French academic painters like Gérôme, who favored "preciseness of detail and . . . a moral or story" as well as "subdued colors" (18).

57. Graham, *Fiction of Frank Norris*, 25.

58. Ibid., 29.

59. Norris, "Why Women Should Write the Best Novels: And Why They Don't," in *Literary Criticism of Frank Norris*, 36.

60. William James, *The Will to Believe*, quoted in Taylor, *William James on Exceptional Mental States*, 139.

5 Dreiser, London, Crane, and the Iron Madonna

1. June Howard demonstrates that within some of these novels the theme of proletarianization, or the fear that one may descend as well as ascend the socioeconomic scale, prevents the reader from assuming that a safe distance exists between himself and the characters being studied: "The gesture of exclusion reinforces the antinomy between human and brute without rendering the image of the brute any less potent, and the assertion of superiority always inscribes a doubt: 'that isn't me (is it?) — that couldn't happen to me (could it?)'" (*Form and History in American Literary Naturalism*, 101).

2. Norris, "Frank Norris' Weekly Letter," *Chicago American*, 3 August 1901; reprinted in *Literary Criticism of Frank Norris*, 75.

3. "A Plea for Romantic Fiction," 77. Norris considered naturalism to be a form of Romance, and he frequently used the terms interchangeably.

4. See, for example, Elaine Showalter, "Syphilis, Sexuality, and the Fiction of the Fin de Siècle" in Ruth Bernard Yeazell, *Sex, Politics, and Science in the Nineteenth-Century Novel* (Baltimore: Johns Hopkins University Press, 1986).

5. Laura Hapke, *Girls Who Went Wrong: Prostitutes in American Fiction, 1885–1917* (Bowling Green, Ohio: Bowling Green State University Press, 1989), 20.

6. Carol Hurd Green, "Stephen Crane and the Fallen Women," in *American Novelists Revisited: Essays in Feminist Criticism*, ed. Fritz Fleischmann (Boston: G. K. Hall, 1982), 234.

7. Wai-Chee Dimock, "'Debasing Exchange': Edith Wharton's *The House of Mirth*," *PMLA* 100 (October 1985): 783–92; reprinted in Harold Bloom, *Edith Wharton*, Modern Critical Views (New York: Chelsea House, 1986), 124.

8. Nell Kimball and "Madeleine" both comment on their customers' interest in this question. Another such source is a collection of letters from a former prostitute, edited and collected by Ruth Rosen and Sue Davidson as *The Maimie Papers* (Old Westbury, N.Y.: Feminist Press, 1977).

9. According to Barbara Meil Hobson's *Uneasy Virtue: The Politics of Prostitution and the American Reform Tradition* (New York: Basic Books, 1987), "One estimate . . . has set the published material on prostitution at one billion pages during this period" (140). In *The Response to Prostitution in the Progressive Era* (Chapel Hill: University of North Carolina Press, 1980), Mark Connelly describes

the basic plot of the white slave narrative: "Typically, a chaste and comely native American country girl would forsake her idyllic country home and family for the promise of the city. On the way, or shortly after arrival, she would fall victim to one of the swarm of panders. . . . Using one of his vast array of tricks—a promise of marriage, an offer to assist in securing lodging, or, if these were to no avail, the chloroformed cloth, the hypodermic needle, or the drugged drink—the insidious white slaver would brutally seduce the girl and install her in a brothel, where she became an enslaved prostitute" (116). Describing the narratives as fulfilling a psychological need much as the Indian captivity narratives had done, Connelly sees the movement as embodying the nation's "ethnocentrism" and nativist fears, its "conspiratorial mentality," and the "illogic . . . and authoritarianism of the Prohibitionist crusade" (134). In *The Lost Sisterhood: Prostitution in America, 1900-1918* (Baltimore: Johns Hopkins University Press, 1982), Ruth Rosen gives much greater credence to the threat posed by the white slave trade. For an examination of these themes in fiction, see Laura Hapke's *Girls Who Went Wrong*.

10. *Madeleine: An Autobiography,* (1919; reprint, New York: Persea Books, 1986), 45; italics in original. The "dissection" of the female body resonates in texts of the period. In "Statistical Persons" (*Diacritics* 17 [1987]: 83-98), Mark Seltzer comments that the realist project of embodiment "of turning the body inside out for inspection, takes a virtually *obstetrical* form in realist discourse" (84; italics Seltzer's) and finds the "body of the monstrously productive mother" a central figure for the slums that becomes "a visual and corporeal model of the social" (87). See also chapter 3 ("A Woman's Case") of *Sexual Anarchy*, in which Elaine Showalter argues that men "open up a woman as a substitute for self-knowledge, both maintaining the illusion of their own invulnerability and destroying the terrifying female reminder of their impotence and uncertainty" (134).

11. David Graham Phillips, *Susan Lenox: Her Fall and Rise* (1917; reprint, 2 vols., Upper Saddle River, N.J.: Gregg Press, 1968), 2:260. Subsequent references will be cited in the text. The one-volume edition published by Southern Illinois Press in 1977 does not reproduce the full unexpurgated text.

12. The phrase is Nell Kimball's, from *Nell Kimball: Her Life as an American Madam,* ed. Stephen Longstreet (New York: Berkeley, 1970), 138.

13. Theodore Dreiser, *Jennie Gerhardt*, ed. James L. West III (New York: Penguin, 1992), 146; italics are Dreiser's. Subsequent references are to this edition and will be cited parenthetically within the text.

14. Carol Schwartz, "*Jennie Gerhardt*: Fairy Tale as Social Criticism," *American Literary Realism* 19.2 (Winter 1987): 17.

15. In his reading of *Jennie Gerhardt* in "Dreiser and the Naturalistic Drama of Consciousness" (*The Theory and Practice of American Literary Naturalism: Selected Essays and Reviews* [Carbondale: Southern Illinois University Press, 1993]), Donald Pizer demonstrates the ways in which Dreiser uses subtle shifts in perspective "as metaphorical reflections of distinctive states of mind, as moments in the drama of a consciousness rather than in generalized philosophical observations" (77). Dreiser's repetition, with variations, of the "good woman" idea suggests a similarly subtle representation of Lester's state of mind.

16. Stephen Crane, *Maggie: A Girl of the Streets*, ed. Thomas Gullason, Norton Critical Edition (New York: Norton, 1979), 20. Subsequent references are to this edition and will be cited parenthetically in the text.

17. Ibid., 21. Chester Wolford in *The Anger of Stephen Crane: Fiction and the Epic Tradition* (Lincoln: University of Nebraska Press, 1983) likens this scene to one of a perverse Ceres destroying the earth after Proserpina's loss (82).

18. Brander Matthews's "Before the Break of Day" (*Harper's New Monthly Magazine* 89 [July 1894]: 222–27), one of his "Vignettes of Manhattan," provides an interesting glimpse into a different possibility for Maggie Johnson. His heroine, Maggie O'Donnell, is also born in the Bowery; suffers beatings at the hands of her drunken parents; takes up with a petty criminal (Jim McDermott) and is consequently locked out despite her innocence; and is subsequently seduced and abandoned by him. Later married to saloon owner Terry O'Donnell, she exacts retribution when McDermott tries to rob the bar. When McDermott pulls a gun, she tells him to "shoot and be damned," and he does. Matthews allows the full drama of this moment to stand before adding that Maggie has received only a flesh wound in the arm.

19. Alan Robert Slotkin, *The Language of Stephen Crane's* Bowery Tales: *Developing Mastery of Character Diction* (New York: Garland, 1993), 44.

20. Hapke, *Girls Who Went Wrong*, 158.

21. Theodore Dreiser, *Sister Carrie*, ed. John C. Berkey, Alice M. Winters, James L. W. West III, and Neda M. Westlake (New York: Penguin, 1981), 192. Subsequent references to this edition will be made in the text.

22. Fisher, *Hard Facts*, 166–67. See also Barbara Hochman on Carrie's acting in "A Portrait of the Artist as a Young Actress: The Rewards of Representation in *Sister Carrie*," in *New Essays on* Sister Carrie, ed. Donald Pizer (Cambridge: Cambridge University Press, 1991). Hochman uses Walter Benjamin's figure of the storyteller to analyze the reciprocal nature of Carrie's (and Dreiser's) exchanges with the audience, finding that "Dreiser's process of composition, especially his involvement with others throughout, partially restored the rewards of the oral storyteller to the work of the latter-day novelist" (58).

23. As Walter Benn Michaels points out, "Selling 'sex attraction' to thousands instead of just one, Carrie leaves the restricted economy of the marriage market for the general economy of show business" ("The Contracted Heart," *New Literary History* 21 [Spring 1990]: 500).

24. The validity of Dreiser's account receives confirmation from an unexpected source. Speaking first of Paul Dreiser, Nell Kimball remarks: "He had a brother who became a writer too, under another name. In New Orleans 1912 some guest gave me one of the brother's books, *Sister Carry* [*sic*], and it was a dandy. The girl was real, for a man writer anyway. . . . I knew men like the saloon manager in the book, who ran off with the safe's money. And I could have been the girl, if I weren't a whore" (*Nell Kimball*, 113).

25. Louis Filler, *Voice of the Democracy: A Critical Biography of David Graham Phillips, Journalist, Novelist, Progressive* (University Park: Pennsylvania State University Press, 1978), 174.

26. Frank Norris, *Vandover and the Brute*, 455. Subsequent references will be cited parenthetically in the text.

27. London, *Letters of Jack London*, 1:263.

28. Jack London, *Martin Eden* (New York: Bantam, 1986), 6. Subsequent references are to this edition and will be cited parenthetically within the text.

29. Like Norris and others of his time, London viewed the Anglo-Saxon "race" as exemplifying the highest product of evolutionary perfection, as he explained to Cloudsley Johns in July 1899:

> [W]e are blind puppets at the play of great, unreasoning forces. . . . These forces generated the altruistic in man; the race with the highest altruism will endure—the highest altruism considered from the standpoint of merciless natural law. . . . The lesser breeds cannot endure. The Indian is an example, as is the black man of the Australian [*sic*] Bush, the South Sea Islander, the inhabitant of the Sub-Arctics, etc. [*Letters of Jack London*, 1:92]

The mixing of races (i.e., London's "Eurasian") was seen as often harmful in itself, especially when the stock of "lesser" races was improved at the expense of "superior" ones. "Lesser" meant "hot-blooded" races given to passion rather than, so the theory went, to reason like the altruistic, temperate Anglo-Saxons. Maria Macapa of *McTeague* is one such "degenerate" product, as is the vicious mixed-blood Spanish woman in Norris's "Case for Lombroso." An interest in "scientific" studies of physiognomy and in genetics gave rise to books like *Our Country: Its Possible Future and Its Present Crisis* (1885), in which the Reverend Josiah Strong "argued that native stock would be adversely affected if the genetic and moral effects of the foreign horde were not stopped in time" (Martha Banta, *Imaging American Women: Idea and Ideals in Cultural History* [New York: Columbia University Press, 1987], 117). Other works, including Joseph Simms's *Physiognomy Illustrated* (1891), V. G. Rocine's *Heads, Faces, Types, Races* (1910), and Henry Dwight Sedgwick's *New American Type and Other Essays* (1908), purported to demonstrate the superior beauty and intelligence of "Aryans."

30. In "Divided Self and World in *Martin Eden*," *Jack London Newsletter* 9 (September-December 1976): 118–26, George Spangler identifies a series of "binary pairs" that inform Martin's view of the world, a view that includes "Martin's tendency . . . to step back from himself, to observe from a corner of his mind some past, present or future image of self, i.e., to divide the self" (123).

31. The submission subplot here reverses Norris's in *Moran of the* Lady Letty. The "Viking goddess" Moran gives up her prodigious strength when Ross Wilbur wrestles her to a draw. Recognizing her love for him, she submits and becomes weak, thus setting the stage for her failure to fight back against the Chinese pirates that kill her. Writing to Cloudsley Johns on 30 April 1899, London approved of *Moran of the* Lady Letty, saying, "It's well done" (*Letters of Jack London*, 1:72).

32. The conflict within the novel has been interpreted variously. Maxwell Geismar sees the tension between George and his mother as a "tragic-comic oedipal love

relationship" resulting in George's self-destruction (*Rebels and Ancestors: The American Novel, 1890–1915* [Boston: Houghton Mifflin, 1953], 94), whereas Agnes Moreland Jackson finds the real source of conflict to be the battle Mrs. Kelcey wages and George loses against alcohol ("Stephen Crane's Imagery of Conflict in *George's Mother*," *American Quarterly* 25 [Winter 1969]: 313–18). Joseph X. Brennan defines the conflict more broadly, with George and his mother representing "larger opposed forces—the Church versus the city of Mammon, the old morality and conformity versus modern license and amorality"; he additionally shows how the pervasive battle imagery is really a "parody of medieval romance literature," specifically recalling the myth of St. George and the dragon ("The Imagery and Art of *George's Mother*," *CLA Journal* 4 [December 1960]: 106–15; reprinted in Wertheim, *The Merrill Studies in* Maggie *and* George's Mother [Columbus, Ohio: Merrill, 1970], 126, 127). In terms of literary sources, Eric Solomon reads *George's Mother* as a parody of temperance tracts, such as those Crane's father wrote, and of Horatio Alger stories (*Stephen Crane: From Parody to Realism* [Cambridge, Mass.: Harvard University Press, 1966]). Finding a source within the text itself, Brenda Murphy identifies the Isaac Watts hymn "Holy Fortitude; or, The Christian Soldier" that Mrs. Kelcey sings in chapter 2 as a commentary on the action of the story. Murphy's thesis depends on an acceptance of Watts's line "Thy saints, in all this glorious war, / Shall conquer, though they die" as confirmation of Mrs. Kelcey's victory over George ("A Woman with Weapons: The Victor in *George's Mother*," *Modern Language Studies* 11.2 [Spring 1981]: 88–93).

33. James B. Colvert, introduction to *George's Mother*, by Stephen Crane, in *Bowery Tales: Maggie/George's Mother*, ed. Fredson Bowers (Charlottesville: University of Virginia Press, 1969), 103, 104.

34. Stephen Crane, *George's Mother* in *Bowery Tales: Maggie/George's Mother*, ed. Fredson Bowers (Charlottesville: University of Virginia Press, 1969), 128, 124. Subsequent references are to this edition and will be cited parenthetically in the text.

35. Mark C. Carnes, "Middle-Class Men and the Solace of Fraternal Ritual," in *Meanings for Manhood: Constructions of Masculinity in Victorian America*, ed. Mark C. Carnes and Clyde Griffen (Chicago: University of Chicago Press, 1990), 38, 42, 43, 45, 47–48.

36. In his unsympathetic interpretation of Mrs. Kelcey in *A Reading of Stephen Crane* (Oxford: Clarendon Press, 1971), Marston La France argues that "for George and his mother the saloon and church represent futile retreats from reality . . . [and] Mrs. Kelcey is as personally dishonest, as wilful in her withdrawal from reality, as George is. She deliberately refuses to accept what her eyes reveal to her because she knows that her vain and lazy son is no king among men, that if her dreams of his greatness were 'worded, they would be ridiculous.' . . . She refuses to see what everyone else in the tenement sees, that she has 'a wild son'" (91).

37. Solomon, *Stephen Crane*, 177.

38. Thomas Gullason, "The Symbolic Unity of 'The Monster,'" *Modern Language Notes* 75 (December 1960): 663.

39. J. C. Levenson, introduction to "The Monster," in *Tales of Whilomville*, ed. Fredson Bowers, vol. 7 of *The Works of Stephen Crane* (Charlottesville: University of Virginia Press, 1969), xv.

40. Frank Norris, "Zola as a Romantic Writer," *Wave* 15 (27 June 1896); reprinted in *The Literary Criticism of Frank Norris*, 72.

41. Stephen Crane, "The Monster" in *Tales of Whilomville*, ed. Fredson Bowers, vol. 7 of *The Works of Stephen Crane* (Charlottesville: University of Virginia Press, 1969), 7–67. Subsequent references are to this edition and will be cited parenthetically within the text.

42. Solomon, *Stephen Crane*, 183.

43. See especially Michael Fried's careful if controversial reading of this section in *Realism, Writing, Disfiguration: On Thomas Eakins and Stephen Crane* (Chicago: University of Chicago Press, 1987).

44. The brusque, telegraphic language here recalls that of the doctor in *George's Mother*, another man whose "knowledgeable" advice is worthless: "'Can't tell,' he said. 'She's wonderful woman! Got more vitality than you and I together! Can't tell! May—may not! Good-day! Back in two hours!'" (176).

45. James Halfley, "'The Monster' and the Art of Stephen Crane," *Accent* 19 (Summer 1959): 159–65; reprinted in Thomas A. Gullason, *Stephen Crane's Career: Perspectives and Evaluations* (New York: New York University Press, 1972), 444.

46. In "Face, Race, and Disfiguration in Stephen Crane's *The Monster*" (*Critical Inquiry* 17.1 [Fall 1990]: 174–92), Lee Clark Mitchell observes that Martha's sympathy stems from "the dream of her pockmarked face of her dead fiancé. The psychology thereby revealed significantly links truth with disfigurement, morality with prosopopoeia, narrative with absence, all in a paradoxical convergence that constitutes the story's plot" (191).

47. Blaming the women for the men's own cowardly evasions rings a prophetic note. Beer reports that when Crane tried to publish "The Monster," Richard Watson Gilder turned it down for the *Century*, saying, "We couldn't publish that thing with half the expectant mothers in America on our subscription list" (Beer, *Stephen Crane*, 164).

48. Levenson, introduction to "The Monster," xv.

49. Oscar Wilde, *The Picture of Dorian Gray* (1891; reprint, Harmondsworth, England: Penguin, 1949), 5.

50. Fried sees this action as a figure for the reader's own impotence at the end, whereas Ronald K. Giles, in "Responding to Crane's 'The Monster'" (*South Atlantic Review* 57.2 [May 1992]: 45–55), views it as an affirmative analogue of Dr. Trescott's "exacting moral vision" (53).

6   Edith Wharton and the "Authoresses"

1. Edith Wharton, *A Backward Glance* (New York: Scribner's, 1934), 147. Subsequent references are to this edition and will be cited parenthetically in the text.

2. Lionel Trilling, "The Morality of Inertia," in *Great Moral Dilemmas in Literature, Past and Present*, ed. Robert MacIver (New York: Harper, 1956), 38.

3. Edith Wharton, *The Letters of Edith Wharton*, ed. R. W. B. Lewis and Nancy Lewis (New York: Macmillan [Collier Books], 1989), 91. Subsequent references will be cited parenthetically in the text.

4. Bernard De Voto, introduction to *Ethan Frome*, by Edith Wharton (New York: Scribner's, 1938); reprinted in Wharton, *Edith Wharton's* Ethan Frome, ed. Blake Nevius (New York: Scribner's, 1968), 92.

5. For example, in "Our Literary Aristocrat" (*Pacific Review*, June 1921; reprinted in *Edith Wharton: A Collection of Critical Essays*, ed. Irving Howe [Englewood Cliffs, N.J.: Prentice-Hall, 1962]), V. L. Parrington complains, "What do the van der Luydens [of *The Age of Innocence*] matter to us; or what did they or their kind matter a generation ago? Why waste such skill upon such insignificant material?" (152). In *On Native Grounds: An Interpretation of Modern American Prose Literature* (1942; reprint, New York: Harcourt Brace Jovanovich, 1970), Alfred Kazin criticizes Wharton more sweepingly, arguing that she was not a great artist because she could not stop telling her own story and "rise above the personal difficulties that attended her career" (77). Like Parrington, he faults her for writing about the destruction of old New York rather than what he considers a greater subject: the "emerging new class of brokers and industrialists . . . who were beginning to expropriate and supplant her own class" (81).

6. Several critics have placed Wharton in the context of local color and naturalism; the more recent of them appear in the body of this chapter. Of the earlier critics, Blake Nevius demonstrates that *The House of Mirth* is her most naturalistic novel, declaring that "Lily [Bart], in short, is as completely and typically the product of her heredity, environment, and the historical moment which found American materialism in the ascendant as the protagonist of any recognized naturalistic novel" (*Edith Wharton: A Study of Her Fiction* [Berkeley: University of California Press, 1953], 57). In "Life among the Ungentle Genteel: Edith Wharton's *The House of Mirth* Revisited" (*Western Humanities Review* 16 [Autumn 1962]: 371–74), Marie Bristol describes *The House of Mirth* as "not a novel of manners, nor a novel of naturalism, but both" (372). Along with *The House of Mirth*, Larry Rubin cites *The Custom of the Country*, *The Age of Innocence*, and *The Fruit of the Tree* as proof of Wharton's adoption of naturalistic conventions such as "sordidness of the spirit" (189), the "molding and determining forces of environment and heredity, the protagonist trapped and crushed by society, and an indifferent, apparently amoral universe" ("Aspects of Naturalism in Four Novels by Edith Wharton," *Twentieth-Century Literature* 2 [January 1957]: 186). Tracing Wharton's links to local color fiction in three of her unpublished New England novels, Nancy R. Leach argues that she "is certainly not a New England writer in the sense that Sarah Orne Jewett and Mary E. Wilkins Freeman are" ("New England in the Stories of Edith Wharton," *New England Quarterly* 30 [March 1957]: 95), concluding that her vision "can best be compared to Eugene O'Neill's" (97). More critical of Wharton's regional fiction than Leach, Abigail Ann Hamblen contends that "Edith Wharton's approach to the Massachusetts 'hill country' savors decidedly of the air of an aristocrat going slumming among the lower orders" ("Edith Wharton in New England," *New England Quarterly* 38 [June 1965]: 240). Alan Henry Rose shows that the "void" or "absence of experiential possibilities in Wharton's New England" prevents her characters from becoming initiated into

"a sound sense of self" ("'Such Depths of Sad Initiation': Edith Wharton and New England," *New England Quarterly* 50 [September 1977]: 424).

7. For a discussion of Ellen Glasgow as a naturalist, see Nancy A. Walker, "Women Writers and Literary Naturalism: The Case of Ellen Glasgow," *American Literary Realism* 18 (Spring-Autumn 1985): 133–46.

8. The plot bears marked similarities with that of Wharton's *Summer*, evoking another (worse) set of possibilities for Charity Royall.

9. Shirley Marchalonis, introduction to *Patrons and Protegées: Gender, Friendship, and Writing in Nineteenth-Century America* (New Brunswick, N.J.: Rutgers University Press, 1988), xi. In "The Traditions of Gender: Constance Fenimore Woolson and Henry James," another essay in the volume, Cheryl B. Torsney demonstrates that Constance Fenimore Woolson was not so fortunate in escaping the stereotype of being "the ash from which the Jamesian phoenix rises" (170). Early in her career, for example, Wharton suffered from her readers' readiness to see her as a less recondite shadow of Henry James who had but imperfectly learned the lessons of the Master; however, when she adopted the style and situation of James, as she did in *The Reef*, her work had a cool reception.

10. Amy Kaplan, *The Social Construction of American Realism* (Chicago: University of Chicago Press, 1988), 73, 71.

11. Ibid., 74.

12. Katherine Joslin, *Edith Wharton*, Women Writers Series (New York: St. Martin's Press, 1991), 39.

13. In *Edith Wharton's Letters from the Underworld: Fictions of Women and Writing* (Chapel Hill: University of North Carolina Press, 1991), Candace Waid suggests that throughout her life Wharton "made no distinctions between local colorists and sentimentalists" (8).

14. In *After the Fall*, Josephine Donovan prefaces her discussion of the mother-daughter estrangement theme in *Ethan Frome* by connecting it in passing with *The Country of the Pointed Firs*: "The barren, frozen world of Starkfield, an obviously symbolic name, could not be farther from the green-world bower of the local-color matriarchs. To read *Ethan Frome* in tandem with Jewett's *Country of the Pointed Firs* (1896) is to realize a study in contrast" (66).

15. Quoted by Millicent Bell in *Edith Wharton and Henry James: The Story of Their Friendship* (New York: George Braziller, 1965), 293.

16. Edith Wharton, "Mrs. Manstey's View," *Scribner's Magazine* 10 (1891): 117. Subsequent references are to this edition and will be cited parenthetically within the text. In *A Feast of Words: The Triumph of Edith Wharton* (New York: Oxford University Press, 1977), Cynthia Griffin Wolff observes that "Mrs. Manstey is revealed to us in a series of reductions" (65), a term that recalls Ann Douglas Wood's characterization of local color as a "literature of impoverishment."

17. R. W. B. Lewis, *Edith Wharton: A Biography* (New York: Harper and Row, 1975), 61; Barbara A. White, *Edith Wharton: A Study of the Short Fiction* (New York: Twayne, 1991), 33.

18. Gwen Nagel, "'This prim corner of land where she was queen': Sarah Orne Jewett's New England Gardens," *Colby Library Quarterly* 22 (March 1986): 43.

19. Examples of stories featuring women artists include Mary E. Wilkins Freeman's "A Poetess" and "A Village Singer" and Sarah Orne Jewett's *Country of the Pointed Firs*.

20. According to *The Oxford Companion to Classical Literature*, 2d ed., ed. M. C. Howatson (New York: Oxford University Press, 1989), Quintus Curtius is the "hero of a Roman Legend invented to explain a depression or pit known as Lacus Curtius, 'Curtius's pond,' in the Roman Forum, which had dried up and was paved over in Sullan times (beginning of the first century BC)" (163). The most popular version of the legend held that "after a cleft had opened in the Forum (supposedly in 362 BC) and an oracle had said that the chief strength of Rome must be thrown into it before it would close, a soldier, Marcus Curtius, understanding the oracle's meaning, rode fully armed into the cleft" (163).

21. In Norris's early sketch "Brute," the eponymous main character shows his appreciation of beauty by solemnly eating a flower that he admires. Wharton's brute does not even display that amount of sensitivity to beauty.

22. Wharton's use of "framing" here anticipates her much more extensive use of it in later works. For a discussion of this device in *Summer*, see Jean Frantz Blackall, "Charity at the Window: Narrative Technique in Edith Wharton's *Summer*," in *Edith Wharton: New Critical Essays*, ed. Alfred Bendixen and Annette Zilversmit (New York: Garland, 1992), 115–26.

23. Edmund Wilson, "Justice to Edith Wharton," in *The Wound and the Bow* (Cambridge, Mass.: Riverside Press, 1941), 204. Elizabeth Ammons reports Wharton's affection for this work in *Edith Wharton's Argument with America* (Athens: University of Georgia Press, 1980), 13.

24. Edith Wharton, *Bunner Sisters*, *Xingu*, 1916; reprinted in *The Best Short Stories of Edith Wharton*, ed. Wayne Andrews (New York: Scribner's, 1958), 187. Subsequent references are to this edition and will be cited parenthetically within the text.

25. In "A Gala Dress" (1891), the two elderly Babcock sisters share a single black silk dress between them, laboriously resewing the trimmings after each wearing to preserve the illusion that they each own a dress. Their gesture does not escape their spiteful neighbor, Matilda Jennings. After Emily steps on some firecrackers and ruins the flounce, the sisters refuse to go out together, allowing tales of their estrangement to spread rather than admit their poverty. The situation is resolved when an aunt dies, leaving them two black silks; they generously give the old dress to Matilda, whose jealousy has caused her to try to expose their ruse.

26. Mary E. Wilkins Freeman, "A Mistaken Charity," in *Selected Stories of Mary E. Wilkins Freeman*, ed. Marjorie Pryse, 44.

27. In *The Social Construction of American Realism*, after noting that R. W. B. Lewis identifies Wharton as the mysterious shopper, Amy Kaplan provides a valuable insight into her role: "the writer and the reader, in the role of shoppers, are implicated in the forces that dispossess the sister and expose her to the streets. By framing the story with shop windows, Wharton implicitly adapts and critiques the class tourism and voyeurism which is presented by her contemporary male naturalists as scientific objective investigation" (84).

28. Elements of this plot occur in some local color stories. Also, the story bears a striking resemblance to Arnold Bennett's naturalistic novel *The Old Wives' Tale* (1908).

29. Ammons, *Edith Wharton's Argument with America*, 13.

30. In *After the Fall*, Josephine Donovan says that this "inappropriately Johnsonian rhetoric" causes the sisters to lose contact "as they engage in patriarchal stylistics" (45). Although she comments that "Wharton's own style [in her earliest work] was much more in the tradition of her New England local-color 'predecessors,' Sarah Orne Jewett and Mary E. Wilkins Freeman" (45), her discussion of both "Mrs. Manstey's View" and *Bunner Sisters* focuses more on Wharton's explorations of the Demeter-Persephone myth than on specific local color connections.

31. Wilson, "Justice to Edith Wharton," 204.

32. Nevius, *Edith Wharton*, 126.

33. Ammons, *Edith Wharton's Argument with America*, 14.

34. Lewis, *Edith Wharton*, 297.

35. Edith Wharton, introduction to *Ethan Frome*, 1922, in *Ethan Frome* (New York: Scribner's, 1970), x. Subsequent references to the introduction and to this edition of the novel will be cited parenthetically in the text.

36. Most of the comments here apply equally to *Summer* (1917), Wharton's other regional novel. Wharton called *Summer* her "hot Ethan" and clearly saw the two as a pair, as evidenced by this comment in the *Colophon*: "My other short novel of New England life, *Summer* . . . deals with the same type of people involved in a different tragedy of isolation . . ." (reprinted in *Edith Wharton's* Ethan Frome: *The Story with Sources and Commentary*, ed. Blake Nevius [New York: Scribner's, 1968], 73).

37. Wolff, *Feast of Words*, 172; Waid, *Edith Wharton's Letters from the Underworld*, 66. Waid reads Wharton's use of frames and interiors ("the woman behind the door") as a key to the novel's pervasive images of silence and infertility.

38. Nevius, *Edith Wharton*, 123; italics are Nevius's. Elsa Nettels notes that of the twenty-three male narrators in Wharton's short fiction, "[o]nly the first-person narrator of *Ethan Frome* has been criticized as unconvincingly masculine" ("Gender and First-Person Narration in Edith Wharton's Short Fiction," in *Edith Wharton: New Critical Essays*, ed. Alfred Bendixen and Annette Zilversmit [New York: Garland, 1992], 246). She characterizes Wharton's male narrators as being "equal or superior to the other characters in social position" (247) and identified primarily with other men in groups. Nettels distinguishes several reasons for Wharton's use of male narrators, among them Wharton's "persistent view of literary creation as a man's vocation" (248), the implicit sanction of tradition, and above all a need to adopt the objectivity and power associated with the male perspective, lest the women's stories they tell be lost.

39. John Crowe Ransom comments that Wharton's reporter makes "slight detective motions at gathering [the story]" ("Characters and Character: A Note on Fiction," *American Review* 6 [January 1936]: 273).

40. Jean Frantz Blackall rejects the readings of Cynthia Griffin Wolff, who argues that the blank is "the author's personal absorption in the narrator's fearful

vision," and of Elizabeth Ammons, who claims that "the ellipses signify a change in genre, from the realistic outer narrative to the fairy tale within" ("Edith Wharton's Art of Ellipsis," *Journal of Narrative Technique* 17 [1987]: 154–55). Blackall contends rather that Wharton uses ellipses here to mark the shift from narrative to drama and back: "The augmented ellipses mark this transition into the critical moment and out of it into enduring time" (155).

41. Marlene Springer, *Ethan Frome: A Nightmare of Need* (New York: Twayne, 1993), 81. The latter point is made in *Harvests of Change* when Jay Martin quotes a passage from Thomas Bailey Aldrich's *An Old Town by the Sea* (1893): "The running of the first train over the Eastern Road from Boston to Portsmouth—it took place more than forty years ago . . . attended by a serious accident. . . . [This] initial train, freighted by many hopes and the Directors of the Road, ran over and killed—Local Character" (135).

42. The extent to which Zeena is seen as an evil force in Ethan's life varies. In *Edith Wharton's Argument with America*, for example, Elizabeth Ammons sees Zeena as a fairy-tale wicked witch (complete with cat) to Mattie Silver's Snow White (63). R. B. Hovey, in "*Ethan Frome*: A Controversy about Modernizing It," describes Zeena as another kind of villain, one who wields her psychosomatic illness as a weapon in the power struggle against Ethan that ends when "[n]eurosis conquers all" (*American Literary Realism* 19.1 [Fall 1986]: 17). Susan Goodman, on the other hand, argues that the narrator, blinded by male preconceptions, lacks sympathy for Zeena in what is obviously an untenable situation for her. In *Edith Wharton's Women: Friends and Rivals* (Hanover, N.H.: University Press of New England, 1990), she reads Zeena as an unfairly maligned figure whose story the narrator ignores because of "what he has been primed to see culturally and literarily. . . . By undercutting his authority and reliability, [Wharton] dissociates herself from his error: telling the wrong story" (68).

43. Diane Price Herndl interprets Ethan's case differently, viewing his lameness as a metaphoric castration and Ethan himself as "stuck at home tending an ill parent . . . feminized, and therefore ill" (*Invalid Women*, 181).

44. The same perversion of "woman as (natural) healer" occurs in the "false hair, the false teeth, the false murderous smile" of Dr. Merkle in Wharton's *Summer* (reprint, ed. and introd. Cynthia Griffin Wolff [New York: Harper and Row, 1979], 225).

45. In "Cold Ethan and 'Hot Ethan,'" Cynthia Griffin Wolff sees this resignation as a different sort of antiheroic act, the consequence of Ethan's own ineffectual, unrealistic romanticizing about his situation: "he explores no avenues that might give their love the adult, social context it requires for survival" (*A Feast of Words: The Triumph of Edith Wharton*, 2d ed. [Reading, Mass.: Addison-Wesley, 1995], 406).

46. The sledding incident itself, although drawn from contemporary sources, suggests also the fatal, forbidden sledding incident in Freeman's *Pembroke*, where Deborah Thayer believes her son Ephraim's death to be due to his forbidden sledding, not to a severe beating that she administered. As it does for Ethan Frome, sledding becomes for Ephraim the only symbol of male freedom from his domination by an all-powerful woman.

In "The Sledding Accident in *Ethan Frome*," Jean Frantz Blackall discusses Wharton's sources for this incident and concludes that Ethan's wish to sit in the front of the sled signifies his desire to protect Mattie by hitting the elm tree first (*Studies in Short Fiction* 21 [1984]: 145–46) .

47. Joseph X. Brennan, "*Ethan Frome*: Structure and Metaphor," *Modern Fiction Studies* 7 (Winter 1961–62): 352; Kenneth Bernard, "Imagery and Symbolism in *Ethan Frome*," *College English* 23 (December 1961): 183.

Afterword

1. Norris, *Literary Criticism*, 42.

2. Elaine Showalter, "Literature between the Wars," in *Columbia Literary History of the United States*, ed. Emory Elliott (New York: Columbia University Press, 1988), 825.

Selected Bibliography

Ahnebrink, Lars. *The Beginnings of Naturalism in American Fiction: A Study of the Works of Hamlin Garland, Stephen Crane, and Frank Norris with Special Reference to Some European Influences, 1891-1903.* 1950. Reprint, New York: Russell and Russell, 1961.

Allen, Grant. "Plain Words on the Woman Question." 1889. Reprinted in Newman, 130-34.

Allen, James Lane. "Local Color." *Critic* 8.106 (9 January 1886): 13-14.

———. "Two Principles in Recent American Fiction." *Atlantic Monthly* 80 (October 1897): 433-43.

Ammons, Elizabeth. *Conflicting Stories: American Women Writers at the Turn into the Twentieth Century.* New York: Oxford University Press, 1992.

———. *Edith Wharton's Argument with America.* Athens: University of Georgia Press, 1980.

———. "Going in Circles: The Female Geography of Jewett's *The Country of the Pointed Firs.*" *Studies in the Literary Imagination* 16.2 (Fall 1983): 83-92.

———. "Material Culture, Empire, and Jewett's *Country of the Pointed Firs.*" In Howard, *New Essays on* The Country of the Pointed Firs, 81-99.

Atherton, Gertrude. "Why Is American Literature Bourgeois?" *North American Review* 178 (May 1904): 770-81.

Austin, Mary. *Stories from the Country of Lost Borders.* Ed. and introd. Marjorie Pryse. New Brunswick, N.J.: Rutgers University Press, 1987.

Bader, Julia. "The Dissolving Vision: Realism in Jewett, Freeman, and Gilman." In Sundquist, 176-98.

———. "The 'Rooted' Landscape and the Woman Writer." In *Teaching Women's Literature from a Regional Perspective*, ed. Leonore Hoffman and Deborah Rosenfelt, 23-30. New York: Modern Language Association of America, 1982.

Banta, Martha. *Imaging American Women: Idea and Ideals in Cultural History.* New York: Columbia University Press, 1987.

Bassan, Maurice, ed. and introd. *Stephen Crane's* Maggie: *Text and Context.* Belmont, Cal.: Wadsworth Publishing, 1966, 3-62.

Baym, Nina. *Woman's Fiction: A Guide to Novels by and about Women in America, 1820-1870.* Ithaca: Cornell University Press, 1978.

Becker, George, ed. and introd. *Documents of Modern Literary Realism.* Princeton: Princeton University Press, 1963.

Becknell, Thomas. "Implication through Reading *The Damnation of Theron Ware.*" *American Literary Realism, 1870-1910* 24.1 (Fall 1991): 63-71.

Beer, Thomas. *The Mauve Decade: American Life at the End of the Nineteenth Century.* Garden City, N.Y.: Garden City Publishing, 1926.

———. *Stephen Crane: A Study in American Letters.* Introd. Joseph Conrad. New York: Knopf, 1926.

Bell, Michael Davitt. *The Problem of American Realism: Studies in the Cultural History of a Literary Idea*. Chicago: University of Chicago Press, 1993.

Bell, Millicent. *Edith Wharton and Henry James: The Story of Their Friendship*. New York: George Braziller, 1965.

———. "Female Regional Writing: An American Tradition." *Revue française d'études americaines* 1.30 (November 1986): 469–80.

Bendixen, Alfred, and Annette Zilversmit, eds. *Edith Wharton: New Critical Essays*. New York: Garland, 1992.

Bernard, Kenneth. "Imagery and Symbolism in *Ethan Frome*." *College English* 23 (December 1961): 178–84.

Berthoff, Warner. *American Trajectories: Authors and Readings, 1790-1970*. University Park: Pennsylvania State University Press, 1994.

———. "The Art of Jewett's Pointed Firs." In *Fictions and Events: Essays in Criticism and Literary History*, 243-63. New York: E. P. Dutton, 1971.

———. *The Ferment of Realism: American Literature, 1884-1919*. New York: Free Press, 1965.

Blackall, Jean Frantz. "Charity at the Window: Narrative Technique in Edith Wharton's *Summer*." In Bendixen and Zilversmit, 115-27.

———. "Edith Wharton's Art of Ellipsis." *Journal of Narrative Technique* 17 (1987): 145-62.

———. "The Sledding Accident in *Ethan Frome*." *Studies in Short Fiction* 21 (1984): 145-46.

Blanchard, Paula. *Sarah Orne Jewett: Her World and Her Work*. Reading, Mass.: Addison-Wesley, 1994.

Bloom, Harold, ed. and introd. *Edith Wharton*. Modern Critical Views. New York: Chelsea House, 1986.

Bloom, Harold, ed. *Stephen Crane*. Modern Critical Views. New York: Chelsea House, 1987.

Borus, Daniel. *Writing Realism: Howells, James, and Norris in the Mass Market*. Chapel Hill: University of North Carolina Press, 1989.

Bowlby, Rachel. *"Just Looking": Consumer Culture in Dreiser, Gissing and Zola*. New York: Methuen, 1985.

Bowron, Bernard R., Jr. "Realism in America." *Comparative Literature* 3.3 (Summer 1951): 268-85.

Boyesen, H. H. *Literary and Social Silhouettes*. Library of American Civilization. New York: Harper and Brothers, 1894.

Brennan, Joseph X. "*Ethan Frome*: Structure and Metaphor." *Modern Fiction Studies* 7 (Winter 1961-62): 347-56.

———. "The Imagery and Art of *George's Mother*." *CLA Journal* 4 (December 1960): 106-15. Reprinted in Wertheim, *Studies in* Maggie *and* George's Mother, 125-34.

———. "Ironic and Symbolic Structure in Crane's *Maggie*." *Nineteenth-Century Fiction* 16 (March 1962): 304-15. Reprinted in Wertheim, *Studies in* Maggie *and* George's Mother, 54-64.

Briggs, Austin. *The Novels of Harold Frederic*. Ithaca: Cornell University Press, 1969.

Bristol, Marie. "Life among the Ungentle Genteel: Edith Wharton's *The House of Mirth* Revisited." *Western Humanities Review* 16 (Autumn 1962): 371-74.

Brodhead, Richard. *Cultures of Letters: Scenes of Reading and Writing in Nineteenth-Century America*. Chicago: University of Chicago Press, 1993.

Burgess, Gelett. "The Ballad of the Effeminates." *Lark* (November 1896): n. p.

Cain, William. "Presence and Power in *McTeague*." In Sundquist, 199-214.

Carnes, Mark C. "Middle-Class Men and the Solace of Fraternal Ritual." In *Meanings for Manhood: Constructions of Masculinity in Victorian America*, ed. Mark C. Carnes and Clyde Griffen, 37-52. Chicago: University of Chicago Press, 1990.

Carrington, George C., Jr. "Harold Frederic's Clear Farcical Vision: *The Damnation of Theron Ware*." *American Literary Realism, 1870-1910* 19.3 (Spring 1987): 3-26.

Carson, Richard G. "Nature and the Circles of Initiation in *The Country of the Pointed Firs*." *Colby Library Quarterly* 21 (September 1985): 154-60. Carter, Everett. *Howells and the Age of Realism*. Philadelphia: Lippincott, 1954.

Carter, Stephen. "'The Field Is the Only Reality': *The Damnation of Theron Ware* and a Physics of Interpretation." *American Literary Realism, 1870-1910* 20.2 (Winter 1988): 43-64.

Cassuto, Leonard. "'Keeping Company' with the Old Folks: Unravelling the Edges of *McTeague*'s Deterministic Fabric." *American Literary Realism* 25.2 (Winter 1993): 46-55.

Clendenning, John. "Stephen Crane and His Biographers: Beer, Berryman, Schoberlin, and Stallman." *American Literary Realism* 28.1 (Fall 1995): 23-57.

Cohn, Jan. "Women as Superfluous Characters in American Realism and Naturalism." *Studies in American Fiction* 1 (Autumn 1973): 154-62.

Colvert, James B. Introduction to *George's Mother*, by Stephen Crane. 1898. In *Bowery Tales: Maggie/George's Mother*, ed. Fredson Bowers, 101-8. Vol. 1 of *The Works of Stephen Crane*. Charlottesville: University of Virginia Press, 1969.

Conder, John J. *Naturalism in American Fiction: The Classic Phase*. Lexington: University Press of Kentucky, 1984.

Connelly, Mark Thomas. *The Response to Prostitution in the Progressive Era*. Chapel Hill: University of North Carolina Press, 1980.

Cooke, Rose Terry. *"How Celia Changed Her Mind" and Selected Stories*. Ed. and introd. Elizabeth Ammons. New Brunswick, N.J.: Rutgers University Press, 1986.

Cooperman, Stanley. "Frank Norris and the Werewolf of Guilt." *Modern Language Quarterly* 20 (1959): 252-58.

Cowley, Malcolm. "A Natural History of American Naturalism." *Kenyon Review* (1947). Reprinted in Becker, 429-51.

Cox, James. "Regionalism: A Diminished Thing." In Elliott, *Columbia Literary History* , 761-84.

Crane, Stephen. *The Correspondence of Stephen Crane*. 2 vols. Ed. Stanley Wertheim and Paul Sorrentino. New York: Columbia University Press, 1988.

———. "Fears Realists Must Wait: An Interesting Talk with William Dean Howells." *New York Times*, 28 October 1894. Reprinted in *Stephen Crane: Uncollected Writings*, 79–82.

———. *George's Mother*. 1898. Reprinted in *Bowery Tales: Maggie/George's Mother*, ed. Fredson Bowers, 113–78. Introd. James B. Colvert. Vol. 1 of *The Works of Stephen Crane*. Charlottesville: University of Virginia Press, 1969.

———. *Maggie: A Girl of the Streets (A Story of New York)*. 1893. Reprint, Norton Critical Edition, ed. Thomas Gullason. New York: Norton, 1979.

———. *The Monster*. In *Tales of Whilomville*, ed. Fredson Bowers, 7–67. Introd. J. C. Levenson. Vol. 7 of *The Works of Stephen Crane*. Charlottesville: University of Virginia Press, 1969.

———. *Stephen Crane: Letters*. Ed. R. W. Stallman and Lillian Gilkes. Introd. R. W. Stallman. New York: New York University Press, 1960.

———. *Stephen Crane: Uncollected Writings*. Ed. and introd. Olov W. Fryckstedt. Uppsala: University of Uppsala, 1963.

Crowley, John W. "The Nude and the Madonna in *The Damnation of Theron Ware*." *American Literature* 45 (November 1973): 379–89.

Davidson, Cathy N., and Arnold E. Davidson. "Carrie's Sister: The Popular Prototypes for Dreiser's Heroine." *Modern Fiction Studies* 23:395–407.

Davis, Rebecca Harding. "In the Grey Cabins of New England." *Century* 49 (1895): 620–23.

De Voto, Bernard. Introduction to *Ethan Frome*. 1938. Reprinted in *Edith Wharton's Ethan Frome*, 91–95.

Dickinson, G. Lowes. "Red-bloods and Mollycoddles." In *Appearances: Notes of Travel, East and West*, 180–86. Garden City, N.Y.: Doubleday, Page, 1914.

Dike, Donald A. "Notes on Local Color and Its Relation to Realism." *College English* 14.2 (1952): 81–88.

Dillingham, William B. *Frank Norris: Instinct and Art*. Lincoln: University of Nebraska Press, 1969.

———. "The Old Folks of *McTeague*." In *McTeague*, ed. Donald Pizer, 344–48. New York: Norton, 1977.

Dimock, Wai-Chee. "'Debasing Exchange': Edith Wharton's *The House of Mirth*." *PMLA* 100 (October 1985): 783–92. Reprinted in Bloom, *Edith Wharton*, 123–38.

Donovan, Josephine. *After the Fall: The Demeter-Persephone Myth in Wharton, Cather, and Glasgow*. University Park: Pennsylvania State University Press, 1989.

———. "Breaking the Sentence: Local-Color Literature and Subjugated Knowledges." In *The (Other) American Traditions: Nineteenth-Century Women Writers*, ed. Joyce Warren, 226–43. New Brunswick, N.J.: Rutgers University Press, 1993.

———. *New England Local Color Literature: A Women's Tradition*. New York: Ungar, 1983.

———. *Sarah Orne Jewett*. New York: Ungar, 1980.

Dooley, Patrick K. "Fakes and Good Frauds: Pragmatic Religion in *The Damnation of Theron Ware*." *American Literary Realism, 1870–1910* 15 (Spring 1982): 74–85.

Douglas, Ann. *The Feminization of American Culture*. New York: Knopf, 1977.

Douglas [Wood], Ann. "The Literature of Impoverishment: The Women Local Colorists in America 1865-1914." *Women's Studies* 1 (1972): 3-45.

Dreiser, Theodore. *Jennie Gerhardt.* 1911. Ed. James L. West III. New York: Penguin, 1992.

——. *Letters of Theodore Dreiser: A Selection.* 3 vols. Ed. Robert H. Elias. Philadelphia: University of Pennsylvania Press, 1959.

——. "The Literary Shower." *Ev'ry Month* 2 (September 1896): 21-24.

——. *Sister Carrie.* 1900. Ed. John C. Berkey, Alice M. Winters, James L. W. West III, and Neda M. Westlake. New York: Penguin, 1981.

——. *Theodore Dreiser: A Selection of Uncollected Prose.* Ed. Donald Pizer. Detroit: Wayne State University Press, 1977.

Eggleston, Edward. Preface (1892) to the Library Edition of *The Hoosier Schoolmaster: A Story of Backwoods Life in Indiana.* New York: Grosset and Dunlap, 1913.

Elliott, Emory, ed. *The Columbia History of the American Novel.* New York: Columbia University Press, 1991.

——. *Columbia Literary History of the United States.* New York: Columbia University Press, 1988.

Fatout, Paul. *Ambrose Bierce: The Devil's Lexicographer.* Norman: University of Oklahoma Press, 1951.

Fetterley, Judith. "'Not in the Least American': Nineteenth-Century Literary Regionalism." *College English* 56 (December 1994): 877-95.

Fetterley, Judith, and Marjorie Pryse, eds. *American Women Regionalists, 1850-1910.* New York: Norton, 1992.

Filene, Peter. *Him/Her/Self: Sex Roles in Modern America.* 2d ed. Baltimore: Johns Hopkins University Press, 1986.

Filler, Louis. *Voice of the Democracy: A Critical Biography of David Graham Phillips, Journalist, Novelist, Progressive.* University Park: Pennsylvania State University Press, 1978.

Fisher, Philip. *Hard Facts: Setting and Form in the American Novel.* New York: Oxford University Press, 1985.

Folsom, Marcia McClintock. "'Tact Is a Kind of Mind-Reading': Empathic Style in Sarah Orne Jewett's *The Country of the Pointed Firs.*" *Colby Library Quarterly* 18 (March 1982): 66-78.

Frederic, Harold. *The Damnation of Theron Ware.* 1896. Reprint, New York: Riverside, 1960.

——. *The Damnation of Theron Ware, or, Illumination.* History of the text by Stanton Garner. Text established by Charlyne Dodge. Vol. 3 of the Harold Frederic Edition. Lincoln: University of Nebraska Press, 1985.

Freeman, Mary E. Wilkins. *Jerome, a Poor Man; A Novel.* New York: Harper and Brothers, 1897.

——. *A New England Nun and Other Stories.* 1891. New York: Harper and Brothers, 1919.

——. *Pembroke.* Ed. and introd. Perry Westbrook. New Haven: College and University Press, 1971.

——. *The Revolt of Mother and Other Stories*. Old Westbury, N.Y.: Feminist Press, 1974.

——. *Selected Stories of Mary E. Wilkins Freeman*. Ed. and introd. Marjorie Pryse. New York: Norton, 1983.

——. *Uncollected Stories of Mary Wilkins Freeman*. Ed. and introd. Mary R. Reichardt. Jackson: University Press of Mississippi, 1992.

French, Alice [Octave Thanet, pseud.]. *A Slave to Duty and Other Women*. Chicago: Herbert S. Stone, 1898.

Fryer, Judith. *Felicitous Space: The Imaginative Structures of Edith Wharton and Willa Cather*. Chapel Hill: University of North Carolina Press, 1986.

Garland, Hamlin. *Crumbling Idols: Twelve Essays on Art Dealing Chiefly with Literature, Painting, and the Drama*. Ed. Jane Johnson. Cambridge, Mass: Belknap Press of Harvard University Press, 1960.

——. *Roadside Meetings*. New York: Macmillan, 1930.

Geismar, Maxwell D. *Rebels and Ancestors: The American Novel, 1890-1915*. Boston: Houghton Mifflin, 1953.

Giles, James R. "Beneficial Atavism in Frank Norris and Jack London." *Western American Literature* 4 (Spring 1969): 15-28.

Giles, Ronald K. "Responding to Crane's 'The Monster.'" *South Atlantic Review* 57.2 (May 1992): 45-55.

Goodman, Susan. *Edith Wharton's Women: Friends and Rivals*. Hanover, N.H.: University Press of New England, 1990.

Graham, Don. *Critical Essays on Frank Norris*. Critical Essays on American Literature. Boston: G. K. Hall, 1980.

——. *The Fiction of Frank Norris: The Aesthetic Context*. Columbia: University of Missouri Press, 1978.

——. "Naturalism in American Fiction: A Status Report." *Studies in American Fiction* 10.1 (Spring 1982): 1-16.

Green, Carol Hurd. "Stephen Crane and the Fallen Women." In *American Novelists Revisited: Essays in Feminist Criticism*, ed. Fritz Fleischmann, 225-42. Boston: G. K. Hall, 1982.

Gullason, Thomas A. "The Symbolic Unity of 'The Monster.'" *Modern Language Notes* 75 (December 1960): 663-68.

Gullason, Thomas A., comp. *Stephen Crane's Career: Perspectives and Evaluations*. New York: New York University Press, 1972.

Halfley, James. "'The Monster' and the Art of Stephen Crane." *Accent* 19 (Summer 1959): 159-65. Reprinted in Gullason, 440-47.

Haller, John S., and Robin M. Haller. *The Physician and Sexuality in Victorian America*. New York: Norton, 1974.

Hamblen, Abigail Ann. "Edith Wharton in New England." *New England Quarterly* 38 (June 1965): 239-44.

Hamilton, David Mike. *"The Tools of My Trade": The Annotated Books in Jack London's Library*. Seattle: University of Washington Press, 1986.

Hapke, Laura. *Girls Who Went Wrong: Prostitutes in American Fiction, 1885-1917*. Bowling Green, Ohio: Bowling Green State University Press, 1989.

Harris, Susan K. *Nineteenth-Century American Women's Novels: Interpretive Strategies*. Cambridge: Cambridge University Press, 1990.

Harte, Bret. "The Rise of the 'Short Story.'" *Cornhill Magazine*, n.s., 7.37 (July 1899): 1-8.

Hartt, Rollin Lynde. "A New England Hill Town." *Atlantic Monthly* 83 (1899): 561-74.

Harvey, Alexander. *William Dean Howells: A Study of the Achievement of a Literary Artist*. 1917. Reprint, New York: Haskell House, 1972.

Hendler, Glenn. "The Limits of Sympathy: Louisa May Alcott and the Sentimental Novel." *American Literary History* 3 (1991): 685-706.

Hicks, Granville. *The Great Tradition*. New York: Macmillan, 1933.

Hobson, Barbara Meil. *Uneasy Virtue: The Politics of Prostitution and the American Reform Tradition*. New York: Basic Books, 1987.

Hochman, Barbara. *The Art of Frank Norris, Storyteller*. Columbia: University of Missouri Press, 1988.

———. "Loss, Habit, Obsession: The Governing Dynamic of McTeague." *Studies in American Fiction* (Autumn 1986) 14: 179-90.

———. "A Portrait of the Artist as a Young Actress: The Rewards of Representation in *Sister Carrie*." In *New Essays on* Sister Carrie, ed. Donald Pizer, 43-64. Cambridge: Cambridge University Press, 1991.

Holstein, Michael E. "Art and Archetype: Jewett's Pointed Firs and the Dunnet Landing Stories." *Nineteenth-Century Literature* 42 (September 1987): 188-202.

Hovey, R. B. "*Ethan Frome:* A Controversy about Modernizing It." *American Literary Realism, 1870-1910* 19.1 (Fall 1986): 4-20.

Howard, June. *Form and History in American Literary Naturalism*. Chapel Hill: University of North Carolina Press, 1985.

Howard, June, ed. and introd. *New Essays on* The Country of the Pointed Firs. Cambridge: Cambridge University Press, 1994.

Howatson, M. C., ed. *The Oxford Companion to Classical Literature*. 2d ed. New York: Oxford University Press, 1989.

Howe, Irving, ed. *Edith Wharton: A Collection of Critical Essays*. Englewood Cliffs, N.J.: Prentice-Hall, 1962.

Howells, William Dean. *Criticism and Fiction and Other Essays*. Ed. Clara Marburg Kirk and Rudolf Kirk. New York: New York University Press, 1959.

———. "Editor's Study." *Harper's Monthly* 74 (1887): 482-86.

———. *W. D. Howells as Critic*. Ed. Edwin H. Cady. Routledge Critics Series. London: Routledge and Kegan Paul, 1973.

Jackson, Agnes Moreland. "Stephen Crane's Imagery of Conflict in *George's Mother*." *American Quarterly* 25 (Winter 1969): 313-18.

James, Henry. *Letters of Henry James*. Vol. 4: 1895-1916. Ed. Leon Edel. Cambridge, Mass.: Belknap Press of Harvard University Press, 1984.

Jewett, Sarah Orne. *A Country Doctor*. Boston: Houghton Mifflin, 1884. Ed. and introd. Joy Gould Boyum and Ann R. Shapiro. Reprint, New York: New American Library (Meridian), 1986.

————. *The Country of the Pointed Firs and Other Stories*. Ed. Marjorie Pryse. New York: Norton, 1981.

————. *Deephaven*. Portsmouth, N.H.: Peter Randall, 1993.

John, Arthur. *The Best Years of the* Century: *Richard Watson Gilder*, Scribner's Monthly, *and* Century *Magazine, 1870-1909*. Urbana: University of Illinois Press, 1981.

Joslin, Katherine. *Edith Wharton*. Women Writers Series. New York: St. Martin's Press, 1991.

Kaplan, Amy. "Nation, Region, and Empire." In Elliott, *Columbia History of the American Novel*, 240-66.

————. "Romancing the Empire: The Embodiment of American Masculinity in the Popular Historical Novel of the 1890s." *American Literary History* 2.4 (Winter 1990): 659-90.

————. *The Social Construction of American Realism*. Chicago: University of Chicago Press, 1988.

Kaplan, Harold. *Power and Order: Henry Adams and the Naturalist Tradition in American Fiction*. Chicago: University of Chicago Press, 1981.

Kazin, Alfred. *On Native Grounds: An Interpretation of Modern American Prose Literature*. 1942. Reprint, New York: Harcourt Brace Jovanovich, 1970.

Kimball, Nell. *Nell Kimball: Her Life as an American Madam*. Ed. and introd. Stephen Longstreet. New York: Berkeley (Medallion), 1970.

King, Kimball. "Local Color and the Rise of the American Magazine." In *Essays Mostly on Periodical Publishing in America: A Collection in Honor of Clarence Gohdes*, ed. James Woodress, 121-33. Durham, N.C.: Duke University Press, 1973.

Kolb, Harold H., Jr. *The Illusion of Life: American Realism as a Literary Form*. Charlottesville: University of Virginia Press, 1969.

Krause, Sydney J. "Harold Frederic and the Failure Motif." *Studies in American Fiction* 15 (Spring 1987): 55-67.

La France, Marston. *A Reading of Stephen Crane*. Oxford: Clarendon Press, 1971.

Leach, Nancy R. "New England in the Stories of Edith Wharton." *New England Quarterly* 30 (March 1957): 90-98.

Lears, T. J. Jackson. *No Place of Grace: Antimodernism and the Transformation of American Culture, 1880-1920*. 1981. Reprint, Chicago: University of Chicago Press, 1994.

Lehan, Richard. "American Literary Naturalism: The French Connection." *Nineteenth-Century Fiction* 38 (1984): 529-57.

Leverenz, David. "The Last Real Man in America: From Natty Bumppo to Batman." *American Literary History* 3 (Winter 1991): 753-81.

Levine, Lawrence. *Highbrow/Lowbrow: The Emergence of Cultural Hierarchy in America*. Cambridge, Mass.: Harvard University Press, 1988.

Levy, Helen Fiddyment. *Fiction of the Home Place: Jewett, Cather, Glasgow, Porter, Welty, and Naylor*. Jackson: University Press of Mississippi, 1992.

Lewis, R. W. B. *Edith Wharton: A Biography*. New York: Harper and Row, 1975.

Lewis, Sinclair. "The American Fear of Literature." Nobel Prize Address, 12 December 1930. In *The Man from Main Street: Selected Essays and Other Writings 1904-1950*, ed. Harry E. Maule and Melville H. Cane, 3-17. New York: Random House, 1953.

"Light Literature of Travel, The." Review of *Country By-Ways*, by Sarah Orne Jewett. *Atlantic Monthly* 49 (1882): 419-21.

Lingeman, Richard. *Theodore Dreiser: At the Gates of the City, 1871-1907*. New York: Putnam, 1986.

London, Jack. *The Letters of Jack London*. 3 vols. Ed. Earle Labor, Robert C. Leitz III, and I. Milo Shepard. Stanford, Calif.: Stanford University Press, 1988.

———. "Local Color." In *Moon-Face, and Other Stories*, 27-55. New York: Grosset and Dunlap, 1906.

———. *Martin Eden*. Introd. Robert Haas. 1909. Reprint, New York: Bantam (Classic), 1986.

———. *The Sea-Wolf*. New York: Grosset and Dunlap, 1904.

Luedtke, Luther S. "Harold Frederic's Satanic Soulsby: Interpretation and Sources." *Nineteenth-Century Fiction* 30 (June 1975): 82-104.

Lutz, Tom. *American Nervousness, 1903: An Anecdotal History*. Ithaca: Cornell University Press, 1991.

MacFarlane, Lisa Watt. "Resurrecting Man: Desire and *The Damnation of Theron Ware*." *Studies in American Fiction* 20 (1992): 127-43.

[Madeleine]. *Madeleine: An Autobiography*. 1919. Reprint, with an introd. by Marcia Carlisle, New York: Persea Books, 1986.

Marchalonis, Shirley, ed. *Critical Essays On Mary Wilkins Freeman*. Critical Essays on American Literature. Boston: G. K. Hall, 1991.

———. *Patrons and Protegées: Gender, Friendship, and Writing in Nineteenth-Century America*. New Brunswick, N.J.: Rutgers University Press, 1988.

Marchand, Ernest. *Frank Norris: A Study*. 1942. Reprint, New York: Octagon Books, 1971.

Martin, Jay. *Harvests of Change: American Literature, 1865-1914*. Englewood Cliffs, N.J.: Prentice-Hall, 1967.

Martin, Ronald E. *American Literature and the Universe of Force*. Durham, N.C.: Duke University Press, 1981.

Matthews, Brander. "Before the Break of Day." *Harper's Monthly* 89 (July 1894): 222-27.

———. "In Search of Local Color." *Harper's Monthly* 89 (June 1894): 33-40.

May, Henry F. Introduction to *Oldtown Folks*, by Harriet Beecher Stowe. Cambridge, Mass: Belknap Press of Harvard University Press, 1966.

McElrath, Joseph R., Jr. "The Comedy of Frank Norris's *McTeague*." *Studies in American Humor* 2 (October 1975): 88-95.

———. *Frank Norris and* The Wave: *A Bibliography*. New York: Garland, 1988.

———. *Frank Norris Revisited*. New York: Twayne, 1992.

———. "Frank Norris's *Vandover and the Brute:* Narrative Technique and the Socio-Critical Viewpoint." *Studies in American Fiction* 4 (Spring 1976): 27-43. Reprinted in Graham, *Critical Essays on Frank Norris*, 177-93.

Michaels, Walter Benn. "The Contracted Heart." *New Literary History* 21 (Spring 1990): 495-531.

———. *The Gold Standard and the Logic of Naturalism: American Literature at the Turn of the Century.* Berkeley: University of California Press, 1987.

Michelson, Bruce. "Theron Ware in the Wilderness of Ideas." *American Literary Realism, 1870-1910* 25.1 (Fall 1992): 54-73.

Miller, Elise. "Jewett's *The Country of the Pointed Firs:* The Realism of the Local Colorists." *American Literary Realism, 1870-1910* 20.2 (Winter 1988): 3-20.

Mitchell, Lee Clark. *Determined Fictions: American Literary Naturalism.* New York: Columbia University Press, 1989.

———. "Face, Race, and Disfiguration in Stephen Crane's *The Monster.*" *Critical Inquiry* 17.1 (Fall 1990): 174-92.

———. "'When You Call Me That . . .': Tall Talk and Male Hegemony in *The Virginian.*" *PMLA* 102 (January 1987): 66-77.

Moers, Ellen. *Two Dreisers.* New York: Viking, 1969.

Morgan, Philip. "The Problems of Rural New England: A Remote Village." *Atlantic Monthly* 79 (May 1897): 577-87.

Mott, Frank Luther. *A History of American Magazines.* 5 vols. Cambridge, Mass.: Harvard University Press, 1930-1968.

Murfree, Mary N. [Charles Egbert Craddock, pseud.]. *In the Tennessee Mountains.* 1884. Reprint, Ridgewood, N.J.: Gregg Press, 1968.

Murphy, Brenda. "A Woman with Weapons: The Victor in *George's Mother.*" *Modern Language Studies* 11.2 (Spring 1981): 88-93.

Nagel, Gwen L., ed. *Critical Essays on Sarah Orne Jewett.* Critical Essays on American Literature. Boston: G. K. Hall, 1984.

———. "'This prim corner of land where she was queen': Sarah Orne Jewett's New England Gardens." *Colby Library Quarterly* 22 (March 1986): 43-62.

Nagel, James, ed. and introd. *Critical Essays on Hamlin Garland.* Critical Essays on American Literature. Boston: G. K. Hall, 1982.

Nettels, Elsa. "Gender and First-Person Narration in Edith Wharton's Short Fiction." In Bendixen and Zilversmit, 245-60.

Nevius, Blake. *Edith Wharton: A Study of Her Fiction.* Berkeley: University of California Press, 1953.

Newman, Louise Michele. *Men's Ideas/Women's Realities:* Popular Science, *1870-1915.* New York: Pergamon Press, 1985.

Norris, Frank. *Blix.* 1899. Reprinted in *A Novelist in the Making: A Collection of Student Themes and the Novels* Blix *and* Vandover and the Brute, ed. James D. Hart, 103-278. Cambridge, Mass.: Belknap Press of Harvard University Press, 1970.

———. *The Letters of Frank Norris.* Ed. Franklin Walker. San Francisco: Book Club of California, 1956.

———. *The Literary Criticism of Frank Norris.* Ed. Donald Pizer. Austin: University of Texas Press, 1964.

———. *McTeague: A Story of San Francisco.* 1899. Reprint, Norton Critical Edition, ed. Donald Pizer. New York: Norton, 1977.

———. *McTeague: A Story of San Francisco.* 1899. Reprinted in *Frank Norris: Novels and Essays*. Library of America. Ed. Donald Pizer. New York: Library Classics of the United States, 1986.

———. *Vandover and the Brute*. 1914. Reprinted in *A Novelist in the Making: A Collection of Student Themes and the Novels* Blix *and* Vandover and the Brute. Ed. James D. Hart. Cambridge, Mass.: Belknap Press of Harvard University Press, 1970.

Oehlschlaeger, Fritz. "Passion, Authority, and Faith in *The Damnation of Theron Ware*." *American Literature* 58 (May 1986): 238-55.

Parrington, V. L. "Our Literary Aristocrat." *Pacific Review* (June 1921). Reprinted in Howe, 151-54.

Pattee, Fred Lewis. *The Development of the American Short Story: An Historical Survey*. New York: Harper and Brothers, 1923.

Petrey, Sandy. "The Language of Realism, The Language of False Consciousness: A Reading of Sister Carrie." *Novel* 10 (1977): 101-14.

Petry, Alice Hall. "Universal and Particular: The Local-Color Phenomenon Reconsidered." *American Literary Realism, 1870-1910* 12 (1979): 111-26.

Phillips, David Graham. *Susan Lenox: Her Fall and Rise*. 1917. Reprint, 2 vols. Upper Saddle River, N.J.: Gregg Press, 1968.

Pinzer, Maimie. *The Maimie Papers*. Introd. and historical editor, Ruth Rosen. Textual editor, Sue Davidson. Old Westbury, N.Y.: Feminist Press, 1977.

Pizer, Donald. "The Masculine-Feminine Ethic in Frank Norris's Popular Novels." *Texas Studies in Literature and Language* 6 (Spring 1964): 84-91. Reprinted in Graham, *Critical Essays on Frank Norris*, 45-52.

———. *The Novels of Frank Norris*. New York: Haskell House, 1973.

———. *Realism and Naturalism in Nineteenth-Century American Literature*. Rev. ed. Carbondale: Southern Illinois University Press, 1984.

———. *The Theory and Practice of American Literary Naturalism: Selected Essays and Reviews*. Carbondale: Southern Illinois University Press, 1993.

Price Herndl, Diane. *Invalid Women: Figuring Feminine Illness in American Fiction and Culture, 1840-1940*. Chapel Hill: University of North Carolina Press, 1993.

Pryse, Marjorie. "'Distilling Essences': Regionalism and 'Women's Culture.'" *American Literary Realism, 1870-1910* 25.2 (Winter 1993): 1-15.

Rahv, Philip. "Paleface and Redskin." In *Image and Idea: Fourteen Essays on Literary Themes*, 1-5. New York: New Directions, 1949. Reprint, Westport, Conn.: Greenwood Press, 1958.

Raleigh, John Henry. "The Damnation of Theron Ware." *American Literature* 30 (1958): 210-27. Reprinted as the introduction to *The Damnation of Theron Ware*. New York: Holt, Rinehart, 1960.

Ransom, John Crowe. "Characters and Character: A Note on Fiction." *American Review* 6 (January 1936): 271-88.

Reichardt, Mary. *A Web of Relationship: Women in the Short Stories of Mary Wilkins Freeman*. Jackson: University Press of Mississippi, 1992.

Riis, Jacob. *How the Other Half Lives: Studies among the Tenements of New York*. New York: Scribner's, 1890.

Romines, Ann. *The Home Plot: Women, Writing and Domestic Ritual.* Amherst: University of Massachusetts Press, 1992.

Roosevelt, Theodore. *Theodore Roosevelt Cyclopedia*, s.v. "Mollycoddles." New York: Theodore Roosevelt Memorial Association, 1941.

Rose, Alan Henry. "'Such Depths of Sad Initiation': Edith Wharton and New England." *New England Quarterly* 50 (September 1977): 423-39.

Rosen, Ruth. *The Lost Sisterhood: Prostitution in America, 1900-1918.* Baltimore: Johns Hopkins University Press, 1982.

Rubin, Larry. "Aspects of Naturalism in Four Novels by Edith Wharton." *Twentieth-Century Literature* 2 (January 1957): 182-92.

Sanborn, Alvan F. "The Future of Rural New England." *Atlantic Monthly* 80 (July 1897): 74-83.

Schwartz, Carol A. "*Jennie Gerhardt:* Fairy Tale as Social Criticism." *American Literary Realism, 1870-1910* 19.2 (Winter 1987): 16-29.

Seltzer, Mark. "Statistical Persons." *Diacritics* 17 (1987): 83-98.

Sergeant, Elizabeth Shepley. "Idealized New England." *New Republic* 3 (8 May 1915): 20-21. Reprinted in *Edith Wharton's* Ethan Frome, 83-85.

Sherman, Sarah Way. *Sarah Orne Jewett, an American Persephone*. Hanover, N.H.: University Press of New England, 1989.

Shorey, Paul. "Present Conditions of Literary Production." *Atlantic Monthly* 78 (1896): 156-68.

Showalter, Elaine. *Sexual Anarchy: Gender and Culture at the Fin de Siècle.* New York: Penguin Books, 1990.

———. "Syphilis, Sexuality, and the Fiction of the Fin de Siècle." In Yeazell, 88-115.

———. "Women Writers between the Wars." In *Columbia Literary History of the United States*, ed. Emory Elliott, 820-41. New York: Columbia University Press, 1988.

Shulman, Robert. "Divided Selves and the Market Society: Politics and Psychology in *The House of Mirth*." *Perspectives on Contemporary Literature* 11 (1985): 10-19.

Silet, Charles L. P., Robert E. Welch, and Richard Boudreau, eds. *The Critical Reception of Hamlin Garland 1891-1978.* Troy, N.Y.: Whitston, 1985.

Simpson, Claude M., ed. *The Local Colorists: American Short Stories, 1857-1900.* New York: Harper and Brothers, 1960.

Slotkin, Alan Robert. *The Language of Stephen Crane's* Bowery Tales: *Developing Mastery of Character Diction*. New York: Garland, 1993.

Solomon, Eric. *Stephen Crane: From Parody to Realism.* Cambridge, Mass.: Harvard University Press, 1966.

Spacks, Patricia Meyer. *Gossip.* Chicago: University of Chicago Press, 1986.

Spangler, George. "Divided Self and World in *Martin Eden*." *Jack London Newsletter* 9 (September-December 1976): 118-26.

———. "The Structure of *McTeague*." *English Studies* 59 (February 1978): 48-56. Reprinted in Graham, *Critical Essays on Frank Norris*, 88-98.

———. "Theron Ware and the Perils of Relativism." *Canadian Review of American Studies* 5 (Spring 1974): 36-46.

Springer, Marlene. *Ethan Frome: A Nightmare of Need*. Twayne's Masterwork Studies no. 121. New York: Twayne, 1993.

Stronks, James B. "Frank Norris's *McTeague:* A Possible Source in H. C. Bunner." *Nineteenth-Century Fiction* 25 (March 1971): 474-78.

Sundquist, Eric. "The Country of the Blue." Introduction to *American Realism: New Essays*, 3-24.

———. "Realism and Regionalism." In Elliott, *Columbia Literary History of the United States*, 501-24.

Sundquist, Eric, ed. and introd. *American Realism: New Essays*. Baltimore: Johns Hopkins University Press, 1982.

Taylor, Eugene. *William James on Exceptional Mental States: The 1896 Lowell Lectures*. New York: Scribner's, 1983.

Terrie, Philip G. "Local Color and a Mythologized Past: The Rituals of Memory in *The Country of the Pointed Firs*." *Colby Library Quarterly* 23 (March 1987): 16-25.

Thompson, Charles Miner. "The Art of Miss Jewett." *Atlantic Monthly* 94 (1904): 485-97.

———. "Miss Wilkins: An Idealist in Masquerade." *Atlantic Monthly* 83 (1899): 665-75.

———. "New Figures in Literature and Art: Hamlin Garland." *Atlantic Monthly* 76 (December 1895): 840-44.

Tompkins, Jane. *Sensational Designs: The Cultural Work of American Fiction, 1790-1860*. New York: Oxford University Press, 1985.

Torsney, Cheryl. *Constance Fenimore Woolson: The Grief of Artistry*. Athens: University of Georgia Press, 1989.

———. "The Traditions of Gender: Constance Fenimore Woolson and Henry James." In Marchalonis, *Patrons and Protégées*, 161-83.

Trilling, Lionel. "The Morality of Inertia." In *Great Moral Dilemmas in Literature, Past and Present*, ed. Robert MacIver, 37-46. New York: Harper, 1956.

Turner, Arlin. "Comedy and Reality in Local Color Fiction, 1865-1900." In *The Comic Imagination in American Literature*, ed. Louis D. Rubin, 167-74. Forum Series. Washington, D.C.: Voice of America, 1974.

Waid, Candace. *Edith Wharton's Letters from the Underworld: Fictions of Women and Writing*. Chapel Hill: University of North Carolina Press, 1991.

Walcutt, Charles Child. *American Literary Naturalism: A Divided Stream*. Minneapolis: University of Minnesota Press, 1956.

Walker, Nancy A. "'Seduced and Abandoned': Convention and Reality in Edith Wharton's *Summer*." *Studies in American Fiction* 11:107-14.

———. "Women Writers and Literary Naturalism: The Case of Ellen Glasgow." *American Literary Realism, 1870-1910* 18 (Spring-Autumn 1985): 133-46.

Warner, Charles Dudley. "Editor's Study." *Harper's Monthly* 86 (December 1892): 148-55.

———. "Editor's Study." *Harper's Monthly* 92 (May 1896): 959-64.

Watson, Charles N., Jr. "Sexual Conflict in *The Sea-Wolf:* Further Notes on London's Reading of Kipling and Norris." *Western American Literature* 11 (Fall 1976): 239-48.

Weatherford, Richard M. *Stephen Crane: The Critical Heritage*. London: Routledge and Kegan Paul, 1973.

Wershoven, Carol. "The Divided Conflict of Edith Wharton's *Summer*." *Colby Library Quarterly* 21.1 (March 1985): 5-10.

Wertheim, Stanley. "Frank Norris and Stephen Crane: Conviction and Uncertainty." *American Literary Realism, 1870-1910* 24 (Fall 1991): 54-62.

———. *The Merrill Studies in* Maggie *and* George's Mother. Columbus, Ohio: Merrill, 1970.

Wertheim, Stanley, and Paul Sorrentino. *The Crane Log: A Documentary Life of Stephen Crane 1871-1900*. New York: G. K. Hall, 1994.

Westbrook, Perry. *Acres of Flint: Sarah Orne Jewett and Her Contemporaries*. Rev. ed. Metuchen, N.J.: Scarecrow Press, 1981.

———. *Mary Wilkins Freeman*. Rev. ed. Boston: Twayne, 1988.

Westra, Helen. "Age and Life's Great Prospects in Sarah Orne Jewett's *The Country of the Pointed Firs*." *Colby Quarterly* 26.3 (September 1990): 161-70.

Wharton, Edith. *A Backward Glance*. New York: Scribner's, 1934.

———. *The Best Short Stories of Edith Wharton*. Ed. and introd. Wayne Andrews. New York: Scribner's, 1958.

———. *Bunner Sisters*. In *Xingu*, 1916. Reprinted in *The Best Short Stories of Edith Wharton*, ed. and introd. Wayne Andrews, 187-263. New York: Scribner's, 1958.

———. *The Collected Short Stories of Edith Wharton*. 2 vols. Ed. R. W. B. Lewis. New York: Scribner's, 1968.

———. *Edith Wharton's* Ethan Frome*: The Story with Sources and Commentary*. Ed. Blake Nevius. Scribner Research Anthologies. New York: Scribner's, 1968.

———. *Ethan Frome*. 1911. Reprint, introd. Edith Wharton (1922). New York: Scribner's, 1970.

———. *Letters of Edith Wharton*. Ed. R. W. B. Lewis and Nancy Lewis. New York: Macmillan (Collier Books), 1988.

———. "Mrs. Manstey's View." *Scribner's Magazine* 10 (1891): 117-22.

———. *Summer*. 1917. Reprint, ed. and introd. Cynthia Griffin Wolff. New York: Harper and Row (Perennial Library), 1979.

———. "The Writing of *Ethan Frome*." *Colophon* 11 (September 1932): n.p. Reprinted in Nevius, *Edith Wharton's* Ethan Frome, 2-73.

White, Barbara A. *Edith Wharton: A Study of the Short Fiction*. New York: Twayne, 1991.

Wilde, Oscar. Preface to *The Picture of Dorian Gray*. 1891. Reprint, Harmondsworth, England: Penguin, 1949.

Williams, Sherwood. "The Rise of a New Degeneration: Decadence and Atavism in *Vandover and the Brute*." *ELH* 57 (1990): 709-36.

Wilson, Christopher. *The Labor of Words: Literary Professionalism in the Progressive Era*. Athens: University of Georgia Press, 1985.

Wilson, Edmund. "Edith Wharton: A Memoir by an English Friend." In *Classics and Commercials: A Literary Chronicle of the Forties*. New York: Farrar, Straus, Cudahy, 1950. Reprinted in Howe, 172-76.

———. "Justice to Edith Wharton." In *The Wound and the Bow: Seven Studies in Literature*, 195-213. Cambridge, Mass.: Riverside Press, 1941.

Wolff, Cynthia Griffin. "'Cold Ethan' and 'Hot Ethan.'" In *A Feast of Words: The Triumph of Edith Wharton*, 397-411. 2d ed. Reading, Mass.: Addison-Wesley, 1995.

———. *A Feast of Words: The Triumph of Edith Wharton*. New York: Oxford University Press, 1977.

Wolford, Chester L. *The Anger of Stephen Crane: Fiction and the Epic Tradition*. Lincoln: University of Nebraska Press, 1983.

Woolson, Constance Fenimore. *For the Major, and Selected Short Stories*. Ed. Rayburn S. Moore. New Haven: College and University Press, 1967.

Yeazell, Ruth Bernard, ed. *Sex, Politics, and Science in the Nineteenth-Century Novel*. Selected Papers from the English Institute, 10. Baltimore: Johns Hopkins University Press, 1986.

Ziff, Larzer. *The American 1890s: Life and Times of a Lost Generation*. New York: Viking, 1966.

Zola, Emile. "The Experimental Novel." 1880. Reprinted in Becker, 161-96.

INDEX

Page numbers followed by n. or nn. refer to notes.